Happiness in World History

Happiness in World History traces ideas and experiences of happiness from early stages in human history, to the maturation of agricultural societies and their religious and philosophical systems, to the changes and diversities in the approach to happiness in the modern societies that began to emerge in the 18th century.

In this thorough overview, Peter N. Stearns explores the interaction between psychological and historical findings about happiness, the relationship between ideas and popular experience, and the opportunity to use historical analysis to assess strengths and weaknesses of dominant contemporary notions of happiness. Starting with the advent of agriculture, the book assesses major transitions in history for patterns in happiness, including the impact of the great religions, the unprecedented Enlightenment interest in secular happiness and cheerfulness, and industrialization and imperialism. The final, contemporary section covers fascist and communist efforts to define alternatives to Western ideas of happiness, the increasing connections with consumerism, and growing global interests in defining and promoting well-being. Touching on the experiences in the major regions of Asia, Africa, Latin America, Europe, and North America, the text offers an expansive introduction to a new field of study.

This book will be of interest to students of world history and the history of emotions.

Peter N. Stearns is University Professor of History at George Mason University, USA. He has written widely both in world history and in the growing field of the history of emotions, and regularly teaches courses in both areas.

Themes in World History

Series editor: Peter N. Stearns

The *Themes in World History* series offers focused treatment of a range of human experiences and institutions in the world history context. The purpose is to provide serious, if brief, discussions of important topics as additions to textbook coverage and document collections. The treatments will allow students to probe particular facets of the human story in greater depth than textbook coverage allows, and to gain a fuller sense of historians' analytical methods and debates in the process. Each topic is handled over time – allowing discussions of changes and continuities. Each topic is assessed in terms of a range of different societies and religions – allowing comparisons of relevant similarities and differences. Each book in the series helps readers deal with world history in action, evaluating global contexts as they work through some of the key components of human society and human life.

Gender in World History
Peter N. Stearns

Neutrality in World History
Leos Müller

Globalization in World History
Peter N. Stearns

Time in World History
Peter N. Stearns

Migration in World History (Third Edition)
Patrick Manning with Tiffany Trimmer

Agriculture in World History (Second Edition)
Mark B. Tauger

Happiness in World History
Peter N. Stearns

Happiness in World History

Peter N. Stearns

NEW YORK AND LONDON

First published 2021
by Routledge
52 Vanderbilt Avenue, New York, NY 10017

and by Routledge
2 Park Square, Milton Park, Abingdon, Oxon, OX14 4RN

Routledge is an imprint of the Taylor & Francis Group, an informa business

© 2021 Peter N. Stearns

The right of Peter N. Stearns to be identified as author of this
work has been asserted by him in accordance with sections 77
and 78 of the Copyright, Designs and Patents Act 1988.

All rights reserved. No part of this book may be reprinted
or reproduced or utilised in any form or by any electronic,
mechanical, or other means, now known or hereafter invented,
including photocopying and recording, or in any information
storage or retrieval system, without permission in writing from
the publishers.

Trademark notice: Product or corporate names may be trademarks
or registered trademarks, and are used only for identification and
explanation without intent to infringe.

Library of Congress Cataloging-in-Publication Data
Names: Stearns, Peter N., author.
Title: Happiness in world history / Peter N. Stearns.
Description: First Edition. | New York: Routledge, 2021. |
Series: Themes in world history |
Includes bibliographical references and index.
Identifiers: LCCN 2020037263 (print) |
LCCN 2020037264 (ebook) | ISBN 9780367561031
(paperback) | ISBN 9780367561055 (hardback) |
ISBN 9781003096436 (ebook)
Subjects: LCSH: Happiness—Philosophy. | Happiness—History.
Classification: LCC B105.H36 S84 2021 (print) |
LCC B105.H36 (ebook) | DDC 302/.14—dc23
LC record available at https://lccn.loc.gov/2020037263
LC ebook record available at https://lccn.loc.gov/2020037264

ISBN: 978-0-367-56105-5 (hbk)
ISBN: 978-0-367-56103-1 (pbk)
ISBN: 978-1-003-09643-6 (ebk)

Typeset in Bembo
by codeMantra

Contents

Acknowledgments	vii
1 Introduction	1
2 Psychological Basics	12

PART I
The Agricultural Age — 21

3 Early Agricultural Society	22
4 From the Philosophers: Happiness in the Classical Period	37
5 From the Great Religions: Happiness – and Hope?	54
6 Popular Pleasures	71

PART II
The Happiness Revolution, 1700–1900 — 87

7 The Happiness Revolution in the West	88
8 The Expansion of Happiness? The New Expectations Encounter Industrial Society	108
9 Global Developments in the 18th and 19th Centuries	134

PART III
Happiness in Contemporary World History — 149

10 Disputed Happiness, 1920–1945	151
11 Communist Happiness	164

vi *Contents*

12 Comparing Happiness in Contemporary Societies   174

13 Western Society in Contemporary History: Even Happier?   188

14 Happiness Goes Global   202

15 Conclusion   213

Index   221

Acknowledgments

A number of people provided great assistance in finding relevant materials: on the history side, Benedict Carton, Joan Bristol, Brian Platt, Marcus Collins, and Peter Mandaville; on psychology, Deborah Stearns, Yulia Chenstova, and Kostadin Kushlev. I am very grateful to Jack Censer and Darrin McMahon for their suggestions on the manuscript; Jack Censer's reading was exceptionally careful; Darrin McMahon's pioneering work in the field has offered real inspiration. Patricia Mikell provided invaluable research assistance and constructive comments, while helping with manuscript preparation. Thanks also to Kimberley Smith, the Routledge editor who encouraged the project. Finally, much of the book was written during the Covid-19 quarantine, which was a bit ironic; and I thank my wife, Donna Kidd, who shared the experience, often fairly happily, and my children and grandchildren who contributed from afar.

1 Introduction

Early in the 18th century, it was common for literate individuals in Britain and North America to emphasize the importance of a "melancholic demeanor" in the face of a rather joyless, judgmental God. Some might actually apologize, in letters or diaries, for moments of laughter, admitting that they should spend their time with "graver people".

Fast forward a few decades toward the middle of the century, and leading intellectuals are proudly proclaiming "Oh happiness! Our being's end and aim" (Alexander Pope) or "the best thing one could do (is) to be always cheerful, and not suffer any sullenness" (John Byrom). And not too long after, a group of American revolutionaries would boldly proclaim "the pursuit of happiness" as a basic human right. The fashionable stance toward happiness was changing dramatically.

Other examples, a bit less striking, suggest other patterns of change. As their religions took hold, Christian and Muslim leaders sought to convince the faithful that full happiness must await the attainment of heaven, deliberately challenging many assumptions about pleasure in this life. Middle-class parents in Britain and the United States, in the mid-19th century, began to establish the custom of regular celebrations of children's birthdays – for several reasons, but primarily because they sought a new way to provide happiness. Communist governments, in the 20th century, worked very hard to promote ideas about happiness that would differ both from religious and from dominant Western concepts, and the process proved quite challenging.

Happiness may be a constant human goal – though that can be debated – but it unquestionably evolves. How it is defined, what expectations and judgments it provokes, and – probably – how happy people actually are, can shift dramatically depending on a combination of ideas and material conditions. Often the change is somewhat gradual, but as the 18th-century example suggests, it can be impressively swift. Opening this process to historical inquiry can reveal a lot about the past but also about how our own commitments to happiness have formed.

This book seeks to extend the evaluation of happiness by asking how major ideas and practices aimed at defining and attaining happiness have altered over time; how different cultures have approached the subject; and

2   Introduction

how concepts and initiatives today can be better understood through analysis of how they have emerged from the past. In the process, we will also periodically address the really challenging question of how happy people "actually" have been, and are today.

★★★

The history of happiness covers many different regions of the world and several distinct periods of time. It involves a mix of formal ideas and more diffuse popular assumptions. It includes explicit efforts to generate happiness, from activities like traditional festivals; to the apparatus of modern consumerism; to broader attempts to improve levels of health and comfort. It traces ways that people have defined happiness, the extent to which they have actively expected happiness in their lives, even the important instances where, for religious or other reasons, apparently popular pleasures were viewed with suspicion. Always, the focus is both on understanding a key feature of the past and applying this understanding to an assessment of the often-eager quests for happiness in society today.

A reasonable first question, however, would simply be: is this a subject with a history at all? Isn't happiness a basic feature in the human emotional arsenal, and not really subject to significant changes or variations? Babies everywhere, for example, regardless of time period or regional culture, learn how to smile by the time they are four weeks old (and some experts argue they actually figure this out even earlier). They are thus able to express this aspect of their mood and also manipulate their parents, many of whom are suckers for an infant's smile. It would be hard to argue that there is much history here. Furthermore, psychologists have demonstrated, in arguing that happiness is a basic human emotion, that people everywhere usually agree on what a happy face looks like.

A variant on this argument, also heavily dependent on psychology, admits that there are lots of gradations in happiness but insists that they are mostly the function of individual personalities. Some people are simply born happier than others. One study claims that as much as 80% of a person's happiness is innate, and therefore that urging someone to be happier is about the same as urging him or her to be taller – there's nothing much to do about it, and certainly no reason to look at history.

Or finally, leaving psychology for what might be regarded as pop philosophy, happiness is simply a bit of a mystery. We often have trouble figuring out whether we ourselves are happy, let alone other people or people in the past. We wonder if certain conditions normally generate more happiness, but we're not sure: hence, the old argument about whether money "buys" happiness (often accompanied by a somewhat wistful hope that it does not). Or we might throw up our hands at the range of individual tastes involved: some people are deeply happy watching their sports teams win, but others, in the same society, could care less about sports.

Introduction 3

Happiness, in this line of thinking, is unquestionably an interesting topic, but it's simply too ill-defined to warrant historical study. Dan Gilbert, a psychologist who has all sorts of interesting things to say about happiness, admits that we will never have a "happymeter" that infallibly indicates how much happiness there is, or even exactly what it is, and if this is true for the present it is even more true for the past.

The historian of happiness can grant all these arguments – up to a point. There are innate features to happiness across time and place; yet, as we will show, even smiling is a social variable, capable of change (at least post-infancy) depending on cultural assumptions and even dentistry. And it is probably true that, in any society, some people are more disposed to happiness than others; but this does not override larger beliefs and assumptions that make some societies, and some time periods, different from others where happiness is concerned.

Finally, we can certainly agree that a precise definition of happiness is really hard to come by and that specific tastes unquestionably diverge – but one reason for this confusion is the fact that a society's ideas about what happiness is, and how much of it we should expect, change over time. All of this is to say, in other words, that the history of happiness is complicated, but historical analysis can nevertheless contribute actively to how we can understand the emotion both today and in the past. The difficulty in offering a single definition of happiness is in a sense an invitation to trace the various conceptions in different regions of the world, how they have changed over time, and how pervasive notions today have emerged from the past. To the extent that a history of happiness not only explains current approaches but also contributes to any personal evaluation of what happiness means, its service is amplified.

∧∧∧

This book further complicates the study of happiness by looking at it in a world history context. The goal is to connect what we know about changes and variations in happiness to a global framework and in turn to introduce regional diversity to the subject at various points in time. This is a tall order, compounded further by the unevenness of available work on the subject: more on Western Europe, for example, than on Latin America, more on China than on Africa. Further as we will see, there may have been more fundamental changes in the Western approach to happiness in modern times than in most other regions, except insofar as they have tried to come to grips with this aspect of Western example. But this does not mean that the modern Western take on happiness is the best version imaginable (it has some built-in disadvantages, as we will see). And it certainly does not suggest that other cultural approaches have somehow disappeared. Indeed, interactions among various happiness standards form an important part of contemporary emotional history.

4   *Introduction*

Huge opportunities exist for further research on the history of happiness even in the Western tradition, and certainly on the world stage. While all sorts of historical research bears on the subject of happiness – from treatments of the great philosophers to work on material conditions or changing levels of health – there is less explicit coverage than one might imagine, partly because the subject can seem so diffuse. Happiness is something of a pioneering historical venture. At the same time, enough spadework has been done on several different societies in several different time periods to venture a brief survey. The results contribute additional perspectives beyond what is available from attention to one region alone and certainly help explain the various contemporary approaches involved. And if they also whet the appetite for further comparative work, all the better.

∧∧∧

Modern Russian adage: "A person who smiles a lot is either a fool or an American."

One way to begin to get a handle on the study of happiness, but also its global complexities, is to look at the fundamental contemporary fact that happiness varies a lot, today, from one region to the next – or, at least, claims about happiness vary greatly. Ever since 2012, the Gallup organization and the United Nations have sponsored an annual international happiness survey, which among other things involves careful polling of a sampling of individuals from each major country around the question of where, on a scale of one to ten, they would rate their own happiness today. (The idea that this kind of attention to international happiness is worthwhile is, itself, a novel and intriguing development.)

The responses demonstrate striking differences. The happiest nations – happiest at least by self-report – are for the most part highly industrialized and Western: leading the list, usually, are the Scandinavian countries along with Iceland, Switzerland, the Netherlands, Canada, and New Zealand. Not too far behind are bigger and arguably more complex societies, like the United Kingdom, Germany, and the United States. At the bottom of the list are societies that are not only extremely poor but also often involved in bitter civil conflicts: South Sudan, Yemen, Afghanistan, and Syria.

With this, the obvious but nevertheless significant point: people's happiness can vary a lot depending on political, military, economic, and epidemiological circumstances. This is true today, and there is every reason to assume it has been true over time as well. Hence, historically, some time periods are likely to have been happier than others: people in the Roman or Han Chinese empires, at their height, with considerable prosperity and internal peace, were almost certainly happier than their counterparts in the same societies once invasions and disease helped topple the

Introduction 5

great imperial structures. And there may be more subtle judgments, about the relationship between circumstance and happiness, that can be applied to the historical record as well, that will help explain not only levels of happiness but also changes in the ways the condition is defined.

But the contemporary polling data harbor one other kind of differentiation that is at least as interesting, and certainly more challenging, than the relationship between happiness and objective circumstance. One set of societies, today, consistently score more toward the middle of the scale than in its upper reaches, despite considerable prosperity, good health, and low crimes rates: Japan, South Korea, and indeed most of East Asia (only Taiwan and Singapore, in the 2019 poll, even placed in the top 35). In contrast, another set, though not at the top of the rankings, often score quite well despite lower levels of economic performance: a number of Latin American or Caribbean countries, headed by Costa Rica, Panama, Mexico, and Trinidad-Tobago.

What's going on here? Pretty obviously, cultural conditions – whether happiness is rated highly as an explicit value – play a major role in determining social response to a pollster's questionnaire. Some cultural systems encourage people to want to portray themselves as happy, and while this cannot overcome desperate material circumstances it can certainly generate surprisingly positive responses when conditions are at least comparatively neutral. In contrast, some societies that rate quite high in larger terms of well-being promote far more measured responses. In all likelihood, differences of this sort go beyond polling responses to basic divergences in personal evaluations of what happiness is all about, and how highly it rates.

This phenomenon has been extensively studied for the United States and Japan, two societies that, objectively, might score rather similarly. American culture is primed for cheerfulness, and although levels have slipped a bit in recent years the ability to convey "positivity" is a deeply ingrained response. Japan, in contrast, is far less individualistic. Personal evaluations depend more on a sense of family and community cohesion, taking comfort in one's place in a group, rather than maximum individual satisfaction. As one study puts it, "the emphasis is on relating to others, fitting in, and harmonious interdependence", which does not easily comport with a questionnaire on purely personal ratings. In contrast, Americans are very comfortable, culturally, with attending to the self. The distinction goes beyond polling, to deeper differences in the way satisfaction is defined. And it shows up, as well, in some of the behaviors associated with happiness in what might, on the surface, seem to be rather similar consumer cultures. Both Americans and Japanese, for example, buy things when on vacation, though Americans are a bit more avid; but Japanese more often buy gifts for family members and others back home, while Americans devote more attention to items for themselves. Different emotional scales are involved.

6 *Introduction*

Distinctions of this sort play a huge role in the history of happiness, because they allow us to trace the origin and evolution of definitions of happiness in different parts of the world, at the level of formal philosophy and religion, but also, at least to some degree, in terms of more popular values as well.

For the kinds of variables that shine through so clearly in the regional differentiations also apply, at least in principle, to probable changes over time. The polling experts themselves are eager to highlight the importance of change, even over the eight years of their global operation: there might be less reason to read their reports if the rankings never shifted. And in fact, recent deteriorations in places like the United States are worth evaluating, along with the striking advance (within the Scandinavian orbit) of Finland, currently the world's happiest place. But far more to the point is a larger historical inquiry, that looks at evolving patterns over a much longer time frame, along the dual criteria of objective conditions and cultural prompts.

To be sure, and this will be obvious in the chapters that follow, we lack the abundant data for the past that are available today. There are no happiness polls, or even precise measurements of Gross National Products or physical and emotional wellness before the contemporary era. Yet a variety of data do exist, often particularly on the cultural side. An increasing number of historians have been exploring various aspects of past emotions and patterns of change, and while attention to happiness has not been at the top of the list a variety of studies are available. A historical focus on happiness, in fact, can help draw together some of the other work in the history of emotion, touching obviously on patterns and changes in sadness or envy and even connecting to aspects of love or fear as well.

The most explicit fulcrum for the historical study of happiness involves the variety of ideas about happiness that began to form a substantial part of philosophical inquiry and religious guidance at least from the classical civilizations onward. This formal intellectual record can be supplemented by other evidence about how people sought pleasure and at times commented directly on their own conceptions of happiness. These wider materials become particularly abundant for the modern period that began to open up in the 18th century, enhanced by more popular guidance as well – as societies began to generate lots of advice to people about how to be happy, as politicians began to fold happiness into their proclamations and as advertisers began to try to sell goods in terms of their potential to contribute to happiness. All this creates a central historical thread: how key societies have tried to define what happiness is and how these ideas and maxims have changed over time. But this book will also, more tentatively, return periodically to issues of "actual" happiness, to talk about how cultural values and objective conditions may intertwine to generate larger trends.

Before turning briefly to the book's organization, it is vital to go back to the most challenging question raised, if only implicitly, by the

Introduction 7

contemporary polling data, where the cultural aspects not only intrigue but baffle. It is important to recognize that Americans are readier to say they are happy than their Japanese or South Korean counterparts, despite having little objective reason to do so. But are they "really" happier, or to put the question more provocatively, are the Japanese despite comparable wealth, less violence and longer life expectancies "really" less happy? Ultimately it is impossible to say, for the differences in each society's cultural criteria preclude a single judgment. This elusiveness bedevils historical evaluations as well, meaning that we can do a lot with the changing values and circumstances relevant to happiness but never claim with absolute certainty that we have captured a truly objective emotional experience. We will deal, for example, with such questions as whether modern people are on the whole happier than their premodern ancestors, and we will establish some probabilities around both cultural assumptions and objective conditions – but there must always be room for debate about whether a common quality has been identified.

While undeniably frustrating, this feature of happiness – the lack of a single objective standard – actually helps justify a historical effort, and one that stretches over a number of regional societies. What follows will not, again, offer a single determination of a complex phenomenon. It will, however, show how various societies have tackled the question of what happiness is and how much of it should be expected, and how contemporary criteria have emerged from earlier, and often very different, formulations.

★★★

Not surprisingly, since this is a historical study, the following chapters proceed roughly chronologically, but with some pauses to deal with comparative issues in a single time period and to venture an initial foray into interdisciplinary considerations.

The first full chapter elaborates on some of the existing findings and claims about happiness, emanating particularly from the discipline of psychology, which have developed around largely contemporary (and mainly Western) evidence. Historians can take issue with some of the arguments, especially those that press too far toward claiming a universal or basic emotional experience, but they can also make use of a number of conclusions. Ultimately, any evaluation of happiness must feature interdisciplinary components, and it is vital to begin, if briefly, on this basis.

Chapter 3 is also interdisciplinary but in a much more specific historical context: here the question centers on happiness levels in the first type of human society – the hunters-gatherers – and the possible decline of happiness when hunting and gathering yielded to agriculture. A number of anthropologists have contributed thoughts here, in what is admittedly a somewhat speculative arena, but a few historians have also taken up the charge.

8   *Introduction*

Several chapters then turn to conditions of happiness in various agricultural societies and periods when happiness was explicitly debated perhaps in part because so many obvious challenges began to emerge. Chapter 4 deals with classic formulations by Greek-Roman and Confucian philosophers, who had a lot to say on the subject, along with some questions about how influential the philosophers were in society at large. Then the focus turns, in Chapter 5, to the major religious formulations, which developed various and influential approaches to happiness while usually arguing that true, durable happiness could only be found beyond this earthly plane. Chapter 6 takes up more popular approaches to happiness, strongly influenced by religion but with somewhat separate efforts to seek happiness in festivals, in opportunities for children's play and, often, through a changing pattern of urban entertainments.

Chapters in Part II turn to more modern conditions, beginning in Chapter 7 with a true revolution in ideas about happiness in the Western world that took shape in the 18th century. Not only the content and range of the new ideas, but also the factors that promoted them, demand assessment. Chapter 8 continues this theme by looking at the ways this revolutionary approach to happiness began to be installed in ordinary life – and some of the constraints and frustrations that could be involved as well, including differences by social class and gender. Chapter 9, still focused on the 18th and 19th centuries, deals with some of the larger complications of the Western ideas about happiness, including responses and objections in other world regions. The Western happiness "revolution" had some wider influences, but it was hardly dominant and it provoked some vigorous debates.

Part III deals with developments in the past century. Chapter 10 deals with various currents during the troubled interwar period: continued exploration of the Western happiness theme, but also deliberate attacks on the same theme in fascist societies, plus some alternative nationalist approaches. Chapter 11 traces the complicated efforts of communist societies, beginning with the Soviet Union, to develop a distinctive approach to happiness, at once recognizing the importance of the goal but disputing the Western approach. Chapter 12 returns to the comparative theme for the postwar decades, elaborating on some of the differences suggested by the international polls. Chapter 13 returns to the West itself, with further efforts to promote happiness but also growing signs of strain, for example in clearer definitions of the problem of psychological depression. Chapter 14 returns more specifically to the comparative and global theme, among other things introducing additional survey data but also the new efforts to promote a new kind of positive psychology and its international influence; happiness was gaining some new global components. A conclusion then turns briefly to the larger questions about happiness over historical time, and the implications of historical findings.

Each major section deals both with ideas about happiness and, to the extent possible, with popular experience, and the interactions between the

Introduction   9

two including probable expectations. Often, ideas will offer the clearest evidence at a given point in time, but it is not always easy to determine their actual influence, particularly before the more modern periods. Ultimately, changes in the values associated with happiness and material conditions broadly construed combine to shape the history of this crucial emotion.

∧∧∧

The growth of historical work on happiness stems from several sources. The subject looms large in many philosophical systems, which has justified a good bit of research and synthesis simply as part of basic intellectual history, particularly for the Greco-Roman tradition and for Chinese Confucianism. As noted, the topic has also gained attention and perspective from the larger advance of study in the history of emotions. This field was proposed several decades ago, as part of a belief that human psychology was itself a historical variable, inviting a greater understanding of different conditions and assumptions that marked periods in the past. Historians of emotions argue convincingly that key emotions are in large part culturally constructed, rather than serving as standard products of human biology: this argument very clearly applies to happiness, and the history of happiness in turn helps illustrate the process of cultural construction. Additionally, a number of other emotions attach to the historical patterns of happiness: several related emotional experiences like boredom and envy have generated considerable research – some of these ancillaries have actually received more attention in the history of emotion than has happiness itself, where opportunities for further research abound. Finally, at a time when many people are anxiously evaluating their own happiness, the need for historical perspective is abundantly clear.

Also it is vital to note (as discussed below in Chapter 14) that many countries, and not just in the West, have picked up a new and explicit interest in happiness in recent years. The mountain nation of Bhutan has pioneered in trying to measure national well-being; the United Arab Emirates has a government ministry devoted to happiness, a theme that also informs its police force. Here, clearly, is another basis for thinking about the evolution of happiness on a global scale.

Finally, though this is a related point, recent attention to the history of happiness has also been linked to the growing interest in positive psychology and human well-being. Understanding how historical conditions and even basic guidelines for well-being have changed over time, and how current interests – including the well-being movement itself – have emerged from the past, can enrich the recommendations and impact of well-being advocacy today. While history does not determine exactly what happiness is, it provides an active basis for assessing some of our own assumptions and limitations. Thinking about the subject historically may contribute to constructive efforts to promote well-being, on a social as well as individual basis.

10　*Introduction*

Appendix

World Happiness Report Selected Rankings 2019

Rank	Country
1	Finland
2	Denmark
3	Norway
4	Iceland
5	Netherlands
6	Switzerland
7	Sweden
8	New Zealand
9	Canada
10	Austria
11	Australia
12	Costa Rica
13	Israel
14	Luxemburg
15	United Kingdom
16	Ireland
17	Germany
18	Belgium
19	United States of America
20	Czech Republic
23	Mexico
24	France
25	Taiwan
31	Panama
39	Trinidad-Tobago
54	South Korea
58	Japan
68	Russia
79	Turkey
93	China
140	India
149	Syria
150	Malawi
151	Yemen
152	Rwanda
153	Tanzania
154	Afghanistan
155	Central African Republic
156	South Sudan

Helliwell et al. (2019).

Further Reading (and Watching)

For a rich overview with a primarily Western focus:
McMahon, Darrin. *Happiness: A History* (New York: Atlantic Monthly Press, 2006).
Several introductions to the growing field of the history of emotion provide a
context for historical work on happiness:

Boddice, Rob. *The History of Emotions* (Manchester: Manchester University Press, 2018).

Matt, Susan J., and Peter N. Stearns. *Doing Emotions History,* (Champaign: University of Illinois Press, 2013).

Oatley, Keith. *Emotions: A Brief History* (Malden, MA: Blackwell, 2004).

Plamper, Jan, and Keith Tribe. *History of Emotions : An Introduction* First edition (New York: Oxford University Press, 2015).

Reddy, William. *The Navigation of Feeling: A Framework for the History of Emotions* (Cambridge: Cambridge Univ. Press, 2001).

Rosenwein, Barbara H., and Riccardo Cristiani. *What Is the History of Emotions?* (Cambridge: Polity Press, 2018).

On the question of Japanese and American culture:

Markus, Hazel R., and Shinobu Kitayama. "Culture and the Self." *Psychological Review* 98 (1991), 224–258.

On issues of defining happiness:

Gilbert, Dan. *Stumbling on Happiness* (New York: Knopf, 2006).

For the international polls:

Bruni, Luigino, and Pier Luigi Porta. *Handbook on the Economics of Happiness* (Cheltenham: Edward Elgar, 2007).

Helliwell, John F., Richard Layard, and Jeffrey Sachs. *World Happiness Report 2019* (New York: Sustainable Development Solutions Network, 2019).

Helliwell, John F., Richard Layard, Jeffrey Sachs, and Jan-Emmanuel De Neve, eds. *World Happiness Report 2020* (New York: Sustainable Development Solutions Network, 2020).

Mathews, Gordon, and Carolina Izquierdo, eds. *Pursuits of Happiness: Well-Being in Anthropological Perspective* (New York: Berghahn Books, 2010).

On historical inputs for the current wellbeing (positive psychology) movement:

McMahon, Darrin, ed., *History and Human Flourishing* (New York: Oxford University Press, 2020).

Stearns, Peter N. "History and Human Flourishing: Using the Past to Address the Present." In Louis Tay and James Pawelski (Eds.), *The Handbook of Positive Psychology on the Arts and Humanities: Theory and Research* (Oxford and New York: Oxford University Press, 2020).

Consult also:

Happy. Directed by: Roko Belic (San Jose, CA: Wadi Rum Films, 2011).

2 Psychological Basics

Happiness is hard to define, even in our own lives. A variety of eminent thinkers, through centuries of human history, have commented on how elusive the emotion is, how much its definition varies from one person to the next. This is a challenge for any student of happiness, but there is one discipline that, particularly in recent decades, has worked hard to gain greater precision. Psychologists have not fully resolved the mysteries of happiness – why for example two people in very similar objective situations report very different levels of happiness – but their work does provide some foundation for the subject. Scholars in the discipline have been trying to define key characteristics of happiness for some time.

To be sure, a movement in recent decades, labeled Positive Psychology, has made the subject a particular priority, arguing that the discipline had been spending too much time on mental health issues and negative emotions; we will come back to this in Chapter 13. But even before this, psychologists had established some parameters for an understanding of happiness, which can contribute to other kinds of inquiry.

They have definitely made some gains. For instance, an early effort in the field assumed that youth and low aspirations were essential prerequisites for happiness. Young people, it was argued, are particularly healthy and perhaps particularly hopeful; not wanting very much makes it easier to be content (a theme that we will encounter at various points in history). However, more careful observation and experiment have cast doubt on both propositions. Young people are often fairly happy, but so, surprisingly, are old people, despite greater health problems and more limited life expectancies. And, depending on personal emotional makeup and the extent of hope, people striving ambitiously for more can be happy as well.

The goal in this chapter, summarizing some psychological work on happiness, is to offer a further initial orientation, on a subject that can be hard to pin down – without pretending that the result is a definitive, once-and-for-all statement. Psychologists themselves still disagree about some key points – for example, the extent of genetic predisposition in the individual experience of happiness. Further, a history of happiness must emphasize the ways the emotion, and even expressions such as smiling or laughing, can vary and change, rather than seizing on a single definition

Psychological Basics 13

of the experience. Psychology, in contrast, often implies a rather uniform human phenomenon, or purely individual variables. Still, the discipline can guide some initial thoughts about the subject, before we turn to the greater complexities of the historical record.

What is happiness for? One good question, which is less obvious than it might seem, simply involves the purpose of happiness. Most people may want it (we will see that representatives of many cultures say this, one way or another), but this does not mean they always know what good it does. However, at least since the work of Charles Darwin, a number of psychologists have been at pains to try to figure out how particular emotions help the human species, and this is a useful first step in thinking about happiness.

Many psychologists argue that there are certain "basic" emotions, innate to the human species (and possibly some other animals as well) that reveal themselves through standard facial expressions. Happiness is on every basics list, if only because there is such a clear way to express it through smiling, and because this expression, in turn, is universally recognized whatever the local culture. Presumably, facial expressions were vital to human interactions well before language was invented, and we still rely on them heavily.

The realization that happiness is basic makes the question of its function all the more compelling. We know what fear is for – to prepare for flight from danger – and we know the basic function of anger; but what about happiness?

The most compelling answer is that happiness helps us realize that something we are doing is working out well and we should keep doing it, at least recurrently, whether the "it" is a personal relationship or some aspect of a job or a rewarding sport or entertainment activity or a particular form of prayer. Happiness provides emotional reinforcement. Happiness results from the achievement of one's goals – again, in a variety of life's categories, and encourages further efforts in the same direction.

By the same token, happiness helps counter other, more troubling emotions, like fear or anger, which are also useful but which are by definition disruptive. Indeed, a key aspect of psychologists' research on varied levels of happiness centers on how different individuals manage to cope with disruptive emotions and keep them in check, generating greater happiness as a result. Another illustration of this balancing function of happiness: it helps lower blood pressure.

Finally, happiness may help individuals relate more successfully with other people; we are a sociable species, and happiness may facilitate the relationships we need. Smiling, for example, can be a useful approach to strangers, predisposing them to constructive interactions. We will see that some cultures emphasize this function of happiness more than others; too much random happiness may seem bizarre, depending on the value system. But it is probably fair to grant some sociability function for happiness.

14 Psychological Basics

Basic definition. Psychologists have tried to push beyond the fairly obvious proposition that happy people "feel good". A happy person manages to maximize certain supportive or positive emotions, like joy and pride, and minimize emotions that are more painful. But that finding, though true, does not necessarily advance understanding very much.

In general, happiness involves a combination of external circumstance and internal, personal reactions. This is one reason that the emotion varies so much from one person to the next. Some people see their lives overwhelmed by bad luck or a particular misfortune, while others figure out active coping strategies. One study examined workers involved in repetitious motions on an assembly line, endlessly repeating procedures that could be extremely boring; some workers, instead of yielding to the boredom, kept experimenting with more efficient hand motions or developed pride in exceeding the expected pace, and were quite happy as a result. "It's better than anything else," one worker reported: "It's better than watching TV."

One approach – actually, a very old one, because philosophers have been working on this for a long time – distinguishes between "hedonic" and "eudaimonic" happiness. The hedonic argument sees happiness simply as maximization of pleasure and greatest possible avoidance of pain; and because each individual has his or her own definitions of pleasure and pain, this approach is fairly subjective. Eudaimonic approaches, in contrast, emphasize a wider definition of what is good for a person, recognizing among other things that some people may think they feel happy doing very harmful things; here, some objective conditions, like positive relationships with others or virtuous activity, go into the real meaning of happiness whatever a person's individual likes or dislikes. Many psychologists, like many philosophers before them, end up seeing happiness as a combination of both approaches.

In recent decades, many psychologists, trying to make happiness more objectively measurable, introduced the idea of "subjective well-being", or SWB. This approach may allow some attention to objective circumstances, like how many friends a person has or how healthy she is, but it focuses primarily on self-reports, what people say about how happy they are or how happy a particular kind of experience makes them. (This approach helps explain the excitement about polling data, which after all depend primarily on whether people say they are happy.) Researchers in this vein admit all sorts of problems about self-report: people may misremember, they may try to please the pollster – a key problem in cultures that place a high premium on seeming to be cheerful; their mood may vary unpredictably. But in final analysis, this approach argues that what people say about how happy they are is an inescapable feature of happiness research.

Some researchers make a distinction between "life satisfaction" and SWB. Here, subjective well-being reflects temporary states, whether a person is feeling happy at any given moment; whereas life satisfaction involves tapping into a longer view, less subject to fluctuation. "Life satisfaction",

Psychological Basics 15

plus the fact that many people learn better coping skills over time – like how to deal with anger – may help explain why, in many societies today, older people are among the happiest age categories.

Psychologists report one other important finding about happiness, though it too is fairly obvious: no one is happy all the time. A "happy life" always involves fluctuations and balances. The emphasis on a person's "coping strategies", as part of SWB, highlights the importance of recognizing and dealing with challenging experiences and emotions and not being overwhelmed by them.

Many leading happiness researchers, such as Ed Diener, also argue that most people are in fact fairly happy, high on a life satisfaction scale – across cultures and objective circumstances, at least in the contemporary world. Most people, in other words, are predisposed to at least mild levels of positive moods and happiness. One study, for example, reports that in 86% of the various countries studied, people self-report at over 50% on a happiness scale. Another way to put this: people have an impressive ability to find a certain amount of happiness even in challenging situations, which helps explain why they are able to keep going. Thus, for example, people paralyzed in a car accident, after initial depression, soon revert to their previous happiness level.

Happiness researchers have also tried to deal with interesting questions about the relationship between happiness and constructive action. It might be possible to argue, for example, that happy people are particularly naïve and selfish, ignoring the world's many overwhelming problems in favor of pursuing their own narrow pleasure menus. In contrast, positive psychologists work to demonstrate that happy people are more productive not just in terms of personal success but in terms of social outcomes as well. They are more altruistic than average. Quite possibly many happy people seek to combine personal pleasure and with social responsibility.

This issue goes back to the wider social functions of happiness. Happy people tend to make the people around them happier – both because happy people usually behave constructively (or even virtuously, to use a word that risks sounding old-fashioned) *and* because their own moods are partially contagious. The idea that happiness involves service to others goes way back to older philosophies and religions, but it seems to have an empirical basis as well.

There is a tension, nevertheless, between viewing happiness as an individual emotion, centered on maximizing individual pleasure and fulfillment, and a more social approach. When happiness tells an individual that goals are being achieved and that he or she should keep going, the individual aspect may predominate. But happiness can also have a basic social dimension, assessed in terms not just of personal goals but effective relationships. In this latter aspect, happiness will tell a person to keep associating with others and show affection. The balance here will reflect personal values but it will also be shaped by the larger culture – the extent

16 *Psychological Basics*

to which the culture is individualistic or collectivist. This is a balance or tension that looms large in the history of happiness.

Genetics. Researchers have spent a lot of time arguing about genetics, or the extent to which a person's capacity for happiness is built into the personality at birth. At an extreme, some genetic determinists argue that telling a person to be happy is a worthless gesture, with the only result making a less-than-happy person feel even worse. It's all in the genes.

Thus studies of identical twins reveal remarkable similarities in emotional moods – including levels of happiness – even when the individuals involved have been raised separately and in very different circumstances. It was a Dutch twins' study that claimed about as much as 80% of happiness potential was genetically determined.

This finding is arguably rather pessimistic, leaving individuals little they can do about happiness, and most psychologists today do not go to such extremes. Even so, the figure of 50% determinism is widely accepted, as a precondition for an individual's potential for happiness, grumpiness or something in between. Some observers have noted that this very contemporary finding is in some ways a modern version of an older belief that happiness depends largely on luck. Genes or luck, nothing much to do about it.

To be sure, the genes involved have not been identified, and in all probability a considerable number of different genes are involved, complicating any systematic claims. Some of the genetic researchers themselves have backtracked a bit, arguing that even people born with gloomier dispositions can and should try to modify their fate. A few have even joined the parade of "how-to" books about happiness, discussed further in Chapter 13. After all, as cynics have noted, it is hard to sell a book that simply tells people they are doomed to their genetic fate. Indeed, there has been a considerable rebellion, since around 2000, against too much genetic pessimism – among other things, people note that modern medicines and other therapies can significantly modify the genetic emotional heritage.

For the historian of happiness, the genetics debate proves interesting but also somewhat distracting or misleading. The importance of individual predisposition can be granted, but it plays little role in an agenda that looks primarily at larger, collective patterns over time. Further, the genetic approach may not take adequate account of the variety of happiness goals that human societies have produced. Might an individual not predisposed to lots of "fun" flourish in a culture that highlights happiness in prayer and contemplation of the divine?

Most current psychologists, certainly, while making a brief bow to the geneticists, devote their primary attention to a how-to approach, emphasizing what we know about how people can achieve greater happiness. Many of their findings repeat ancient wisdom, as the more erudite and generous contemporary practitioners admit. Some may be more culturally or historically specific than the psychologists realize – when it comes to matters like consumerism, for example; this is a problem to which we must return.

Psychological Basics 17

But the conventional list can nevertheless be helpful, both as an indication of the state of current psychological knowledge and as a checklist which, with due caution, may serve as a useful historical guide as well.

Desires and state of mind. As psychologists debate the best options to achieve happiness, they grapple with several approaches. One tack, called desire theory, amplifies the hedonist explanation of happiness. People who figure out how to maximize their desires, and limit frustration of desire, are the happiest. This approach is popular with many economists, who use standard of living measurements to determine social good. It also seems to resonate in modern, consumer-oriented societies. And it may appeal to a popular belief as well, that the best way to be happy is to get more of what one wants. This approach, further, places great stock in external circumstance, like levels of wealth, marital status, and so on.

Against this, and again reflecting many earlier philosophical and religious emphases, other authorities tout the importance of internal disposition. They point to studies showing how different individuals register very different happiness levels despite the same objective conditions – for example, students reacting to the same grade for a course. Here, within reason, happiness depends less on what happens to us than on how we respond. And, the argument goes on, there are many things that people can do to improve their mental outlook – including, as positive psychologists insist, learning to pay more attention to the good things that happen in life.

A preliminary list. The catalog of those factors contributing to happiness over which individuals have some discretion is neither long nor, in the main, very surprising, but it is worth keeping in mind before diving into the history of happiness.

Health is a vital component, with all the usual accompaniments in terms of eating habits, sleep, and appropriate levels of exercise. Next on the list is self-esteem, a positive outlook, a willingness to forgive one's own mistakes. But, quite apart from the fact that this is not necessarily an easy category to work on, there are also warnings about too much attention to the self – an old problem for many religions as they sought to emphasize a different, more spiritual kind of happiness.

Healthy relationships with others figure high on the list, involving friendships and (often) family plus positive emotional links, extending also to emotional emphases such as love and gratitude. Loneliness is an enemy here, though some historians are pointing out that some cultures see loneliness as a positive attribute; this is complex territory. Most psychologists also believe that "virtuous" behavior – an altruistic outlook toward others, outright generosity – captures an important component of happiness as well, in contrast to arguments that stress a more selfish approach.

The factor of religion, or what one happiness psychologist called the "connection to a larger beyond", also enters into the equation. Studies in the United States often find that people with religious beliefs and practices are happier than others. On the other hand, most of the polled happiest

18 *Psychological Basics*

countries in the world, like the Scandinavian nations, are unusually secular. Here is another conundrum that warrants historical attention – including, obviously, the type of religion involved. We will return to this tension in Chapter 15.

Hope and aspiration. Most happiness psychologists believe that a demonstrable connection exists between hope and happiness. Certainly, many people are able fairly cheerfully to go through uncomfortable periods in life armed with a firm hope that things will be better at some later point. The ability to trade short-term denial for longer-term happiness is an important attribute. On the other hand, hope can be vulnerable, and when frustrated can lead to greater unhappiness. Further, the nature of hope is very much a historical variable: hope for salvation in a life to come? Hope for a better society? Hope for personal fame and fortune?

Psychologists have also demonstrated, somewhat accidentally, that the relationship between happiness and hope depends not just on personality, but on social class. A famous experiment in 1972 presented children with the choice between having a marshmallow immediately, and waiting ten minutes with the marshmallow available but not consumed – after which the prudent child would get two. The results showed that some children could use hope to override short-term satisfaction and gain greater happiness in the long run. These children were arguably destined for greater life success. But in fact more recent work shows this was not what the experiment proved. Rather, lower-class kids consumed the marshmallow right away because life had already taught them to seize happiness whenever possible, because it might not be available later on. The nature and possibility of hope, in other words, constitute a social and not just a personal variable – like other aspects of happiness.

Aspiration levels pose a similar conundrum. Many cultures have urged people to be content with what they have, and some psychologists, also, wonder if low aspirations help avoid disappointment and therefore contribute to happiness. On the other hand, a sense of building for the future, sometimes not just for oneself but for one's children, can be a powerful component of happiness. In some cultures, lack of aspiration may be seen as an unhappy characteristic. Here, as with hope, we are almost certainly dealing with a cultural and historical variable, though possibly with some individual personality factors folded in as well.

Hope and aspiration may be social as well as individual factors. Some cultures not only define distinctive hopes but may depend on different levels of hope, which in turn affect the way individuals within the culture assess their own happiness. Here, individuals are urged to sustain their happiness in the belief that the whole society or group will gain greater justice or greater religious enlightenment later on. Indeed, most of the factors on the list of contributions to happiness have a social as well as personal dimension, as in the extent, for example, to which particular societies actively encourage health or promote familial affection.

The downsides of happiness. Psychologists who work on happiness offer a few cautions, along with their attempts to figure out how to promote more positive outcomes. These, too, reflect some peculiarly modern and Western characteristics, but they are worth noting and may have some value in assessing historical developments.

For happiness, like all emotions, requires some constraints. An unthinking commitment to happiness, particularly short-term, sensual happiness, can lead to risky behavior. Excessive happiness may dampen creativity; while happiness usually improves responses to a social environment it may also promote routine behaviors, rather than encouraging innovation. On another front, happiness can simply be inappropriate, for example in situations that call for displays of grief.

But the greatest caution applies to what many psychologists see as an unrealistic effort to seek happiness too regularly and too explicitly, inviting disappointment. Too much attention to happiness and unduly frequent questioning about whether one is happy or not are actually counterproductive. Somewhat ironically, many of the researchers who devote themselves to understanding happiness urge that many people make their lives more difficult by thinking about happiness too often.

A further agenda. Many specialists in this branch of psychology urge that there is still much to learn. Tensions in the field, for example between the hedonistic and the more altruistic approaches, have not been fully resolved; what balance generates the more genuine happiness? A number of experiments lead to some truly dubious conclusions. For example, some researchers recently tried to demonstrate that happiness involves careful attunement to the surrounding emotional context. "Feeling right", or being in tune with the relevant group, might be more important than feeling personal pleasure, and some experiments have supported this conclusion. But there is an obvious problem: what if the group involved is dominated by fear or hatred? Conformity to this type of emotional context might be a very destructive kind of happiness, perhaps making a mockery of the whole concept.

But the main agenda of psychological research on happiness currently centers on building more empirical evidence for the attitudes and behaviors that will most predictably enhance individual happiness – around qualities like curiosity (good), resilience (good), gratitude (good), trying to correct one's weaknesses (probably bad, if not balanced by even greater attention to one's strengths). Some of the ongoing findings are fairly predictable, but others strike out in unexpected directions. Here, psychological research becomes part of the larger contemporary, and increasingly global, approach to happiness, as more and more groups and even governments seek not only to measure but to generate happiness.

Psychology and history. Psychological and historical inquiries into an emotion like happiness have an uneasy but potentially productive relationship. To a historian, some psychological findings seem far more limited by a specific time and place than psychologists themselves often realize.

20 *Psychological Basics*

Thus it may be true that too many people, today, spend too much time asking themselves if they are happy or not; but it is unlikely that this was a significant problem in many periods in the past, or in many other cultures today, where happiness is simply less frequently discussed. Happy people, today, are more likely to enjoy personal success, which in turn supports happiness; but was this true, say, in the 17th century, or in India today when happiness is less routinely expected or defined in other ways? Historical approaches to happiness introduce more realistic complexity into some psychological findings, and they also explain how some current psychological patterns have emerged from a somewhat different past. In this sense, they provide greater understanding than psychology alone can offer.

On the other hand, there is no question that historians can also benefit from many of the findings and clarifications concerning happiness that recent psychological research has provided. And, in the end, the two disciplines share many of the same basic questions about this elusive phenomenon.

Further Reading

Biswas-Diener, Robert, Todd B. Kashdan, and Laura A. King. "Two Traditions of Happiness Research, Not Two Distinct Types of Happiness." *The Journal of Positive Psychology* 4, no. 3 (May 1, 2009): 208–211.

Diener, Ed, Eunkook M. Suh, Richard E. Lucas, and Heidi L. Smith. "Subjective Well-Being: Three Decades of Progress." *Psychological Bulletin* 125, no. 2 (1999): 276–302.

Diener, Ed, Satoshi Kanazawa, Eunkook M. Suh, and Shigehiro Oishi. "Why People Are in a Generally Good Mood." *Personality and Social Psychology Review* 19, no. 3 (August 2015): 235–256.

Diener, Ed, Samantha J. Heintzelman, Kostadin Kushlev, Louis Tay, Derrick Wirtz, Lesley D. Lutes, and Shigehiro Oishi. "Findings All Psychologists Should Know from the New Science on Subjective Well-Being." *Canadian Psychology/Psychologie Canadienne* 58, no. 2 (May 2017): 87–104.

Diener, Ed, Richard E. Lucas, and Shigehiro Oishi. "Advances and Open Questions in the Science of Subjective Well-Being." *Collabra: Psychology* 4, no. 1 (May 1, 2018): 15.

Fredrickson, Barbara L. "Positive Emotions Broaden and Build." In E. Ashby Plant & P.G. Devine (Eds.), *Advances on Experimental Social Psychology*, 47, 1–53. (Burlington: Academic Press, 2013).

Gruber, June, Iris B. Mauss, and Maya Tamir. "A Dark Side of Happiness? How, When, and Why Happiness Is Not Always Good." *Perspectives on Psychological Science* 6, no. 3 (May 2011): 222–233.

Lykken, David. *Happiness: The Nature and Nurture of Joy and Contentment* (New York: St. Martin's, 1999).

Myers, David. *The Pursuit of Happiness: Who Is Happy, and Why* (New York: Morrow, 1992).

Ryff, Carol D. "Happiness Is Everything, or Is It? Explorations on the Meaning of Psychological Wellbeing." *Journal of Personality and Social Psychology* 57 (1989): 1069–1081.

Part I

The Agricultural Age

Agricultural economies began to emerge about 11,000 years ago, and while they gained ground only gradually they ultimately encompassed the bulk of the world's population. As a result, at least 6,000 years of the human experience can legitimately be grouped under the heading of an agricultural age, when most major societies were shaped by the nature of the agricultural economy. Only about 300 years ago did the hold of agriculture begin to yield to the rise of an industrial alternative.

Many world history surveys divide the long Agricultural Age into several main segments: a formative period; the emergence of initial, river-valley civilizations; a classical period, when expanded cultural and political zones developed in China, India, the Middle East, and the Mediterranean, from about 600 BCE to 500/600 CE; a postclassical period after the collapse of the great classical empires, dominated by the vigorous missionary religions but also growing trade; and finally an early modern period, 1450–1750, characterized by still further commercial growth and the inclusion of the Americas in interregional commerce.

This conventional periodization contributes to what we know about the history of happiness, but does not fully define it. The chapters that follow simply focus instead on three very rough chronological divisions: the emergence of agriculture itself; the classical period, where several major philosophical systems grappled with the definition of happiness; and finally (with two chapters) the substantial impact of the great religions but also the fuller development of popular entertainments – extending from about 300 CE through the 17th century.

3 Early Agricultural Society

Here's the possibility: early humans, living in hunting and gathering societies, were not only probably pretty happy, but also happier than many people in societies that arose later, amid more complex economies. Most specifically, the rise of agriculture, though it gradually displaced hunting and gathering in many areas, probably worsened the human condition in a number of measurable ways, creating new possibilities for unhappiness. And if this is so, it may explain two kinds of developments later on: first, compensatory arrangements that sought to create new opportunities for happiness, usually outside the constraints of ordinary daily life. And second, a new need to talk about what happiness really means, which would become a considerable preoccupation of intellectual and religious leaders in many rising civilizations.

Here's the complication, before we turn to the evidence: we simply cannot conclusively prove this hypothesis, for we have no direct records of humans' emotional state before the invention of writing or more elaborate art. It is indeed quite likely that these early societies did not generate an explicit idea of happiness at all, since, while there were many specific problems, the normal conditions of life could be judged to be fairly satisfactory, with little need to single out particularly happy circumstances. No special effort or formal concepts were required. This is also the conclusion of a number of anthropologists who study some of the hunting and gathering groups that still survive: they lack words or beliefs about happiness, but they live in conditions, and with expectations, that are consistent with considerable happiness in fact.

This is not the first time we've confronted the dilemma of trying to figure out if people are happy even though they may not say so very directly: interpreting contemporary Japanese satisfaction, despite rather modest happiness polling ratings, involves a bit of a leap of faith. Contemporary Western standards lead to expectations that happy people should be willing to talk about their happiness, and when they do not, as least as vigorously as Westerners do, there is something of a dilemma. Yet it was suggested, briefly, in Chapter 1 that the Japanese may well be about as happy as Westerners are, given the objective conditions of their lives, despite different polling results. It's culture, not "reality", that

Early Agricultural Society 23

creates a different impression – though those cultural differences make it difficult to be sure.

The same dilemma, but on a much wider scale, applies to evaluating happiness in hunting and gathering societies, when we are trying to assess conditions and attitudes vastly different from our own. It is vital to remember the amount of sheer speculation involved, in arguments about a group's emotional experience even where explicit claims, or even explicit vocabularies, are lacking. But a number of historians, and certainly many anthropologists, find a happiness assessment plausible, and if it is, it puts the later history of happiness, and efforts to define happiness, in a really new light.

Again, the basic argument is simple: many hunting and gathering groups, though lacking clear concepts or vocabularies around happiness, were and are in fact quite happy, often freer from some of the challenges to happiness that more complex societies experience.

A First Cut

We can begin with the historical speculations (derived from work in several disciplines). Here are some of the advantages of hunting and gathering societies, from what we can glean from archeological and anthropological records. Their populations enjoyed relatively good nutrition, high in protein and free from refined carbohydrates – thus better than the average diets both in agricultural and industrial societies. The popularity of "paleo" diets by health-conscious people today testifies to the advantages involved (which also raises the issue of why so many modern people, who can afford alternatives, find that unhealthy diets make them happier). Evidence from skeletal and dental remains show that hunters and gatherers were less likely to suffer from malnutrition than their peasant counterparts once agriculture arrived. They were also, on average, taller. Life expectancy wasn't bad if one survived infancy – admittedly, a darker spot; people living into their sixties were common. Infectious diseases did not seriously affect these groups that moved around in small bands, and outright epidemics were rare to nonexistent. To be sure, medical interventions were not available when illness did strike, though knowledge of herbal remedies was extensive. Wars were also rare, though there is some debate about this. The first clear evidence of war dates from only 14,000 years ago, toward the end of the hunter-gatherer period when crowding may have begun to increase in a few regions: a cluster of skeletal remains, all in one spot, suggest violent conflict in one location in northeastern Africa. Ordinarily, hunter-gatherers responded to the threat of violence by simply moving away – they operated amid abundant space. Really long-distance displacements would be challenging, but often a shift to an adjacent territory was possible. After all, on the eve of agriculture there were only about 10 million people scattered over the entire world. Most groups also

24 The Agricultural Age

developed a number of explicit practices aimed at keeping peace with their neighbors: formal gift exchanges and frequent intermarriage headed the list. While usually scattered, hunting and gathering bands in some societies might meet annually for some collective ceremonies, usually around heralding the sun either at its lowest or highest points in the year. Yearly festivals of this sort, with some feasting, were common around sites like Stonehenge, in England. Here was another way to promote positive relationships. Good nutrition; fairly good health; considerable and indeed probably normal peace – not a bad list.

The societies were also relatively egalitarian. A few distinctions may have existed for some leaders; some skeletons have been discovered with ornamental jewelry, probably not available for most people. But there were few social distinctions and little economic inequality overall. This could well have minimized envy and resentment – and one of the topics to consider in later societies, including our own, is the extent to which inequality causes active unhappiness in more complex structures, not an easy issue. Men and women had different economic roles, but both were extremely important to the food supply and were recognized as such. On this basis women had some voice in group affairs. Gender issues almost certainly less troubling than they would become later on.

Some scholars go on to speculate that considerable freedom existed as well. Certainly there were few constraints on individuals who decided to leave a group and strike out on their own, though survival might be an issue. Among Australian aborigines, a tradition of "walkabout" covered individuals who decided to travel around for a while, for whatever reason, then returning to their kin. Group norms might constrain behavior in these small clusters, though some have argued that shaming – so common in more complex societies – may have been less intense. Sexual habits, at least in some cases, were less constrained than would be the case later on.

Three obvious caveats to all this: first, there's a lot we don't know, though this historical sketch is substantially confirmed and amplified by more purely contemporary anthropological studies, discussed below. We can assume for example that these groups normally spent relatively little time at work, given normal availability of food, but we do not know directly.

Second, there were certainly drawbacks in hunting-and-gathering life. Individual violence was not infrequent: while the collective graves caused by war seem rare (though this may of course mean they simply have not been found), individual skeletons with heads bashed in are not uncommon. To be sure, specific implements designed primarily for violence do not emerge until, again, very late in the hunter-gatherer period (the first explicit weapon, not much use for hunting, was a mace), but obviously hunting apparatus or found objects like rocks could be used earlier on. There was also danger from animals, though the invention of fire and the domestication of dogs – both occurring well before the end of this

Early Agricultural Society   25

period – undoubtedly helped a bit. Depending on the region, getting through harsh winters could be challenging, though the nutritional evidence suggests considerable success. This society, in other words, had a number of measurable advantages but it was not a paradise, which legitimately complicates speculations about happiness.

And finally: we don't know that these people were happy. There is no direct evidence available to deal with this question. We can surmise that they were reasonably satisfied and probably had little sense of alternatives, which may be a component of a certain kind of happiness. The historians who have painted the brightest pictures of these societies generally assume that their inhabitants were largely content but probably lacked any explicit concept of happiness, for there was no need for one. Conditions were normally fairly good, and there was no active sense of alternatives and hence little frustration. But this picture rests on informed guesswork.

More from Anthropologists

A number of anthropologists, looking at the small groups of huntergatherers still existing today, say much the same thing as historians do, but since they can observe more directly they have some additional bits of evidence.

Here are the key conclusions from a study of the Khoisan or Bushman people of the Kalihari desert, in contemporary Namibia and Botswana, based on years of observation. The first point emphasizes the balance between work and other activities: these people work about 15 hours a week on average, leaving the rest of the time free for socializing with family and friends, loafing and napping, and pursuing various hobbies. Children, too, are relatively free from formal obligations, leaving lots of time for relatively unsupervised play; they learn some skills and social habits, of course, but on an informal basis.

Life is not trouble-free. There are personal tragedies and sadness, including death. Fighting occasionally occurs, particularly after drinking. Some seasons are more challenging than others, in a region where there are considerable periods without rain.

But there are relatively few needs, and most of them, normally, can be taken care of rather easily. The society has developed great skill in hunting and in identifying the plants that are useful for food and medicine. The people are well adapted to their environment and comfortable with it. They also strongly emphasize group solidarity and deliberately play down individual achievement or blame. When a hunter returns from a productive hunt, for example, he will minimize his success rather than trying to go one-up on his colleagues: hence, arguably, few problems with envy or resentment. The society is also relatively unstratified, with few gradations in wealth. While men and women are seen as different, women's contributions are clearly recognized and their opinions valued.

26   *The Agricultural Age*

Much of this, not surprisingly, echoes the conclusions of historians we have already examined. But the anthropologists can add in a few other points, concerning the attitudes involved. There is little sense of striving. These people do not think in terms of improving their lives, and in fact they don't think much about happiness. They have words for joy or sadness, but not for "being happy" in any long-term sense. The constancy of life, not aspiration, is the dominant theme. Everything is oriented to the present, on meeting immediate needs. The people don't wonder if they are doing better than their ancestors did – in fact there is little interest in ancestors at all. Nor do they compare themselves to other groups or individuals. The key, obviously, is a distinctive culture that provides a fairly steady sense of contentment without the formal apparatus other societies, including our own, commonly associate with happiness.

Other anthropologists extend this argument in additional ways. Much has been made, for example in dealing with Australian aboriginal culture, of the deep connections to nature expressed in animist religions – connections that many later, more sophisticated religions would lose sight of in developing ideas about more remote, and sometimes angrier and demanding, gods. Anthropologists also comment further on the importance of group solidarity and a sense of belonging.

These overall characterizations are not uncontested. First, some anthropologists shy away from characterizations about one type of society being happier than another, arguing that the judgments involved are too complex and that most societies forge some valid notions of happiness. Second, and more specifically, some scholars stress the hardships of life, the constant struggles against predators – both animal and insect, the periodic bouts of collective violence that some contemporary groups engage in. (Given greater constraints on space, war may well be more common in contemporary hunter-gatherer societies than it was earlier on, though there are some contemporary groups that avoid it completely.) Many recent studies emphasize the complexity of some hunting and gathering societies, as against generalizations that imply a standard primitive simplicity. It is quite possible, indeed, that generalizations about *all* current hunting and gathering groups are off the mark, that some are markedly happier and more peaceful than others. The subject, clearly, is complicated. And it is vital to remember that even in the most positive arguments about happiness, we are assuming emotional experiences that the groups themselves do not articulate, and this carries some risk.

Nevertheless, it does seem clear that old assumptions about the predominant nastiness and brutality of our hunting and gathering past are really mistaken. Life could be fairly good, particularly because definitions of needs were kept modest. Material conditions had positive features and, perhaps even more important, a culture could be developed that promoted satisfaction over aspiration. As the more optimistic anthropologists suggest, modern people, casting about for ways to make themselves feel

Early Agricultural Society   27

happier, have undoubtedly created a false sense of early humanity, with arguments about life being (in the words of the English philosopher Thomas Hobbes) "rude, brutish and short." It is time to reconsider that prop and to base our ideas about the history of happiness on a less linear, more complex foundation.

Characteristics of Agricultural Societies

This, then, brings us back to history, and the basic question: what happened to happiness when, about 12,000 years ago, some groups began to turn away from hunting and gathering and develop agriculture, a dramatically new economic system that would, though very gradually, gain ascendancy in many parts of the world and that certainly began to support the largest concentrations of people.

For the record, agriculture arose separately in at least three places (Black Sea region, south China, Central America), which certainly suggests that some real needs for change must have developed in several previously hunting and gathering regions. And from these three centers agricultural systems would fan out widely; innovations on the southern edge of the Black Sea, for example, ultimately reached not only the entire Middle East, but also North Africa, the Indian subcontinent, southern Europe (and then from these spots ultimately further still). But the spread was arguably surprisingly slow; it would be several thousand years, for example, before southern Europe was drawn in, despite being reasonably close, geographically, to the initial agricultural center. Undoubtedly one key explanation for this involves the still-limited level of interregional contact and the difficulties of long-distance transportation. Arguably, however, the frequent lags reflected conscious resistance of many hunting and gathering groups who were aware of agriculture and simply did not want to make the conversion. Resistance, of course, could simply reflect stubborn attachments – as among men who did not want to give up the excitement and prestige of relying on hunting for a farming life that might seem prosaic by contrast. But it also could express a real understanding that agriculture, in many ways, could make life worse (possibly including an inchoate sense that it would reduce human contentment).

For there were, in fact, a number of drawbacks, as against the characteristics of hunting and gathering. On the most basic level, diets deteriorated for most people (whose stature, as a result, declined). Agriculture produced more food than hunting and gathering did, but it was of lower nutrient quality – more carbohydrates from grains and (in the Americas) potatoes, but far less protein – even with the domestication of some animals. Levels of disease went up: most agriculture involved settled communities that were, as well, somewhat larger than hunting and gathering bands. Hence more opportunity for contagion and local pollution. As most agricultural societies also came to engage in some long-distance trade – which had its

28   *The Agricultural Age*

advantages, in terms of expanding the variety of goods available – periodic plagues became a normal feature of life as well. And all this involves not only changes in material existence, but emotional life as well, most notably in expanding opportunities for fear and grief.

Work was harder. Farming requires longer hours than hunting, though there is downtime in winter. In some cases, the physical demands of planting and harvesting might be more intense as well. This is a huge distinction.

Wars became more common. Agricultural societies accumulated some surplus, which meant targets for raiding. When (ultimately) formal states emerged as well, this brought professional soldiers and, in some cases, rulers eager to make their mark through conquest. Of course there were countervailing impulses: many agricultural communities worked hard to build defenses, many rulers sought peace. Agriculture itself suffered from war. This was one reason, in the early centuries of the new economic system, that troops would cease battle during harvest time, to go home to help – a nicety that was fairly soon abandoned in favor of military goals.

Agriculture everywhere massively increased inequality, creating growing gulfs between a wealthy upper class and the masses of the laboring population (which might in some cases also be burdened by compulsory systems such as slavery or serfdom). Gaps also developed between urbanites (though they were relatively small in number) and the rural population. Gender inequality was at least as intense, and perhaps an even more vivid contrast with hunting and gathering conditions. For several reasons, all agricultural societies introduced patriarchal systems that held women to be markedly inferior to men, tended to emphasize their domestic roles and confinements, and barred them (with individual exceptions) from any public or political functions.

Small wonder that some recent scholars have argued, with Jerrod Diamond, that the transition to agriculture was "the worst mistake in the history of the human race". Small wonder as well that some of the historians who have focused on happiness contend that in all probability, the transition also reduced the level of human contentment – making happiness more problematic than it had been with hunting and gathering.

Causes and Complexities

The downsides of agriculture were very real, but they were not of course the whole story. The bleak picture sketched here raises the obvious question: if agriculture created so many problems, why did people turn to it in the first place? This then leads to the second, more subtle issue: what opportunities did people have to adapt, to seek and find happiness in these new conditions?

A third issue can be noted: some of the drawbacks of agriculture, particularly in terms of nutrition and disease, would be addressed subsequently,

Early Agricultural Society 29

with industrialization, when on average the material framework for human existence clearly began to improve. But this is for later, when we turn to the complex issues concerning happiness and modernity.

On agricultural society itself, there are several questions. First, why turn away from hunting and gathering at all? Early agricultural systems may have developed in part out of necessity, with no great thoughts about long-term impacts on material or emotional life. In some regions, climate changes may have reduced the amount of large game available for hunting; over-hunting itself might have contributed, for while hunter-gatherers were sensitive to the environment, they were capable of killing more animals than the system could bear. And as gatherers, women at least would have learned the potential of deliberately planting seeds rather than simply picking from the wild – an option that could help address any hunting crisis.

Then, whatever the initial spur, agriculture did bring one huge set of advantages: agricultural economies could produce a much greater quantity of food than hunting and gathering groups could provide, which led quite quickly to an unprecedented increase in human population. There is an irony here of course: the system generated larger numbers of people who may have faced far more problems than their ancestors had, and food supply itself could falter in periodic famines. But there is no doubt about the basics: in terms of sheer numbers of people, there was huge gain.

And this leads to two further factors that help explain the gradual spread of the system (despite continuing holdouts in regions that simply did not buy in). First, population numbers could generate force. We know that agriculture spread in Europe in part simply because groups from the Middle East, needing more space, migrated in and compelled adoption of the new system, converting or subduing hunting and gathering rivals. (This would also occur in North America, of course, much later on.) There was no conversion, no careful weighing of pros and cons, involved.

Second, it was quite possible that many people could take pride in the advancement of the species and, more specifically, in their own larger families. Boasting about reproductive prowess – and casting shame on the families that could not reproduce – was a common feature of agricultural societies, though men were more likely to brag than the women whose lives were more directly involved.

(It is worth noting that agricultural economies also facilitated the production of alcohol, and a few scholars, not entirely frivolously, have claimed this may have played a role in easing the burdens of the new economic system, particularly for men. Recipes for producing beer and fermented spirits unquestionably commanded some of the first uses of writing in several early civilizations. And the complex relationship between drinking and happiness becomes an issue from the early agricultural society to the present day.)

Down the line, agriculture also generated possibilities for creating small cities and supporting a fraction of the population available to do

30 *The Agricultural Age*

other kinds of work, producing tools, ornaments, even fine art. These possible advantages do not explain agriculture's first arrival – they lay in the future; but some preliminary innovations might factor in. More immediately, some scholars argue that in providing opportunities to settle down, to build more solid houses and amenities such as wells, even the earliest agriculture could have attracted some converts; but it is not clear that people accustomed to wandering a bit would find this advantageous.

Necessity; compulsion; some advantages clearly combined both to generate agriculture and to facilitate its dissemination. Where happiness levels fit into this equation remains elusive; no explicit comment is available, at least until much more recently when we can trace the tremendous discomfort experienced by some groups, for example among indigenous Americans, when pressed to abandon the hunt in favor of settled farming.

Adaptations and Inequalities

Most of the history of happiness from about 9,000 BCE until the 17th or 18th century CE involves trying to figure out how agricultural populations dealt with the constraints of their situation, capitalized on the advantages, or – in between – tried to figure out compensations. Still focused on the early stages of agriculture's introduction, two points stand out: new class distinctions and the impressive capacity of people to adapt.

First, early on, a minority of individuals – physically bigger, more forceful and aggressive, able to take over more land – began to carve out an upper class life that was, on average, measurably different from the conditions of the bulk of the population – even deliberately different. A decisive recent historical study has emphasized how, since the early days of agricultural civilization, a distinctive upper class has been an almost invariable feature of the social experience.

Food supply was better for this small group, particularly in terms of meat and protein. As one result, aristocrats and landlords were physically larger than their lower-class counterparts, taller by several inches on average. This size distinction would persist, in places like Great Britain, into the 1930s. And the difference could generate other advantages: bigger people could see themselves, and be seen, as naturally superior.

Disease was a problem for upper classes too; issues here were less easy to evade. But early on, wealthy groups had some opportunities to flee plagues; and their housing, more capacious, might provide a slight shield against the worst forms of contagion. They could also afford fancier tombs, if these offered some comfort.

This upper class routinely took greater advantage of the opportunity for large families; here is where male pride in substantial breeding showed through most clearly. In contrast, ordinary folk, without the means to

Early Agricultural Society 31

support too many offspring, faced greater tension. They wanted enough children to provide family labor and carry on the family line, and there could be pride here as well. But too many offspring would be disastrous, potentially ruining the family economy. Hence, in most agricultural societies, ordinary families had six to eight children (up to half of whom would die in infancy) and cringed at the prospect of exceeding this level (which in turn was about half of what an average family CAN breed, if it goes at the process without constraint). Periods of sexual abstinence were almost essential to keep numbers manageable, given the absence of control devices. But still, many families could overshoot; a clear response to this tension, again in many agricultural societies at least until the past millennium, was a high rate of infanticide.

It was the upper class, of course, that could also take the fullest advantage of new opportunities to acquire jewelry, fine artisanal products, and the most elaborate entertainments – though ordinary folk, particularly in the cities, might gain some access as well.

But this first reaction is, overall, fundamental: the constraints and opportunities of agriculture generated massive social distinctions. A minority was able to take special advantage and, surely, despite a host of problems, its members were far more likely to be and feel actively happy than their inferiors. Indeed, the opportunity to feel superior might itself generate a new sense of pleasure.

The second point, about adaptation, as we focus attention on the masses of the population, is trickier, and in some sense it will preoccupy us through several of the following chapters. Here is a basic analytical challenge: some of the problems we can identify, in our retrospective judgment and informed by what we know about the contrasts with earlier, hunting and gathering existence, may not always have appeared to be problems to those involved. More elaborate religions could also factor into popular calculations, in explaining the woes of ordinary life, as we will see in Chapter 5. (And we must not forget the possible pride in raising large numbers of children and a sense, however vague, of contributing to the species or the family lineage.)

The issue of nutritional quality, for example, is a problem we can see clearly in hindsight, but it was probably not consciously realized except amid outright famines. And we will see that agricultural people generated periodic opportunities, in festivals, to eat better and more abundantly than was normally possible, and the contrast may have been truly sweet. (Periodic rather than more routine pleasure may have been an important feature of agricultural life, and it might support an active sense of happiness through anticipation and recollection.)

Work could certainly be seen as a huge burden, though active memory of the greater leisure in hunting and gathering probably faded fairly quickly. But while the burden could not be denied, almost every agricultural society designed some holidays when work could recede and, above

32 The Agricultural Age

all, introduced some form of weekend – every five, or seven, or ten days, the length of the week varied. This was an entirely artificial unit of time, with no relation to any natural cycle. But it provided a recurrent day in which people could shift greater attention to worship, or to marketing, or simply to relaxing.

Growing and persistent inequality can sound ominous, and it would generate periodic social protest and individual unhappiness. But it could also prove acceptable, for a number of reasons. The idea that aristocrats were better than other folk, and deserved their relative good fortune, might be surprisingly widely accepted if the message was driven home persistently; the same held true for the idea of male superiority, which many children began learning literally from infancy. Or people could manage simply to ignore radical inequality in day-to-day life, tending to their own affairs; aristocrats, most obviously, were often distant figures, and women sometimes figured out ways to keep men away from their daily routines.

The main point is that human beings are surprisingly adaptable, and often find reasons for satisfaction and even dignity that they prefer to nagging discontent. Clearly, most people were certainly happy enough to seek to have children, to carry on – and from a species standpoint, this was the main requirement. It is important not to force our own value system on the past, and to assume unhappiness or dissatisfaction that people at the time did not experience.

To be sure, as we will see, there were plenty of observers, in many early civilizations, who talked about the whimsical balance between fortune and misfortune, and the lack of control most people had over their own fate. This certainly suggested some degree of uncertainty about the availability of happiness. The Chinese, particularly, frequently discussed the randomness of luck (while acknowledging that people should enjoy good luck if they found it). And there were darker visions still. A Persian thinker in the 6th century BCE voiced a sentiment that may well have been widely shared:

> Short as human life is, there is not a man in the world, here or elsewhere, who is happy enough not to wish – not only once but again and again – to be dead rather than alive. Troubles come, diseases afflict us, and this makes life, despite its brevity, seem all too long.

While we lack the direct evidence, on either side of the introduction of agriculture, to prove the claim that people were less happy than their counterparts had been in the simpler hunting and gathering economy, the probabilities are clear. At the least, it seems safe to claim that happiness became increasingly problematic, which is one reason that so many early intellectuals and religious figures would come to believe that they had to address the topic directly.

Early Agricultural Society 33

The Lure of a Past Golden Age

Amid the undeniable uncertainties and the amount of speculation required, given lack of explicit evidence of how the people who experienced the transition actually compared their agricultural lives to those of their near ancestors, there is one final type of data that may be particularly suggestive of an awareness of loss.

Almost all agricultural societies, as they developed oral and then written stories about human origins, created a deep belief in a past Golden Age, vastly superior to ordinary life in their own time and, in many renditions, clearly supremely happy – an age from which present-day society had deteriorated.

The Greek writer Hesiod, in the late 6th century BCE, painted the picture clearly in his book, *Works and Days*. Humanity's first age, which he called golden, featured people and gods mingling peacefully. People indeed lived like gods, without "sorrow of heart" "remote from toil and grief." They feasted joyfully, and grew old without losing their youthful appearance; when death occurred, it too was peaceful, as if going to sleep. "And they had all good things, for the fruitful earth unforced bore them fruit abundantly."

But the age did not last, and Hesiod described a steady decline to silver, bronze, heroic, and iron (his present day); Gods abandoned cohabitation with man after the silver age, because human greed and folly became too much to bear. Here was a clear descent in the quality of life and the availability of happiness.

Many later Greek writers, including Plato, picked up on the Golden Age idea, and it was also central to some of the writings of the leading Roman poet, Virgil. For Virgil, the first age, when people had just descended from the gods, also featured ease, but there was more. There was no private property – any boundary lines were "impious", because the earth gave its bounty freely. Another Roman writer, Ovid, added that this blissful period required no government or punishments, because people pursued the good naturally.

Somewhat similar visions emerged in other cultures. Hindu teachings also saw a procession of ages for humankind, though here there was a belief that they might recur in a cyclical fashion. A "First and Perfect" age was described in the great early Hindu epic, the *Mahabarata*. There was no buying and selling, there was "neither poor nor rich". Disease was absent, "there was no lessening with the years", "no sorrow, no fear". And people were supremely virtuous, readily abandoning earthly desires (a spiritual theme not present in the Greek and Roman visions). "It was the time when all people were happy."

A number of Native American peoples, such as the Cree and the Navajo, also ventured ideas of a past age when the gods moved among people and laid out basic truths about harmony with nature, peace, and equality. Here, the tone was more optimistic, holding that at some future point these virtues would be recaptured, as people came together to realize the ancient teachings.

34 *The Agricultural Age*

African creation stories often featured, again, the idea of an early existence that was prosperous and peaceful. Some added particular emphasis on the initial harmony between people and animals, which was then disrupted by human acts such as the invention of fire.

Confucius, writing in a time of internal strife and political disarray in China, also looked back to a better past, emphasizing that crucial ideas of harmony and balance had been developed centuries before. His vision was less grandiose than the Greek or Hindu golden age notions, focused more on the belief that an earlier political dynasty had established a just and peaceful order from which his own society has deteriorated. In this view, while it was vital to turn back to the ideas and models of a superior past, these might be recaptured by proper imitation in the present.

Traditions in the Middle East emphasized the perfection, but also the loss, of a golden age. Persian mythology generated the belief that in the earliest time, the world had been populated by gods who lived in prosperity and peace – another image of a lost golden age. Humanity initially flourished in a prosperous, divinely established garden that was a kind of paradise. Some scholars believe that this notion was then picked up by early Judaism and translated into one of the most influential of all, the fall-from-perfection scheme: the Garden of Eden and the human inability to sustain this perfection because of greed – a classic image of how happiness can be spoiled by irrational dissatisfaction. The word "Eden" itself may have been derived from an ancient Hebrew word for pleasure, suggesting the dominant theme involved.

For the idea of Eden, which would be transmitted from Judaism to the other Abrahamic religions, Christianity and Islam, emphasized the ease and abundance of this first human phase. Material goods flowed from nature without effort. Interestingly, in contrast to visions in other cultures that stressed harmony with nature, the Biblical account placed humankind atop the rest of the natural order, commanding lesser creatures to provide abundance. (In the Qu'arnic version however, early humans were simply told that they could "eat of the bountiful things, therein, as ye will." For our purposes, however, the result was the same as with the other visions of a Golden Age: a life of ease, freedom from worry.) Furthermore, other negative emotions, such as shame, were absent as well. Only the human inability to accept this contentment without wondering if there might be more, disobeying divine orders, forced people out of this ideal state and into the burdensome existence that followed.

★★★

The idea of a lost Golden Age, impressively ubiquitous in the cultures that arose in agricultural societies, does not of course prove that people actually remembered that their conditions had deteriorated in so many respects with the move away from hunting and gathering. Indeed a few hunting

Early Agricultural Society 35

and gathering societies themselves generated ideas of an earlier ideal. And the whole notion may have been an impulse to conceive what perfection might be like, to give free rein to imagination and also, possibly (as with the Biblical story) find ways to chide people into better behavior

But the pattern is at least suggestive. In many of the stories, several of the probable deteriorations noted by historians and anthropologists are specifically addressed, particularly the changes in work and equality. People who had to work harder with agriculture may have preserved some vague recollection of an earlier time when this level of exertion had been less necessary. The same could apply to the need for new concern about disease, or the existence of greater inequality. It is not implausible to read the Golden Age stories not just as flights of fancy but a flickering remembrance of better things past.

Without question, finally, the stories certainly encouraged people to think of their own existence as flawed in many ways, well beneath imagined perfection and possibly, as well, a punishment for human arrogance. References to a Golden Age were not designed to highlight the happiness available in daily life.

★★★

The transition to agriculture occurred, for most societies, several millennia in the past. Modern societies, while they have not renounced all the Golden Age stories entirely, tend to think about the past very differently, assuming that progress, not deterioration, is the true historical trajectory. (Though some people are still tied to a belief that there must have been more happiness "back then", as frequent references to "the good old days" suggest.) The first formal history of happiness, written in 1772 by the Marquis de Chastellux, was built around this confident assumption: what he called "public felicity" had clearly increased since humankind's earliest days. This dramatic recasting was part of what Darrin McMahon calls the "revolution of expectations" associated with a very different view of happiness from the characteristic approach of writers in the agricultural age.

Yet, as we have seen, the assumption of linear progress from the earliest human societies is, at the least, highly questionable. People in agricultural societies, faced with a number of problems almost certainly more acute than those encountered in hunting and gathering groups, at least vaguely aware of deterioration, had to think about happiness more explicitly than their ancestors had done. Few of them, particularly in the lower classes, could expect it with confidence. Ideas of luck or pure chance loomed large in most of the formal discussions of happiness in the agricultural civilizations. Indeed, the word happiness in the English language, deriving from an old Norse term for luck and emerging in the 14th century, emphasized chance, being favored by fortune, gaining a broader meaning of contentment only somewhat later.

36   *The Agricultural Age*

Further, ideas and word meanings aside, agricultural people had to generate some new ways to mitigate some of the constraints most of them faced, or to find some kind of compensation. All this was quite different from the implicit experience of happiness characteristic of many hunting and gathering groups. The kind of writing about happiness that emerged in the agricultural civilizations – a clear legacy from this long phase of the human experience – was in part simply the result of this new means of expression, available to none of the hunting and gathering groups. But it was also the product of the new need to grapple with constraints, to wonder about alternatives, almost certainly in ways that would have seemed unnecessary before agriculture's advent.

Further Reading

For two superb sketches of the historical argument:

Harari, Yuval N. *Sapiens: A Brief History of Humankind* (Toronto: Signal, 2014).

McMahon, Darrin. "From the Paleolithic to the Present: Three Revolutions in the Global History of Happiness." In E. Diener, S. Oishi, and L. Tay (Eds.), *Handbook of Well-Being* (Salt Lake City, UT: DEF Publishers, 2018).

On issues of inequality:

Boehm, Christopher. *Hierarchy in the Forest: The Evolution of Egalitarian Behavior* (Cambridge, MA: Harvard University Press, 1999).

Flannery, Kent V., and Joyce Marcus. *The Creation of Inequality: How Our Prehistoric Ancestors Set the Stage for Monarchy, Slavery, and Empire* (Cambridge, MA: Harvard University Press, 2012).

Scheidel, Walter. *The Great Leveler: Violence and the History of Inequality from the Stone Age to the Twenty-First Century* (Princeton, NJ: Princeton University Press, 2017).

For relevant anthropological work:

Hill, Kim, and A. Magdalena Hurtado. *Aché Life History: The Ecology and Demography of a Foraging People* (New York: Aldine de Gruyter, 1996).

Poirier, Sylvie. *A World of Relationships: Itineraries, Dreams, and Events in the Australian Western Desert* (Toronto: University of Toronto Press, 2005).

Sahlins, Marshall. *Stone Age Economics* (Chicago, IL: Aldine-Atherton, 1972), especially the first chapter on "the original affluent society".

Suzman, James. *Affluence without Abundance: The Disappearing World of the Bushmen* (New York: Bloomsbury USA, 2017).

On complexities in evaluating contemporary groups, see for example:

Diamond, Jared. "The Worst Mistake in the History of the Human Race." *Discover Magazine* (May, 1987).

Pascoe, Bruce. *Dark Emu: Black Seeds: Agriculture or Accident?* (Broome: Magabala Books Aboriginal, 2014).

On the issue of war:

Kelly, Raymond C. (Raymond Case). *Warless Societies and the Origin of War* (Ann Arbor: University of Michigan Press, 2000).

See also:

Briggs, Jean L. *Never in Anger; Portrait of an Eskimo Family.* (Cambridge, MA: Harvard University Press, 1970).

4 From the Philosophers

Happiness in the Classical Period

There is simply no real record relevant to happiness in the many centuries after agricultural economies first took shape. We can surmise, as discussed in the previous chapter, but that's about it. We know that grain yields were fairly high in the early centuries of agriculture, at least in northern Middle East, which may have produced some satisfaction along with the higher birth rate. Modest agricultural surplus also permitted the establishment of the first small cities (though the vast majority of the population remained rural); these too had some advantages but they could also be targets of raids and their health conditions were bad, with mortality rates notably higher than the average. (This rural-urban disparity would last until about a century ago.) But all of this is scattered and vague in terms of levels of happiness or the criteria involved.

Early Civilization

Evidence begins to expand once early civilizations began to form in a few centers from about 3,500 BCE onward – generating more elaborate art, writing, and formal governments. Civilizations had their own drawbacks, with even greater inequality and, sometimes, increased warfare, but they could offer some compensations even aside from the enjoyments of the upper classes.

Indications from ancient Egypt are particularly interesting, along with the possibility that this society offered more support for happiness than most of the early civilizations. Here is a case where objective conditions and value systems seem to have intersected to support expectations of happiness. There's an interesting comparative challenge here, among the various river-valley civilizations, so long as the lack of extensive direct evidence is recognized.

Egyptian society offered several objective advantages: relatively long periods of peace, for the region was rarely invaded and did not consistently attempt further conquests. The Nile River provided a fairly reliable source of irrigation, which in turn bolstered the food supply. And while Egypt featured considerable inequality, including the patriarchal gender system, its slave population was relatively limited and women were treated somewhat

38   *The Agricultural Age*

more favorably than was the case in many other early civilizations. Here, at least potentially, was a hospitable environment for the experience of happiness – and a warning as well that we should not be too sweeping in our generalizations about the disadvantages of agricultural societies.

Egyptian culture encouraged a sense of gratitude to the gods for the basic qualities of life, including family and children, adequate health and material support, and assurance of a proper burial. One Egyptian ruler encapsulated this idea of happiness by citing "Life, Prosperity and Health" after signing his name on official documents. An inscription on a tomb read,

> He who keeps to the road of the god, he spends his whole life in joy, laden with riches more than all his peers. He grows old in his city, he is an honored man in his home, all his limbs are young as those of a child. His children are before him, numerous and following each other from generation to generation.

And an ordinary Egyptian was cited as saying, when asked what he would most miss when he died, "My wife, my son, beer, my dog, the river." Egyptians also devised a wide range of diversions, though more for the upper classes than others: archery, sailing, swimming, and several imaginative board games.

The most interesting testimony to an Egyptian belief in happiness was a distinctive idea of death and the life thereafter, always assuming a proper burial and a favorable judgment by the gods. The afterlife was perceived as an extension of patterns already experienced, just without illness, sadness, or death. A tomb inscription conveyed the message: "May I walk every day on the banks of the water, may my soul rest on the branches of the trees which I planted, may I refresh myself under the shadow of my sycamore." The notion that eternity was in some ways a continuation of life, though without the frailties of the body, was an unusual suggestion that one did not have to wait on death to find a reasonable amount of contentment. Finally, common scorn for non-Egyptians and a general lack of interest in traveling outside of Egypt reflected a belief that Egyptians themselves were living the best life possible.

What we know about the most comparable river-valley civilization, in Mesopotamia, suggests considerable contrast, again probably reflecting more frequent warfare and a less reliable environment for agriculture. Mesopotamian gods, often angry, inspired fear and obedience, requiring service and sacrifice rather than promoting an emphasis on the positive qualities of earthly existence. To be sure, appropriate cultivation of one's personal god could produce benefits in this life, but on the whole the religious culture inspired a considerable sense of gloom and apprehension. And again in contrast to the Egyptians, life after death was a perpetual time of darkness, rather than some kind of affirmation. To be sure, like the Egyptians the Mesopotamians developed a variety of games and

Happiness in the Classical Period 39

diversions, so the negative impressions should not be pressed too far, but a noticeable degree of pessimism does characterize many accounts of the basic culture.

All of this is suggestive at best. We know even less about approaches to happiness in other early civilizations, though it is worth remembering that in China, Confucius would look back at a formative period in which rulers provided harmony and balance. What we can take from the impressions of Egypt and Mesopotamia does suggest ways in which objective conditions and ideas could combine to produce different regional approaches to happiness, within the larger constraints of agricultural societies.

The Classical World

The situation changes considerably in the next major period in civilizational history, though still within the basic framework of an agricultural economy. The societies that began to take shape in the eastern Mediterranean and in China after about 800 BCE generated far more extensive records than their predecessors and, in all probability, a more active intellectual life overall. Most important, in these centers and also in India, philosophical or religious systems began to be developed that would spread widely within each region and would provide a cultural legacy that proved surprisingly durable in these areas and often in neighboring countries as well.

Debates about the nature of happiness were central to the cultures of the classical world. It is important to remember that these same classical societies were the first to build elaborate pictures of a prior Golden Age, suggesting already some sense that available levels of happiness had, through human folly, somehow deteriorated. And these same societies tended to tie personal happiness to a strong element of sheer luck, another interesting constraint.

But there more was involved. The two great philosophical traditions that formed in the classical period, both in the 6th–5th centuries BCE, devoted explicit attention to the problem of defining and attaining happiness. (More purely religious approaches will be taken up in the next chapter.) Both traditions, in turn, strongly influenced later regional patterns, though particularly in China and its neighbors. Confucian values, broadly construed, still help shape expectations and responses in East Asia. Greek and Roman traditions are less salient, but they are still consulted as part of Western and East European intellectual life and they wielded extensive influence at the time.

The Social Framework

It may seem self-evident that once more formal intellectual inquiry began to develop, discussions of the nature of human happiness would gain a prominent place. After all, it's a great and vital topic. It is also possible that

40   *The Agricultural Age*

the vague sense of deterioration from a prior Golden Age would inspire commentary – most obviously with the Confucian idea of the past.

There was another source of inspiration, directly attached to basic features of agricultural civilizations as they had developed by this point, that would shape philosophical discussion in both these major centers: the lifestyle options now available to upper-class males.

For whatever the limitations of conditions for the majority of the population, the upper classes carved out some distinctive opportunities for enjoyment. There was the attraction of pursuing still-greater wealth, symbolized by legendary rulers like Croesus in Greece. High living could also include unusual indulgence in wine or sexual pleasures. The Greeks even had gods that represented this kind of excess, like Dionysius. Opportunities of this sort, in real life as well as mythology, inevitably raised questions about their relevance to true happiness – particularly in societies where the upper classes also sought to justify their existence by offering constructive political leadership. Both Chinese and Greek philosophers grappled fairly directly with the issues involved, reaching somewhat similar conclusions around this specific focus. Some scholars indeed see their efforts as essentially a rebellion against the kinds of values that had defined upper-class life to that point, in an effort to reach a higher level of happiness, one that was less dependent on luck or circumstance and one that had deeper human meaning.

This social framework would also raise questions about the applicability of these philosophical concepts to life beyond the reaches of the upper class. Here, Greek and Chinese approaches diverged somewhat, in ways that might also affect their wider social impact.

The Greek Approach

Beginning with foundational figures like Socrates and Plato, Greek philosophers sought to make it clear that a largely material focus could not serve as the core of human happiness. A certain degree of physical comfort and support, along with good health, provided important preconditions, but the main emphasis was different. In working to clarify this distinction, Greek thinkers established one of the first attempts to define a field of knowledge around the nature and achievement of happiness.

Socrates made it clear that happiness was a primary human goal: "What being is there who does not desire happiness?" But Socrates, and in his wake Plato, quickly stipulated that material or sensual pleasure, however widely sought, was not the substance of real happiness. Desire in fact must be carefully limited, carefully directed away from sheer sensuality in a process that would require real discipline. Happiness does not consist – as the Greek upper classes had long believed – in wealth, or drink, or even power, but rather in "the better elements of the mind". Pursuit of wisdom might make true happiness available regardless of physical hardships or the

Happiness in the Classical Period   41

whims of fortune. For Plato, it was Socrates himself, pursuing wisdom and harmony, who had managed to live "like a god" and find true happiness.

Aristotle, following on the heels of Socrates and Plato, wrote even more extensively on happiness, in work that would prove particularly influential over time. While Aristotle was somewhat more tolerant of earthly pleasures than his predecessors, he was equally insistent that true happiness could only be found in the attributes that distinguish humans from all other creatures: reason and virtue. Happiness was in fact nothing more than an "activity of the soul expressing virtue."

In this vision, pursuit of mere physical pleasure was essentially a form of slavery, more akin to "grazing animals" than true qualities of human beings. Wealth, comforts, even friends and family, though valid to a point, were not the stuff of true happiness, whose pursuit might require some truly difficult choices.

In his most influential work on the subject, *Nicomachean Ethics*, Aristotle set about trying to define the ultimate purpose of human existence. He was at pains to distinguish true happiness from the kind of fleeting pleasures that might result in sensual satisfactions or even interactions with friends. Rather, happiness was a culmination of a whole life devoted to living up to one's full potential as a rational human being. "For as it is not one swallow or one fine day that makes a spring, so it is not one day or a short time that makes a man blessed and happy." For this reason children, among other things, cannot be considered happy, because their potential for a flourishing human life has not been realized.

Aristotle consistently emphasized the distinction between humans and animals in his definition of happiness. This was why he saw pursuit of pleasure as an unworthy basic goal, because it was common to animals as well as man. Rational capacity is what constitutes the human essence, and perfecting that capacity is the core of happiness. The goal is not to deny physical urges, but to channel them in ways appropriate to the exercise of reason. As he said in the *Ethics*,

> The function of man is to live a certain kind of life, and this activity implies a rational principle, and the function of a good man is the good and noble performance (of this principle), and if any action is well performed it is performed with the appropriate excellence.: if this is the case, then happiness turns out to be an activity of the soul in accordance with virtue.

In the short term, pursuit of virtue can seem painful, for it can require a sacrifice of more superficial pleasures. Developing a good character requires effort, but it is moral character – what Aristotle called "complete virtue" – that is essential to true happiness. "He is happy who lives in accordance with complete virtue and is sufficiently equipped with external goods not for some chance period but throughout a complete life." Even

42 *The Agricultural Age*

friendship, which Aristotle esteemed as part of happiness because it combines intellectual and emotional satisfactions, must be rooted in virtue, wanting the best for friends regardless of mere pleasure and seeking to join with them in goodness and morality.

Aristotle's emphasis on rational virtue as the essence of happiness involved the capacity not only to think about doing the right thing, but actually doing it; this could not be a merely passive quality. But the philosopher also stressed the importance of pure intellectual contemplation for a truly happy life. The ultimate expression of our rational natures is rational reflection, including lifelong curiosity. This capacity, along with promotion of virtuous character, should be the true goal of education.

In all this Aristotle, more than Socrates and Plato, had to acknowledge the wider Greek belief in the importance of chance or luck: the mere desire to achieve virtue and exercise reason was not enough. Even moderate living, another Aristotelean emphasis, might not suffice. A person could pursue virtue all his life and still encounter some disaster in old age that would spoil the whole effort. And it was essential to have adequate economic means, good health, and even physical attractiveness to pursue the cultivation of virtue and reason. People cannot do "fine actions" without resources, and they cannot have the "character of happiness" if they look "utterly repulsive" or if they are alone or childless. While Aristotle was optimistic in some moments about opportunities to achieve happiness, he also emphasized a number of constraints. The necessary preconditions could not be created by the individual alone, there had to be some good fortune. There is no escaping the ambiguity here. Ultimately Aristotle hoped that it would be happy people – virtuous and rational (and lucky) – who would lead society, but he had to admit that they might be few in number.

Aristotle's greatest achievement, though clearly building on his predecessors, was to establish happiness and its achievement as a central philosophical goal and to distinguish it from merely physical satisfaction. His influence – for many centuries he would be known as "The Philosopher" – would extend around the Mediterranean and beyond, affecting work on happiness in the Middle East as well as Europe, eastern Europe as well as western.

A Darker View: Greek Tragedy

The Greek cultural legacy was not of course philosophical alone. The powerful dramatic tradition contributed as well, among other things, setting up a division between comedy and tragedy that would have enduring implications. While performances of comedy loomed large, it was really the tragic tradition that deserved particular emphasis, contributing to a sense of ambivalence about happiness that was on the whole lacking in Chinese culture in the same period.

Happiness in the Classical Period 43

For the themes in tragedy elaborated on the sense of the unpredictability of happiness that even Aristotle had conceded – but with far more vivid specifics. A son mistakenly kills his father and blinds himself as punishment, or a man sleeps with a woman who turns out to be his mother, who then kills herself in remorse. In some of these dramas, gods simply toy with hapless mortals. Revenge is another common theme, another way plans can be thwarted and happiness denied. In some cases human folly causes the problems, but more often the situation spins out of control without any wrongdoing. As the messenger in one Euripides play proclaims, "no man is happy". Another play bemoans humankind as an "unhappy race" "doomed to an endless round of "sorrow, and unmeasurable woe."

The notion of a powerful series of dramas completely devoid of what, in modern terms, we might call happy endings was a striking reminder that the happiness the philosophers sought was often denied in Greek culture. The role of luck or chance was undeniable, painfully driving home one of the themes we have already noted as characteristic in agricultural societies.

Beyond this basic point about lack of control, some scholars have speculated that public performances of the tragedies served as emotional release for the audience – as catharsis, particularly by allowing harmless expressions of fear or pity and by offering dramatic contrasts that might make daily life a bit more palatable: at least most people did not have sons who had to blind themselves. It is also true that many performances were capped by a brief but more amusing play – and that the audiences frequently drank a good bit of wine during the show. The overall impact on the actual experience of or expectations for happiness is not easy to calculate.

Greek and Roman Successors

Later Greek and then Roman philosophers maintained many of the emphases of the founding figures, but added some significant emphases. Several writers argued that people should be responsible for their own happiness, rather than serving as puppets to mere chance or to be doomed to tragic ends. Happiness is, or should be, the one possession humans can be sure about. A second emphasis related closely to this issue of control: philosophy should not only guide to happiness but should help deal with human pain and suffering. Cicero, the Roman politician and writer, compared philosophy to medicine: just as doctors aided the ailing body, so philosophy should address an ailing soul.

One school of thought, launched by Epicurus in the 4th century, broke further with the earlier tradition by emphasizing the importance of physical pleasure: "pleasure is the beginning and goal of a happy life". Epicureans argued then that rather than fighting this aspect of human nature, people should indulge it. But this did not mean the simplest kind of hedonism – Epicureans in fact were not so radical, though their ideas

44   *The Agricultural Age*

could be abused. Epicurus blasted "sensuality" – "continuous drinking and revels, nor the enjoyment of women and young boys". Rather, people should base their lives on reasoning and sober virtue, carefully thinking through every choice in life. Avoidance of unnecessary pain was a key goal, and Epicureans worked hard to dispel needless fears about death or angry gods. Short-term satisfactions must be weighed against the possibility of longer-term suffering. People's basic needs were actually very few: avoiding cold, hunger, and thirst. If these requirements are taken care of, a person can be as happy as the gods. It was vital to keep things simple: "He who is not satisfied with a little, is satisfied with nothing."

The other main philosophical school that passed from the Greeks to the Romans, the Stoics, even more obviously urged the importance of limiting desire. Many Stoic writers actually narrowed Aristotle's teachings to emphasize virtue alone as the key to happiness. Riches, beauty, honor were really irrelevant. As the Roman writer Seneca urged, "The happy man is content with his lot, no matter what it is" – though in other passages Seneca admitted his own delight in wealth and luxury. Cicero went so far as to argue that a perfectly virtuous man could be happy even under torture.

This heightened emphasis on the importance of limiting human desires – an impulse that would be carried further in major religions such as Christianity – arguably responded to two or three factors. The emphasis might certainly recall, implicitly, some of the limitations on life in agricultural societies, where urging the importance of making do with little could make good sense, More specifically, both the Epicureans and the Stoics were trying to deal with the obvious problems in the earlier Greek approach: the fact that true happiness, a life of virtue that assumed prosperity and good health, was available only to a very few, as even Aristotle had ultimately admitted. It was important to open a path to happiness to people less blessed by good fortune. Finally, both of these philosophical schools developed after the Greek city states had fallen into disarray, and life became more unpredictable. It seemed vital to develop an approach that was less vulnerable to the external world – and here, clearly, there would be many similarities to other, later approaches to happiness that sought to limit the individual's dependence on the larger environment.

This approach might widen philosophy's social appeal. One Stoic writer, Epictetus, was a Greek enslaved to a wealthy Roman in the 1st century CE, allowed by his owner to study extensively. He picked up on the Stoic belief that by limiting desires, an individual can achieve happiness regardless of external conditions. "That which is happy," he wrote, "must possess in full all that it wants" – and that means stifling all cravings and appetites. These ideas certainly reduced dependence on the trappings of upper-class life, though they appealed as well to many privileged people like the Roman emperor Marcus Aurelius. But, in narrowing the purview of happiness, this form of Stoicism also required unusual self-discipline.

Epictetus was quoted as saying "We have no power over external things, and the good that ought to be the object of our earnest pursuit, is to be found only within ourselves", and he himself, even after gaining freedom, lived a rigorously simple life.

Despite some obvious and significant disagreements, a basic consistency joined the Greek and the Roman approach. Happiness remained a primary human goal; it was not dependent on purely subjective interpretations, but was at base the same for all (however hard to attain); it depended on virtue and rational control; and it was to be achieved over a lifetime, not in momentary or purely sensual pleasures. This was a powerful vision that exercised real influence beyond the ranks of philosophers; and it stands in obvious contrast to many of the ideas of happiness that would develop much later, in the modern world, and that seem to predominate today.

Happiness in Chinese Philosophy

As in Greece and Rome, classical China generated a number of schools of thought, both in philosophy and religion. There were pessimists who claimed that human beings are evil, requiring discipline from a powerful state; happiness might be almost irrelevant in this vision, where the leading challenge was assuring some kind of social order. A major religious strand developed with Daoism, that urged simplicity, frugality, and attunement to the basic rhythms of the universe. Daoism remains one of the main recognized religions in China today. Ultimately, however, it was Confucianism that came particularly to shape the Chinese approach to happiness (often combining with the Daoist emphasis on harmony) and would ultimately influence cultures in other parts of East Asia. Confucianism itself was elaborated over time, as later philosophers such as Mencius embellished the early writings; but a basic approach remained fairly stable.

Confucius and his followers shared much of the Greek interest in defining human happiness and would reach several similar conclusions. Like the Greek philosophers, Confucius and indeed the early Daoists were highly critical of the life they saw around them, arguing that too many people pursued hollow goals, vaunting purely sensual satisfactions over true happiness. Like the Greeks as well, Confucianists and indeed Daoists believed that, properly conceived, happiness can be found in this world and that it is a valid and worthy goal. In contrast to the Greeks, however, Confucianists placed greater emphasis on the importance of linking individuals and wider communities, yielding a somewhat different overall approach.

The core concept, for Confucianism and Daoism alike, centered on being in harmony with the natural order, perceiving and following "the Way" (Dao). When life was in accord with heavenly patterns and processes, it could be filled with satisfaction and joy; Confucianists emphasized that happiness was both an objective condition, in terms of balanced patterns in life, and a deep emotional experience.

46 *The Agricultural Age*

Confucius himself offered the profound pleasure available in listening to music as an example of the kind of harmony he sought. Engaged in music, the feet begin to move in rhythm, hands move as well in response to the patterns, and the individual is embraced in this larger experience. Both mind and body are engaged. A disciple claimed that Confucius was once so wrapped up in music that he simply forgot about more worldly things: "for three months he did not eat meat."

Another practical example of how an individual could find a wider harmony involved the Confucian fascination with manners and rituals. As with music, there was a basic order here that transcended personal concerns.

The problem with most people, in the Confucian view, was that they became so consumed with distracting worries that they lost sight of the basic alignment, which in principle was widely available. With harmony, however, other concerns faded away; "He did not allow his joy to be affected" by lesser concerns.

This approach created considerable ambiguity about the role of material conditions in happiness – a conundrum similar, in broad outline, to problems Greek philosophers had tried to deal with. On the one hand, a person focused on alignment with the Way should not be bothered by hunger or cold. A happy person is not concerned about poverty but "anxious lest he should not get to the truth." On the other hand, Confucius also made clear that a good government should strive for general prosperity. Enriching the population took priority over providing education – implying, clearly, that happiness might be hard to achieve for people lacking basic material standards. By the same token, while Confucianists were quite certain that blatant pursuit of wealth was a false goal (and there was great suspicion of merchants on that basis, who ranked low in the social hierarchy), there was nothing wrong with enjoying creature comforts. "Eating coarse rice and drinking water – there is joy to be found in such things." They simply should not displace the more basic goals.

The good life did not involve fulfilling all desires or attaining the greatest power, but centers on achieving ethical desires. Prudence and moral constraint were essential components.

The Chinese approach placed great emphasis on virtue and a love of learning. "Those who are not virtuous cannot maintain themselves for long either in a state of want or joy", for they have no basic anchor in life. A person who followed the Way, in contrast, would always do what is right and proper. Moral action should be like music, drawing the individual into a larger harmony in which the self was subsumed in a greater good. Devotion to study and learning about humanity helped align with the Way and provided direct satisfaction as well: "isn't it a joy to study and practice regularly?" "Eager pursuit of knowledge" allowed a person to forget about sadness or even physical discomfort. It was not enough simply to do the right thing, as many ordinary people tried to do: it was important to cultivate understanding, to seek the kind of virtue that underlay correct behavior.

Happiness in the Classical Period   47

Achieving the kind of alignment that produced true pleasure took a great deal of experience; it did not come easily, and it was far more profound than any transient experience. A person can't really know happiness "until you catch the sense after a long time of practice" – another similarity to the claims of the Greeks (and a fascinating contrast with modern Western beliefs that children can and should be happy).

The Confucian approach also involved deep connections with other people. Greek and Roman writers had also placed great emphasis on the importance of friendship, but the centrality of interactions with others was arguably even stronger in the Confucian system. Attunement to the Way itself involved attunement with humanity.

This emphasis on others, in turn, showed up in two respects. First, it was vital to treat others fairly. The famous Confucian phrase, anticipating later Christianity, urged "do not do unto others as you would not want them to do to you." In political life, as well, Confucianism insisted that those in power treat the general population with respect and consideration. Good behavior, not mere laws, provided the basis of the Confucian social system (and it sometimes worked).

The other aspect, more directly linked to happiness, emphasized the importance of friendship. "Is it not delightful to have friends come from different quarters?" Pleasure was far greater in groups than when experienced alone, and indeed true happiness could not be found in isolation. Mencius added, "The argument for enjoying together is based on the fact that all men share the same feelings." Confucianists also believed that group pleasure could be enhanced by a bit of wine, which could contribute to the sense of harmony, though they characteristically warned against excess. More broadly, Confucian happiness was deeply connected to the idea of a shared community culture.

The philosophical approaches to happiness generated, entirely separately, in classical China and the classical Mediterranean offer an intriguing mix of similarities and differences. The concept of the Way was unquestionably distinctive, and the Greeks placed much more emphasis on the superiority of humankind over nature. Confucian insistence on the links to humanity and the importance of participation in a group for the achievement of happiness suggested an even more important distinction in practice, which arguably carries over into East Asian culture even today – as later chapters will suggest. Greek interest in friendship as a component of happiness simply did not match Confucian valuation of the role of community.

Clearly, regional differences in basic concepts of happiness enrich and complicate historical analysis, and the comparative challenge began to emerge early in the history of civilization.

But the similarities are marked as well, as both philosophical schools worked to distinguish true happiness from superficial pleasure or indulgence and also, tentatively, to offer an approach that might override life's miseries. Shared emphasis on virtue and learning, and the distinction

48   *The Agricultural Age*

between truly happy people and the many who wasted lives on more trivial goals, provided another vital linkage. It might be argued that, on balance, the commonalities were more impressive than the differences – including the belief in the importance of happiness and the human capacity to find it on this earth.

Impact: Where Does Philosophy Fit?

There are several reasons to pay attention to the rise of philosophical interest, in a larger history of happiness. The conclusions of people who spent a great deal of time trying to sort out the components of happiness can certainly stimulate thinking today; even areas of disagreement can contribute to better understanding. The main lines of classical thought, both from China and from the Mediterranean, certainly deserve comparison with ideas that came later, as a way to calculate change or continuity over time.

One key conundrum, however, involves a set of questions that warrant more extensive comment: how influential were these ideas in their own day? How do they contribute, or do they contribute, to an evaluation of the larger experience of happiness in these two great classical societies? There are several angles to explore here.

The Philosophers and Ordinary People

We have seen that both in Greece/Rome and in China, the writers on happiness attacked many of the common perceptions of happiness they saw around them, finding them tragically off the mark. In both societies also, they grappled with questions about the extent to which happiness was even conceivable among the bulk of the population, almost by definition less likely to enjoy the material conditions that while not the core of happiness, at least established a suitable context. Both Confucianists and the Greek thinkers operated in a highly hierarchical society, which they found entirely natural, even essential to the proper conduct of the state. Did they even think that their ideas were relevant to the bulk of the population?

We have seen that thinkers in both societies, aware of the issue, suggested considerable ambivalence as they built concepts of happiness that went well beyond basic physical pleasures. Plato and, even more, Aristotle, were fairly candid in arguing that probably only a few people would have the combination of wisdom and virtue, on the one hand, and good health and prosperity on the other, to achieve happiness. Slaves were out of the question; both philosophers viewed many slaves as a basically inferior species. Women did not come into play at least for Aristotle, again too intellectually stunted to measure up. And even in the upper classes, distraction by lower pleasures or sheer bad luck would keep many from happiness. Plato was almost vicious in his characterization of how most people

Happiness in the Classical Period 49

behave: living "day by day", often indulging in "sensuous pleasures" like drinking or playing music, sometimes exercising but often idling, with no sense of virtuous direction at all. Plato's only real hope, and Aristotle largely agreed, was that some elements of the aristocracy could rise above all this and find happiness through a clearer purpose in life.

Other Greek and Roman thinkers were less categorical, particularly when, as with the Stoics, they sought the kind of happiness that might coexist with poverty. Even here, however, it was widely assumed that happiness depended on some level of abundance.

Confucian writers were similarly conflicted. They wrote of the possibility of virtue and learning even in the lowly born. But they also pointed out how often ordinary people chose to seek inferior goals or merely simulated good behavior without really exploring virtue and the Way. And while some degree of comfort was not essential to happiness, it could certainly play a role so long as it did not deflect from the basic priorities.

Despite what we might call elitist assumptions, the classical concepts of happiness certainly could appeal beyond the ranks of the upper classes. We have seen the deep impression on the slave Epictetus (who would go on to teach philosophy in his own right). Connection might be difficult however, particularly in societies where the vast majority of people were both rural and illiterate. And even for the upper classes, who might indeed encounter the ideas through school or tutoring, it is not clear how far the influence went.

Competing Options

Given these limitations, and the lack of much direct evidence about the emotional experience of nonintellectuals in the classical period, it is hard to claim great insight into "actual" happiness in this early period – particularly given what we know about the limitations of agricultural society.

What is clear, however, is that the classical societies did develop a number of opportunities for pleasure and enjoyment that differed considerably from the recommendations of the philosophers. Indeed, it was this very context that inspired people like Aristotle and Confucius to come up with what they saw as more meaningful values. Outlets were far greater for the wealthy than for the vast majority, but there was some overlap.

The most interesting development – though Egypt and Mesopotamia had provided precedents – was the spread of popular forms of entertainment that provided some contrast with the ordinary routines of life. Most of them were recurrent, offering special occasions periodically during a year rather than on a daily basis. People might look forward to them even though, from week to week, regular work routines predominated.

Thus in China, the creation of a traveling circus dates back well over 2,000 years ago – emerging, in fact, shortly after the life of Confucius. There is some debate about where the popular circus began – some argue

50   *The Agricultural Age*

that it started in the courts of the wealthy – but most scholarship suggests an origin among ordinary peasants and artisans. Among other things, proficiency in juggling tools such as hammers or knives began to translate ordinary diversions into opportunities for entertainment. Acrobatics and pole balancing were also introduced early on, along with other variety acts. What began as local performances, often associated with the celebration of the lunar new year, evolved gradually into the establishment of professional troupes which traveled around the country, ultimately providing entertainment for royal courts as well.

Athletic festivals, designed to honor the gods as well as to provide entertainment, developed widely in classical Greece, capped of course by the periodic Olympic games. Romans built even more elaborate stadiums throughout the empire, for races and other athletic contests including some brutal clashes among gladiators. Even more important, perhaps, were the kinds of local festivals that periodically sought to honor the gods, usually involving feasting, opportunity to drink, and entertainments by musicians and others.

We do not know, of course, whether these occasions made people happy, but they surely had that goal at least in part. In a backhanded way they confirmed some of the limitations of agricultural societies, by suggesting that only departures from the normal routine were capable of providing real pleasure (a notion largely absent from the rhythms of hunting and gathering cultures). Their existence nevertheless suggests a fairly explicit realization of the need for pleasure.

For the upper classes, opportunities for enjoyment were far greater and, on the whole, more regular – though these groups participated in recurrent festivals and games as well, as participants and spectators alike. Sexual pleasure stood high on the list, for people who had some time to spare and funds to support their interests. In China, many upper-class men took concubines to supplement their official wives. The number of these concubines long depended simply on the man's ability to support, but toward the end of the classical period numbers were limited by law, varying depending on wealth and rank. Roman celebration of sexual indulgence was suggested by vivid representations of the phallus that adorned many wealthy homes at least by the time of the Empire – suggesting the importance of fertility but also male pleasure. In Greece and to a lesser extent Rome, upper-class men frequently took young boys as lovers, sometimes developing passionate attachments. Upper-class life also involved enjoyment of abundant food and drink. Famously, Greek and Roman religion directly celebrated the importance of indulgence through gods like Dionysius and Eros who provided example and inspiration.

Romans actually developed a term, "Felicity", that incorporated some of this delight in earthly pleasures, though it also involved fertility and prowess in war. The word originated – characteristically – in the idea of good luck, but it came to acquire a larger meaning. Romans might

Happiness in the Classical Period 51

shout "felicity" at a wedding, expressing hope for good fortune, fecundity, prosperity – and happiness. The twin notion was that worldly pleasures offered opportunities for happiness and that they depended on the blessings of the gods.

Back to the Philosophers – and Legacies

The importance of hopes for pleasure, and the variety of institutions and customs that sought to provide it at least periodically, returns us to the question of the relevance of the classical philosophies. The Roman spectator, shouting his hopes that an ill-favored gladiator should die, or the Chinese circus fan, did not reflect any particular awareness of the formulas of the Stoics or the Confucianists. There was clear disjuncture between the demanding definitions of happiness offered by philosophy and the wider interest in pleasure. This in turn leaves the issue, what did happiness really mean in the classical period, difficult if not impossible to resolve.

Yet it would be rash to dismiss the philosophers too glibly. In the first place, the philosophers themselves recognized the importance of wealth, abundant children, and sheer luck as components in happiness – Aristotle called these "features that people look for in happiness". We have seen that both the Greeks and the Chinese wrestled with the balance between these components and the more demanding qualities of virtue or harmony – they did not dismiss them entirely.

Second, the strictures of the philosophers – that too much emphasis on earthly pleasures was misplaced – had some impact beyond their limited readership. Emperors, like Marcus Aurelius, could buy into their ideas and seek restraint and virtue in their own lives. Chinese leaders often frowned on excessive indulgence and periodically punished upstart business tycoons who flaunted their wealth. Criticisms of excess also abounded during the early centuries of the Roman Empire, when indulgent aristocrats were seen, correctly enough, as losing the virtuous quality of their ancestors.

Entertainers themselves, though they won audiences, were characteristically held in low regard. In China, entertainers (and prostitutes) were part of the category called "mean people", ranked below all the productive groups and in principle required to wear green scarves to designate their humiliating status. Successful Olympic athletes won fame in Greece (one of the reasons they often tried to cheat in the games), but most entertainers were similarly near the bottom of the social order and treated accordingly. Here, the tension between larger concepts of propriety and true happiness, and the provision of popular entertainment, was clearly expressed. (And it would be a long time before entertainers fully escaped this status hierarchy, and when they did, it would suggest that ideas about happiness themselves were changing.)

52 *The Agricultural Age*

It would be wrong, then, to dismiss the philosophers' approaches to happiness too readily. They had impact at the time, even though they did not monopolize the search for happiness. And their ideas could shape or affect attitudes toward happiness later on, among intellectuals and possibly beyond.

Here, however, a final distinction emerges, familiar enough in world history after the classical period. Confucianism, eagerly promoted by some of the most successful Chinese dynasties, came to outlast the classical empire, resurfacing and extending its legacy well into modern times. This, along with the interest among some Confucianists in guiding ordinary people as well as the wealthy toward a true concept of happiness, arguably had a lasting impact on the Chinese approach to happiness – not a monopoly, but a strong influence that ultimately extended beyond the elites. In the Mediterranean, the ideas of the philosophers lived on as well; they would revive and be reread at several points. But their hold was shaken by the partial collapse of the Roman Empire and their popular influence, limited at best, would be further redefined by the rise of Christianity or Islam.

★★★

When the Athenian leader Pericles vaunted the great achievements of his city-state, just a few years before its tragic collapse, he talked about democracy and freedom. He touted opportunities "for the mind to refresh itself from business," with "games and sacrifices all the year round", with elegant buildings that "form a daily source of pleasure and help to banish spleen." When the 18th-century British historian Edward Gibbon termed the heyday of the Roman Empire the point in time "when the human race was most happy and prosperous", he pointed to leaders who ruled with "virtue and wisdom". Were these historical junctures – Athens and Rome at their height, along with the successful Han dynasty period in China – indeed some of the happiest in the human experience? If so, by what criteria, and what role did the careful philosophical explorations of happiness play? Here are some crucial, and difficult, questions to consider in trying to evaluate the history of happiness over time and place. And why (a question that bedeviled Gibbon) did the achievements not last?

Further Reading

On ancient Egypt,

David, A. Rosalie. *Handbook to Life in Ancient Egypt* (New York: Facts on File, 1998).

Mark, Joshua J. "Daily Life in Ancient Egypt." *Ancient History Encyclopedia* (September, 2016).

Happiness in the Classical Period   53

For an overview of the formation of classical cultures,

Bellah, Robert N., and Hans Joas. *The Axial Age and Its Consequences* (Cambridge, MA: Belknap Press of Harvard University Press, 2012).

On Greek and Roman concepts of happiness,

Annas, Julia. *The Morality of Happiness* (New York: Oxford University Press, 1993).

Haidt, Jonathan. *The Happiness Hypothesis: Finding Modern Truth in Ancient Wisdom* (New York: Basic Books, 2006).

Hughes, Gerard J. *Routledge Philosophy Guidebook to Aristotle on Ethics* (London: Routledge, 2001).

McMahon, Darrin. *Happiness a History* (New York: Atlantic Monthly Press, 2006).

Mikalson, Jon D. *Ancient Greek Religion*, 2nd ed. (Chichester: Wiley-Blackwell, 2010).

Nussbaum, Martha C. (Martha Craven), 1947–. *The Therapy of Desire: Theory and Practice in Hellenistic Ethics* (Princeton, NJ: Princeton University Press, 1994).

White, Nicholas P. *A Brief History of Happiness* (Malden, MA: Blackwell Pub., 2006). ★which focuses largely on Greek thinkers.

For Confucianism,

David, Susan, Ilona Boniwell, and Amanda Conley Ayers. *The Oxford Handbook of Happiness* (Oxford: Oxford University Press, 2013).

Chen, Shaomin. "On Pleasure: A Reflection on Happiness from the Confucian and Daoist Perspectives." *Frontiers of Philosophy in China* 5, no. 2 (2010):179–195.

Hsu, Becky Yang, and Richard Madsen, eds., *The Chinese Pursuit of Happiness; Anxieties, Hopes and Tensions in Everyday Life* (Oakland: University of California Press, 2019).

Ivanhoe, Philip J. "Happiness in Early Chinese Thought." In S. A. David, I. Boniwell, and A. C. Ayers (Eds.), *The Oxford Handbook of Happiness*, 263–278 (Oxford: Oxford University Press, 2012).

Shaoming, Chen. "On Pleasure: A Reflection on Happiness from the Confucian and Daoist Perspectives." *Frontiers of Philosophy in China* 5, no. 2 (2010): 179–195.

On popular entertainments,

Gunde, Richard. *Culture and Customs of China* (Westport, CT: Greenwood Press, 2002).

Swaddling, Judith. *The Ancient Olympic Games*. Rev. and enl. ed. (London: British Museum, 1999).

5 From the Great Religions
Happiness – and Hope?

The ideas of the philosophers, and the challenges of assessing their impact on the history of happiness, center on the period that runs from about 600 BCE to the collapse of the classical empires between about 200 and 450 BCE – though their legacies would extend beyond this point. As we turn to the role of the largest religions in the history of happiness, we embrace a more diffuse time period. Two religions that gained and retain wide influence, Hinduism and Buddhism, originated in India by the 5th or 4th century BCE (Hinduism a bit earlier). Christianity and Islam came later, in the 1st and 7th centuries CE respectively. This chapter, as a result, ranges over a wide and varied chronological span, though it is fair to note that overall, it was in the centuries running from about 300 to about 1,400 CE that religions and their missionary expansion wielded particularly strong influence in much of Asia and Europe and in several regions in Africa.

Religion and concerns about happiness had long intertwined. In earlier agricultural societies religion had often shaped beliefs about propitiating the gods to prevent calamities or promote good fortune. Egyptian religion, more distinctively, sought to enhance the possibility of earthly happiness and carry it over into life after death. Greek and Roman religion certainly emphasized the importance of divine favor, but also used religion to highlight the lack of human control and to exemplify certain kinds of pleasure.

The great religions that arose in India and the Middle East were somewhat different, certainly more elaborate and ultimately capable of winning far wider adherence. Each of the four was distinctive in many ways. The Abrahamic religions of the Middle East differed from the Indian faiths in the emphasis on a single God and a clear concept of heaven. Buddhism attacked Hindu reliance on priestly ritual and its emphasis on social inequality.

From the standpoint of happiness, however, the four religions had one key point in common: they all insisted that true or complete happiness was not to be found in earthly existence but rather, at least for the truly fortunate, after life, in another spiritual plane. Only Buddhism left the door open to some earthly fulfillment. Arguably, the religions constituted one of the most sweeping compensations for the limitations agricultural

The Great Religions: Happiness – and Hope? 55

societies imposed on work, health, and material conditions, by arguing that current problems might be surmounted in a later phase of existence. The religions all introduced a clearer role for hope, in balancing recognition of the shortcomings in daily life with an expectation that there were better things to come. They might provide particular consolation for those who most suffered from inequality and deprivation. For some people, at least, the religions also offered new glimpses of happiness even in life on earth – through spiritual happiness and joy, even a sense of rebirth – in ways less clearly available in earlier, polytheistic faiths. Finally, all the religions could provide their faithful with a vivid sense of fellowship and belonging, another way in which, despite the emphasis on rewards beyond this life, they could contribute to happiness here and now.

All the major religions proved capable of attracting wide followings, usually across other political and cultural boundaries – in contrast to other interesting religions that confined themselves more exclusively to a particular group or region. This unusual appeal had something to do with the religions' complicated role in defining paths to happiness. It also helps explain why these religions would continue to play a major cultural role well into modern times and foster expansion into additional parts of the world.

The major religions certainly repeated a number of the recommendations of the classical philosophers, with some direct borrowing from the Greeks in Christianity and Islam. All four of the religions, seeking to appeal to a diverse audience, worked to balance the ultimate spiritual aims with practical recommendations about gaining some happiness and relieving anxiety in ordinary life. All, however, introduced new elements into the idea of happiness and, for some at least, significantly redirected attention to new uncertainties concerning the proper goals for life on this earth.

Hinduism

Traditional Hindu approaches to happiness, as the religion evolved in classical India, were complicated by the relationship to the caste system. The religion made it clear that members of each caste should live up to the duties of the caste – warriors should be good warriors, artisans good craftsmen – and that this would prepare for spiritual advancement in the next, reincarnated life. This framework provided a sense of direction, but it did not directly refer to happiness.

There was, however, a larger approach, more widely relevant though particularly for the upper castes. Hinduism distinguished among three levels of happiness. Physical pleasures came first, from comforts and sensual enjoyments; then mental, focused on a sense of fulfillment and freedom from sickness and anxiety. But finally spiritual happiness, or *atmanandam,* which involves freedom from the cycle of births and deaths and ultimate union with the Self as a soul in the highest heaven – obviously,

56 *The Agricultural Age*

unobtainable in this life. The happiness available to mortals should not however be pursued for its own sake, for this leads to attachment or bondage. Rather, it can be accepted as part of a life in which ultimate liberation remains the highest goal. Doing one's duties on earth – back to the caste obligations – provides some temporary happiness, hoping for later, permanent liberation later on.

Hinduism established something of a tension between fulfilling earthly goals while recognizing the larger hope for the future, and striving for some glimpse of greater spiritual fulfillment. In all cases, selfishness and desire should be avoided. And it was quite acceptable to seek some prosperity and comfort, and certainly to enjoy family life including sexual pleasure. But it was also tempting, particularly in later age after social and family obligations had been fulfilled, to seek seclusion and contemplate the ultimate purposes of human life and the nature of liberation, renouncing other goals including earthly knowledge. Suffering is unavoidable in this life, not only because of illness and aging but also because of the attachment to impermanent things – an attachment that cannot be easily escaped. Temporary happiness, through sensuality or even friendship, is always a trap, because it binds people to misleading and impermanent goals. Ultimately, both minds and bodies must be restrained, lessening dependence, and with careful discipline some of this liberation can be achieved even during life. Physical self-discipline and even deprivation – there was great respect for holy men who had no worldly goods and depended on charity – can be enhanced by prayer and meditation. But the results are only an approximation of the final goal. The ultimate bliss is incomparably greater than any happiness that mortals gain on this earth.

In working the tension between duties and liberation, Hinduism early on adopted a number of practices that could establish a path toward happiness. Yoga routines were developed to discipline the body and promote meditation, helping a person distinguish between impermanent attachments and true, transcendent reality. Suffering could be set aside in favor of an inner peace. The exercises also lifted an individual from self alone, and into a sense of coexistence with everyone and everything. Various forms of yoga developed over time, continuing well after the classical period and ultimately spreading to other cultures as well – but always in the interest of reaching toward a distinctive kind of happiness.

Several contemporary versions of Hinduism in India tend to downplay the idea of happiness in favor of a larger concept of well-being. Their practitioners continue to argue that it is almost impossible to free oneself from the burdens of life, though children can briefly enjoy a time of innocence and then, in later age, people can gain a greater sense of inner coherence. But they see earthly happiness as a misleading concept, in favor of perhaps a somewhat more modest set of emotional goals attached to well-being. We will return to some of these distinctions in the final main chapter.

Buddhism

Buddhism built on many Hindu beliefs and practices, but established an even more striking stance on happiness and the worldly condition – in some ways, the most radical of any of the major religions. For Siddhartha Gautama, who became known as the Buddha, was deeply impressed with the miseries and impermanence of life around him and sought a path to happiness that would free people from the limitations of ordinary existence. Further, in attacking Hindu reliance on the caste system, he offered an approach that was in principle applicable to everyone, regardless of social position.

The story is that Buddha, raised in an affluent family that tried to shelter him from normal concerns, once ventured out into the real world and was appalled at the poverty, disease, and death that surrounded him. This led him to question the transience of life and its pleasures.

For Buddhism went beyond most commentary in commentating on the various miseries that surrounded life, to emphasize that even achievements that many people esteem, that seem superficially to provide happiness, are miseries as well. Buddhist writings devoted considerable attention to the various and misleading forms of apparent happiness, from sensual pleasures to the achievement of wealth or power, from family life to education. All were ultimately found wanting, which means that most people badly misconstrue the real source of happiness. To be sure, Buddhist writings often discussed more limited forms of happiness, notably in terms of avoidance of disease, but the main emphasis always rested on spiritual goals.

Thus many wealthy and educated people are miserable. The reasons? Worldly achievements of this sort are often fleeting, and those who have attained them feel great anxiety about simply holding on. Even more, the people involved fall into the trap of always seeking more, developing a kind of desire that can never be fully satisfied. As the *Dhammapada* – the great collection of Buddhist sayings – stipulates: "There is no happiness greater than the perfect calm."

> To live unafflicted amid the afflicted is to be happy. To live without ambition among the ambitious is to be happy. To live without possession is a happy life like that of the radiant gods. To live without competition among those who compete is to be happy.

Buddhist writings seek to distinguish between affliction and suffering: affliction, such as a physical disability, comes from external sources, beyond human control; but suffering is something people do to themselves.

At first glance, Buddhism is sometimes assumed to offer a markedly pessimistic view of life, particularly through the insistence not only on the many common misfortunes but also on the fundamental misery inherent in apparent pleasures and achievements. In fact, Buddhism urged that

58 The Agricultural Age

there were clear, if demanding, paths to happiness and that every individual could, though with great effort, pursue these paths. To be sure, the ultimate goal was Nirvana, or freedom from the cycles of death and rebirth, which in some versions of Buddhism would come only through reincarnation. But approaches to Nirvana, or even for some, such as Buddha himself, achievement of Nirvana in this life were possible through careful cultivation of the mind.

"All we are is the result of what we have thought. It is founded on our thoughts. If one speaks or acts with a pure thought, happiness follows one, like a shadow that never leaves." "One should know what happiness is, (and) having known what happiness is, one should be intent on inward happiness."

It goes without saying that Buddhism emphasized the need for a moral life and renunciation of impulses that only lead to further misery, like hatred or violence. Ethical conduct – in speech and action – is an essential category in the eightfold path to happiness. Buddhism also urged the importance of compassion, for consideration for all life. To an outsider, a certain tension may seem to exist between the Buddhist emphasis on withdrawal and personal contemplation and obligations to the rest of humanity but in principle Buddha saw personal happiness as deeply related to the happiness of other beings in the natural world.

Beyond this, Buddhism emphasized the importance, though also the difficulty, of achieving peace of mind, by detaching oneself from all craving, achieving a mental state free from the passions, needs, and wants of life. "If by leaving a small pleasure one sees a great pleasure, let a wise person leave the small pleasure and seek the great." Buddha urged his followers to pursue "tranquility and insight" as the mental qualities that would lead to Nirvana, or the ultimate reality. The goal was a capacity simply to exist in the present.

The effort would be demanding. Buddhism insists that achieving proper mental discipline comes only from great effort, over an extended period of time. A first step is simply learning to avoid negative or unwholesome thoughts; in a later stage, the mind is cleared from such thoughts and becomes ready for wholesome tranquility. "Mindfulness", or the capacity for deep concentration through meditation, is central to this effort. A person "who with tranquil mind has chosen to live in a bare cell knows an unearthly delight in gaining a clearer and clearer perception of the true law." All excitements cease, giving way to a perfect calm. Buddhist writings set forth a series of achievements toward perfect contemplation: first, mental barriers and impure intentions disappear, yielding a sense of bliss; then, activities of the mind cease, and only bliss remains; in the third stage, bliss itself begins to disappear leading to the final achievement – a total peace of mind, which Buddha described as a deeper sense of happiness.

From the outset, Buddhism established several complicated tensions, many of which persist in Buddhist practice today. The injunction of

The Great Religions: Happiness – and Hope? 59

compassion might press against the emphasis on passivity, on withdrawal from things of this world. Buddha's own example, in renouncing wealth and comfort – indeed, learning how to abandon all craving – and seeking a life of privation, suggested the importance of embracing poverty and celibacy as preconditions for a life of true contemplation. Fairly quickly, groups of monks and nuns formed that depended on charity for their daily survival. But what of others, for whom such a radical renunciation did not seem possible? Buddhism was, at base, truly optimistic about the possibility of achieving the kind of happiness that was indeed the proper goal for humankind; but the emphasis on the effort required might, for many, temper the optimism.

As Buddhism spread from India to other parts of Asia, a host of variants developed, with different specific practices and, in a few cases, some startling redefinitions of certain practices; at one extreme, a group of monks actually urged extensive sexual indulgence as a means of seeking greater spiritual fulfillment. Always, however, there was a deep interest in stressing the goal of human happiness and establishing paths toward its achievement.

Christianity

Christianity, emerging initially as an effort toward radical reform within Judaism, originated entirely independent of Buddhism, yet it developed many similar features, particularly in seeking a happiness far different from the fleeting pleasures of material life. A tension emerged around the extent to which withdrawal from the world was essential to spiritual fulfillment that bore some resemblance to Buddhism as well. The religion placed less emphasis, however, on the possibilities of achieving more than a glimpse of true happiness in this life, pointing more exclusively on the hope of achieving salvation and an eternal life in heaven.

The ultimate goal for Christians centered on gaining entry into Heaven, or what Jesus termed the Kingdom of God, vastly different from and vastly superior to life on earth. Jesus described heaven as a place where "the last will be first and the first will be last," implying a reversal of the kind of social hierarchy that left the majority of people powerless and poor. Most Christians came to see heaven as a place (either real or metaphorical) where Christ sat on the right hand of God, surrounded by angels and those people who have gained salvation. One Catholic pope described heaven as "neither an abstraction nor a physical place in the clouds, but a living, personal relationship with the Holy Trinity. It is our meeting with the Father through the mediation of Christ and the Holy Spirit".

This emphasis on a final goal, a deep contrast with ordinary life, meant that many Christians placed unusual reliance on hope. Many early Christians, in fact, believed that a new order was imminent, that Christ would soon return to establish a Kingdom of God on earth. But even

60 The Agricultural Age

after these expectations faded, Christians periodically generated millennial movements – in Europe, later in Latin America and elsewhere – that saw paradise right around the corner, often in response to particularly acute social problems that called out for a radical alternative. Seeking a "new heaven and a new earth", these movements elaborated on a theme in the Book of Revelation in the Bible, that referred to a "holy city, a New Jerusalem, coming down from God out of heaven, prepared as a bride adorned for her husband." More consistently, Christians would pin personal hopes on their own access to paradise after death, and in some cases organized much of their life around this goal by minimizing attachment to worldly things and fulfilling religious obligations.

Visions of heaven – whether personal or part of a larger millennial thrust – could themselves be deeply satisfying, taking their beneficiaries far from any ordinary cares or concerns. One early Christian, describing an ecstatic dream and its taste of the future, simply exclaimed: "And then I woke up happy." At an extreme, many early Christian martyrs, suffering torture or death, were sustained by the belief that their suffering would take them directly to their celestial goal.

Many Christian writers were quite explicit in their contention that ascension to heaven and access to the presence of God was true happiness. Boethius, a sixth-century writer, put it this way:

> Since men become happy by achieving happiness, and happiness is itself divinity, clearly they become happy by attaining divinity.... Hence every happy person is God. God is by nature one only, but nothing prevents the greatest possible number from sharing in that divinity.

All of this, of course, could dramatically reshuffle normal priorities. For if the purpose of life lay beyond life, experience on earth was almost, by definition, of secondary importance. This meant that the problems people encountered, in sickness or economic distress, might in principle be endured through the hopes for a better life to come. This might particularly apply to the poor or, as Christ put it, the "meek", who would have the readiest opportunity to gain salvation precisely because they were not distracted by worldly achievements. For the Christian framework also meant that what seemed to be the pleasures of life must also be reevaluated, for they were of lesser importance and might indeed, as with Buddhism, distract from the true goals.

Many Christian leaders embellished this recalibration of normal life with a deep sense of the sinfulness of mankind and the basic misery of human existence. As the most influential early Christian theologian put it, "count no man happy until he is dead." Augustine of Hippo, the author of this stark phrase, had a life experience not totally different from that of Buddha earlier on. He lived his early adulthood amid considerable luxury and sensuality, but he could find no fulfillment in this pattern.

The Great Religions: Happiness – and Hope? 61

He kept wanting more, finding himself never fully satisfied. At one point he encountered an impoverished beggar who was laughing and joking, clearly expressing a "peaceful happiness" that Augustine himself had never achieved. Augustine's own conversion to Christianity, in 386 CE, finally gave him what he saw as the true perspective on the meaninglessness of worldly pleasures and the capacity to aspire to true happiness.

Armed with this basic realization, Christian leaders endlessly urged their followers not only to endure life's problems with their hopes for salvation, but to realize the dangers of apparent pleasures that would distract them from their true goals. Overindulgence, or gluttony, became a basic sin. Many Christians paid unusual attention to the snares of sexuality, and indeed the Catholic Church, in ultimately mandating priestly celibacy, made it clear that complete sexual abstention was the clearest path to salvation. Even within marriage, where procreation was an appropriate goal, too much enjoyment might be dangerous. Other worldly goals were also suspect: pursuit of fame or wealth could easily lead people astray, for they could not provide true happiness. Christ himself had emphasized that it might be very difficult for a rich man to enter heaven – like passing a camel through the eye of the needle. Augustine, writing as the Roman Empire was beginning to collapse, was also aware of the dangers of leaders' lust for power, which could lead to unspeakable acts of violence, to the "vast mass of evils" that he saw around him.

And there was a final issue, on which Christians frequently disagreed: granting the importance of downplaying worldly attachments, were there positive things that the faithful could do, in this life, that would enhance their opportunities for access to the true happiness of salvation? Many Christians, leaders and ordinary believers alike, believed that some combination of moderation and discipline, plus good and virtuous works, plus adherence to the rituals of the Church and faith itself in Christian teachings would do the trick.

Others, however, were not so sure. Augustine himself came to emphasize the magnitude of human sin that led to the expulsion from the Garden of Eden: all people thereafter were cursed with this burden, this original sin. And only God's grace, not their own actions or beliefs, could save them. People could not by themselves achieve real faith or virtue; they constantly fell short. Even the classical philosophers, or perhaps particularly the philosophers, who believed that people could set themselves straight and achieve a virtuous happiness, had simply been wrong. But God had predestined some for salvation, it was His choice, not the result of any human effort. This was the true "happiness of hope", in Augustine's words, that would allow the saved finally to see God and realize – after death – all their true desires.

This emphasis on divine predestination, which would be picked up later by Protestant leaders, was clearly double-edged. It did offer hope, which was sorely needed since there was nothing people could do to find real

62   *The Agricultural Age*

happiness in this life. But it could also create deep doubt – for who could be sure he or she was predestined, since simply trying hard was pointless? Christianity could create a truly existential anxiety.

Most Catholic leaders, though never renouncing Augustine, offered a somewhat less rigorous vision. People could, by moral conduct, restraint, and faithfulness to the Church, advance their opportunities for salvation. Thomas Aquinas, the great 13th-century theologian who was arguably the most important Catholic writer after Augustine, actually went a bit further still, to claim that people could actually, through their own efforts, achieve some taste of happiness in life – what he called "imperfect happiness" – even though true fulfillment could only come after death.

Aquinas was working after the rediscovery of Greek and Roman thought following centuries of intellectual disarray precipitated by the fall of the western Roman Empire. Deeply impressed with Aristotle's insistence on human reason as the path to truth and happiness, Aquinas sought to blend this with Christian teaching. He devoted a whole section of his great work, the *Summa Theologica*, to the knotty problem of happiness. Like Augustine, and indeed like virtually all Christian thinkers, Aquinas emphasized that true happiness could not be attained in life: people naturally sought it, but they were plagued by too many unfulfilled desires to achieve their goal. For true happiness, the direct knowledge of God, was available only to a purified soul. Then the ultimate pleasure is available, obliterating all sadness and fulfilling all true desire.

In the meantime, however, people can use their reason to gain some elements of the ultimate truth – hence an imperfect happiness on earth. Even here, it is vital to be aware of the snares of worldly goods; physical pleasures may yield "enjoyments", but these will be very short-lived, leaving people unhappy, aware that they were missing something. But through reason, aiming toward a contemplation of truth, and virtue, this partial happiness – what Aquinas called "felicity" as opposed to perfect happiness or beatitude – is available.

The great Christian achievement was to recast the definition of happiness and remove it from life on earth. The result confirmed the attacks on lesser pleasures that Greek and Roman philosophers had already emphasized, while more vividly highlighting the misery of human existence. While Christians were urged to be content with their lot in life and grateful to God for what they had, hope was the true beacon. Left for debate was the question of whether some glimpse of happiness was possible before death, and whether any human effort could help provide this glimpse.

Islam

The Prophet Muhammad and later Muslim thinkers worked on many of the same issues that preoccupied Christians, and came up with many similar conclusions – including the attainment of true happiness only in Heaven.

The Great Religions: Happiness – and Hope? 63

But they also offered a more positive view of some aspects of earthly existence, and while this did not suggest a fundamental difference in the ultimate definition of happiness, it did raise some distinctive issues.

The *Qur'an* and later Muslim writers made it clear that happiness in the hereafter, or everlasting felicity, is the goal of the believer. All the joys that people experience in this world are a means to the basic goal, and Muslims should express their gratitude to God for the blessings granted to them. "And as for those who are happy, they will be in Paradise, abiding there so long as the heavens and the earth endure."

Purely physical pleasures exist, but in and of themselves they are shared with the animals. Health, wealth, even friendships are transient, they cannot provide permanent happiness. As the *Qur'an* states: "Are you content with the life of this world, rather than with the hereafter? Yet the enjoyment of the life of this world compared with the hereafter is but little." At the same time, if taken in the right spirit, and not as ends in themselves, earthly joys are bounties from God and should be gratefully received. Those who have done good in this world, and believed in God, will merit otherworldly happiness on the day of judgment.

Heaven itself, in the Muslim view, offers "a happy life, in an exalted garden...Eat and drink to your satisfaction in consideration of what you had left in previous days." The basic quality of eternal happiness is the presence of God: the faces of true believers will be "fresh with joy and will be looking at their Lord." But there is a material aspect to Heaven that is noteworthy as well: an abundance of food and drink, beautiful surroundings and clothing, the company of one's family. Negative emotions have vanished.

In this world, believers should put their faith in God and be satisfied. This is the basis of true contentment, which is a prelude to the joys of Heaven. But, taken in the right spirit and not as ends in themselves, some worldly goods can be enjoyed. Wealth, for example, is acceptable, and Muhammad particularly praised the calling of merchants. If the wealthy strove for virtue, if they gained their wealth ethically and used it properly including contributing the required amount to charity, and if they focused ultimately on spiritual rather than selfish ends, there was nothing wrong with enjoying their achievement.

To be sure, some distracting pleasures were banned to faithful Muslims, notably the consumption of alcohol. Gluttony might be attacked directly as well: the *Qur'an* specifically noted, "Do not waste; God does not love the wasteful", and a later commentator added pointedly: "God does not love overeating." But the image of heaven, and aspects of Muslim ritual, suggested some appreciation of good food. Attitudes toward sexuality were particularly revealing. There was great concern about regulating sexual behavior, punishing violations, and making sure that sexual urges – what the theologian Al-Ghazali called "carnal desire" – were kept within bounds. This was one reason that sexual activity was restricted during the

64   *The Agricultural Age*

holy month of Ramadan. And a few versions of Islam were even more restrictive: in the 9th century, a separatist section, the Kharji, urged the spiritual value of celibacy. Overall, however, Islam accepted and even valued sexual pleasure within marriage, with wives expected to make themselves attractive and husbands offering adequate foreplay to assure their partners' pleasure. The emphasis on women's right to sexual fulfillment – noted specifically by Al-Ghazali – was a distinctive feature.

As with Christianity, Islam saw life as a constant struggle with sin. But there was no original sin; people were born good. By the same token, if properly directed and controlled, the pleasures of life were meant to be enjoyed. One writer put it this way: "Whoever works righteousness – whether male or female – while he (or she) is a true believer (in the one true God) verily, to him We will give good life" – meaning material provision and contentment – as well appropriate reward in Paradise.

Misguided people, along with lacking the proper faith in God, simply overdo the pursuit of earthly goals for their own sake. They seek too much wealth, too much "play and amusement", too many children, too much "show and boasting." A true believer accepts all that God bestows, including material goods, but uses them toward the real objective of pleasing God. "Those who desire the life to come, and strive for it as it ought to be striven for...they are the ones whose strivings find acceptance and reward."

Ultimately, while Islam did not require the level of rejection of pleasure that Christianity implied or suggest the same level of human incapacity, it did establish a clear tension with daily desires. It was vital to keep clear focus on the ultimate goal, the only source of true happiness – by qualifying for Paradise. This meant attending to God's requirements, beginning with faith, and constantly struggling to keep base impulses in check.

This was the message of the later theologian who most specifically addressed the question of happiness, the Persian Al-Ghazali, writing in the 11th and early 12th centuries. The goal in his work was to revive the basic truths of the faith but also to reconcile the spiritual thrust of Islam with some of the thinking of philosophers like Aristotle – a combination not entirely unlike that of Aquinas later on where Christianity was concerned. His book, *The Alchemy of Happiness,* emphasized the point that "ultimate happiness" could be achieved only in the hereafter, when people were freed from their bodies and gained what Al-Ghazali called "active intellect". By using his reason in this life, man could be spiritually transformed, weaning his soul from worldliness to a complete devotion to God. For his part, God has sent thousands of prophets to earth to teach men how to purify their hearts from baser qualities "in the crucible of abstinence". Al-Ghazali's alchemy is described as "turning away from the world", with four components: knowledge of self, knowledge of God, knowledge of the world as it really is, and "knowledge of the next world as it really is."

The Great Religions: Happiness – and Hope? 65

Here, explicitly, pursuit of the goal of eternal happiness required a clear head and rigorous discipline in this world – a formula that, in broad outline, was shared by all the great religions.

The Question of Impact

The religious approach to happiness invites the same kind of tests as those applied to the philosophers in the previous chapter: what was its ultimate impact on the expectations and experiences relevant to happiness? How might religion shape happiness beyond the sphere of prophets and theologians, priests and monks?

Here, the importance of the question is magnified by the fact that all the major religions sought, and achieved, a massive response, as literally hundreds of thousands of people, particularly after about 300 CE, converted from polytheism to one of these powerful faiths. To be sure, some of the leading writers, like Aquinas, addressed a more limited audience of students and fellow theologians. But the larger messages reached a huge following, clearly shaping popular approaches to happiness and continuing to wield substantial influence still today. How can their impact be assessed? How fully did the religions reshape wider definitions of happiness, and how much happiness – new or old – did they provide?

The question is complicated by the differences among the religions, and by divisions and changes within the religions themselves. Nevertheless, there are several valid lines of inquiry.

The Holy Option

Some people devoted their lives to seeking, and often finding, religious joy, and while this approach to happiness may not have been entirely new – after all, there had been priests in other religions – it almost certainly became more widespread under the aegis of the great faiths. And while the people involved were most likely to serve religion directly, as priests or imams, as monks and nuns, individuals from other walks of life might participate as well.

What were the components of a happy/holy life? Typically, first, considerable asceticism in disciplining and limiting bodily desires, usually well beyond what was regarded as religiously essential. Long periods of abstinence, often complete celibacy, helped prepare the individual for concentration on the divine. But with this preparation, over time, a person might at least glimpse the infinite, or as one description of a Christian saint put it, rise above "every visible and invisible creature, soar over all understanding and, deified, enter into God who deifies him." This kind of mystical rapture emerged in all the religions, and surely provided a deep kind of happiness – an anticipation, indeed, of the larger happiness that awaited after death.

66 *The Agricultural Age*

Deep spiritual joy lends itself to a number of psychological interpretations, but it clearly constituted a distinctive kind of happiness (though that may be too mild a term). Hildegard of Bingen, one of a number of female Christian mystics in the 12th and 13th centuries, talked about a "vision of the soul" she had experienced even in childhood.

> In this vision my soul…rises up high into the vault of heaven and into the changing sky and spreads itself out among different peoples…The light which I see thus is not spatial, but it is far, far brighter than a cloud which carries the sun.

This was a transcendent experience, which supported Hildegard through many periods of illness by allowing her to glimpse the divine.

The encounter with religious joy could come both to individuals and to groups. Clusters of monks and nuns supported each other's quests, in Buddhism and in Christianity alike. In Islam, gatherings of Sufi mystics sought contact with the divine. Some discovered that coffee, imported from Ethiopia, could promote their transcendence when consumed in group sessions meeting through the night – thus establishing the first use of this beverage outside of Africa. A number of Christian monastic gatherings deployed music to facilitate a higher experience; indeed, some mystics, like Hildegard, contributed compositions directly.

Deep religious joy was not necessarily a goal for all or even most who became religious officials. Many Christian monks became known for their gluttony. A few groups of Buddhists actually experimented with a variety of forms of sexuality. And even individuals who sought religious ecstasy might not find it.

On the other hand, some ordinary people, not part of any kind of officialdom, might seek and gain a sense of oneness with the divine, at least periodically in their lives. Buddhism and to an extent Hinduism, indeed, suggested that with practice deep spiritual satisfaction might be more widely available. Here was one way in which the great religions not only redefined happiness, but provided direct access even on earth.

The Faithful

For the many people for whom the special experience of religious ecstasy was not relevant or not available, the great religions unquestionably provided other opportunities for happiness, some of them rather new.

Awareness of the existence of a holy minority might be one such source. Some versions of Buddhism argued that the lives and experiences of the saints brought holy credit and benefit to other believers. In Christian festivals, contact with holy relics might provide a brief sense of transcendence and the experience of awe.

The Great Religions: Happiness – and Hope? 67

All the religions – though this was by no means entirely new – encouraged satisfaction through shared fellowship with other believers, as in the daily communal prayers in Islam. Crucial rituals offered opportunities for special sacrifice, which could offer a sense of purification, sometimes associated with certain earthly pleasures as well. Thus Ramadan enforced a month of privation during the day – shared with others – while offering special feasting particularly when the month drew to a close. In Christianity, the renunciation of certain foods during Lent, again a shared experience, was preceded by more earthy celebrations of Holy Tuesday. Religion also motivated new forms of group travel, in pilgrimages to holy sites. This was particularly marked with the ambitious pilgrimage to Mecca encouraged for Muslims, but Christians and Buddhists had targets as well. Chaucer's *Canterbury Tales* describes a pilgrimage that, despite the fundamentally religious purpose of visiting a great cathedral, had the air of a spring vacation with a host of worldly elements. The fact that the pilgrimages were available to women (again, in all the major religions) was another interesting feature.

Prayer itself, private and communal alike, could comfort, though it more commonly sought to ward off trouble than to promote positive happiness. For some, a sense of the closeness, even companionship of God was deeply reassuring, possibly inhibiting loneliness. None of this is explicitly attached to happiness, but it could provide a relevant context.

All the religions encouraged charity. This was a very specific element in Islam, but prominent in Christianity (including Orthodox Christianity) as well; Hindu and Buddhist ascetics depended extensively on alms. This could provide a deep sense of satisfaction to those who gave, most obviously to the wealthier groups whose life purposes might otherwise seem somewhat suspect.

For many, finally, religion offered opportunities to reconsider goals during the course of life. While the major religions did not the place the same degree of emphasis on maturity that the philosophers had – religious joy might come to people at various ages, as with Hildegard – the fact was that many people redoubled their commitment to religion in later life, as part of spiritual and emotional preparation for death. Buddhism, in stressing the long experience required for spiritual advancement, identified an age factor directly. In Christianity, many merchants, pious during life but pursuing profits as well, underwent a conversion experience later on, often giving their wealth to charity and joining a religious group.

The various sources of satisfaction, religious or religiously linked, could produce a sense that life itself should be filled with a sense of joy. To be sure, there was some skepticism attached, since purely worldly happiness could be so deceiving. In the Catholic Church, St. Francis, who took such obvious pleasure in nature and religion alike, urged that "it is not right for a servant of God to show sadness and a dismal face." Buddha, as many faithful have pointed out, was almost always represented with a

68 *The Agricultural Age*

smiling face. The Prophet Muhammad was known for his cheer; as one companion noted, "I have never seen anyone who smiles more than the Prophet does." Muhammad also urged the importance of meeting others "with a cheerful face". In Christianity, Protestant leaders picked up on the importance of happiness. Martin Luther contended that "all sadness is from Satan," a sign of the absence of God's grace. John Calvin insisted that the praise due to the Lord could only come from a "cheerful and joyous heart". An English poet put it this way: "Rejoice always, in your prosperity ... and in your adversity too."

The Darker Side

Religion could also promote a sense of anxiety and despair, particularly when the readiest compensations, in the earthly pleasures that might be available, were held to be flawed at best, and at worst positively dangerous – or as the Buddhists put it, yet another form of misery.

A number of historians have described the acute sense of fear and guilt that ran deep among many Christians. Preachers, Catholic and then even more Protestants, hammered home the sinfulness of mankind and the perils of life after death. For, after all, for Muslims and Christians alike, the hope of eternal happiness in paradise was balanced by the horrors of hell for those judged unworthy. Real-world disasters, like a plague, could be taken as signs of God's wrath. While Christian leaders might officially urge joy, ordinary sermons more commonly played up the miseries and terrors of this life and the risks of damnation.

Paintings and sculptures, many widely visible, emphasized pain and death. Church doors were surrounded by depictions of ladders – some rising up toward the heavens, but others plunging downward, into the very physical and grotesque torments of the damned. Evidence of death was widespread, with cemeteries, placed in churchyards, a daily reminder of the transience of life and the sinfulness of mankind.

To be sure, Buddhist and Muslim art displayed less fascination with death and the macabre, but some of the overall judgments of human frailty and the perils of ordinary life were not totally dissimilar. Indeed when Buddhism arrived in China, from contacts with India, many Confucianists were deeply and unfavorably struck by what seemed to be a very negative view of ordinary familial or political life, the extent to which happiness could be found – with difficulty – only by turning away from normal engagements.

All of this was meant to be balanced by hope, as well as the joys that might respond to divine grace. But for some, at least, religion might be a source of more pain than comfort. The tension could be very real. And there was a strain, in both Christianity and Islam, that looked forward to the end of the world, when the sinners would be damned once and for all and the perils of earthly existence would give way to the full reign of God.

Religion in Historical Time

The major religions originated in very different specific times and circumstances. They resulted from the inspiration of particular prophets – though Hinduism emerged more gradually – and their influence cannot be neatly pinned to a single historical period.

It is true, however, that the great age of religious conversion in Asia, Europe, and parts of Africa occurred as the great classical empires were collapsing, as epidemic diseases made new inroads in China and Europe, and as nomadic invasions and internal warfare increased. People turned to one of the new faiths for a host of reasons, but surely in part because they seemed to acknowledge the miseries of this world and offered some hope that greater happiness might be available when earthly life ended. Scattered evidence suggests that the periods of greatest dislocation caused genuine psychological discontent. Thus tombstones around Rome increasingly carried the inscription, "I was not, I was, I am not", hardly an ode to joy. The religious definitions of happiness were not caused by new levels of distress, but they surely responded to them in part.

In a few cases, indeed, the distinctive religious age yielded somewhat when conditions improved. Most obviously in China, the popularity of Buddhism came under new attack when, under the Tang dynasty, political and economic stability had returned.

In most instances, however, the religious approach to happiness would outlast any particular period of time, continuing to shape or at least deeply influence the definitions and experience of happiness into the modern age and indeed to the present day. No religious monopoly on happiness resulted, but there was no denying the force of the religious message or the hopes and anxieties it entailed.

Further Reading

On history of hope,

Burke, Peter. "The Dawn of Hope." *The Furrow* 64, no. 11 (November 1, 2013): 620–624.

Cohn, Norman. *The Pursuit of the Millennium: Revolutionary Millenarians and Mystical Anarchists of the Middle Ages*, Rev. and expanded ed. (New York: Oxford University Press, 1970).

For general orientation:

Armstrong, Karen. *A History of God: The 4,000 Year Quest of Judaism, Christianity and Islam* (New York: Random House, 1993).

Coomaraswamy, Ananda. *Hinduism and Buddhism* (Mountain View, CA: Golden Elixir Press, 2011).

On Hinduism and Buddhism,

Bercholz, Samuel, and Sherab Kohn, eds. *The Buddha and His Teachings* (Boston, MA: Shambhala, 1993).

70 *The Agricultural Age*

Ricard, Matthieu. "A Buddhist view of Happiness." In David, Susan, Ilona Boniwell, and Amanda Conley Ayers (Eds.), *The Oxford Handbook of Happiness* (Oxford: Oxford University Press, 2013).

Selin, Helaine, and Gareth Davey, eds. *Happiness across Cultures Views of Happiness and Quality of Life in Non-Western Cultures* (Heidelberg: Springer Netherlands, 2012).

On Christianity and happiness,

Baumgartner, Frederic J. *Longing for the End: A History of Millennialism in Western Civilization* (New York: St. Martin's Press, 1999).

Davies, Brian. *Aquinas* (London: Continuum, 2002).

Dupre, Louis, and James Wiseman. *Light from Light: An Anthology of Christian Mysticism.* (Mahwah, NJ: Paulist Press, 2001).

Emerson, Jan Swango, and Hugh Feiss. *Imagining Heaven in the Middle Ages: A Book of Essays* (New York: Garland Pub., 2000).

McCready, Stuart, ed. *The Discovery of Happiness* (Naperville, IL: Sourcebooks, 2001).

McMahon, Darrin M. *Happiness: A History*, 1st ed. (New York: Atlantic Monthly Press, 2006).

Newman, Barbara. *Voice of the Living Light: Hildegard of Bingen and Her World* (Berkeley: University of California Press, 1998).

On Islam,

Corbin, Henry. *History of Islamic Philosophy* (London: In Association with Islamic Publications for the Institute of Ismaili Studies, 1993).

Esposito, John L., and Yvonne Yazbeck Haddad. *Islam, Gender, and Social Change* (New York: Oxford University Press, 1998).

Keddie, Nikki R. *Women in the Middle East: Past and Present.* (Princeton, NJ: Princeton University Press, 2007).

Leaman, Oliver. *An Introduction to Classical Islamic Philosophy*, 2nd ed. (Cambridge: Cambridge University Press, 2002).

Watt, William M. *Al Ghazali: The Muslim Intellectual* (Chicago, IL: Kazi Publications, March 2003).

On religious fear and guilt,

Delumeau, Jean. *Sin and Fear: The Emergence of a Western Guilt Culture, 13th–18th Centuries* (New York: St. Martin's Press, 1990).

Muchembled, Robert. *Popular Culture and Elite Culture in France, 1400–1750* (Baton Rouge: Louisiana State University Press, 1985).

6 Popular Pleasures

The basic dilemma is worth repeating. We do not know how happy people were during the "religious age" (or how many were made anxious by the thundering sermons); or how they defined happiness; or even whether happiness would have been a relevant concept in their communities. There is no evidence to measure how many found inner peace through one of the religions (or perhaps even greater spiritual bliss), or indeed how many people would have said that inner peace was the core of their idea of happiness. We know that religion had an influence: we have direct records of some, like Hildegard, who gained a taste of the divine, and we know that they had colleagues; but it is impossible to be more precise.

This chapter, building on the kinds of activities more briefly discussed alongside the classical philosophies in Chapter 3, talks about another kind of satisfaction – possibly in some cases deep satisfaction – that developed concurrently with the religions and that attracted wide popular participation – sometimes, indeed, cutting across lines of social class and gender. Many of the people involved may also have shared religious joy and hope. But it is also true that many of the activities discussed in this chapter drew considerable concern from religious authorities, as being too frivolous and distracting.

Even here, we cannot measure happiness. We can make some plausible assumptions, because people often suggested how important the activities were and how much they enjoyed them. Even art work helps here: Just take a look at some of the village scenes pained by the 16th-century Dutch artist, Pieter Breughel, for a sense of – sometimes bawdy – popular merriment. We can argue that along with religion itself, some of these activities helped people compensate for the notorious downsides of agricultural life, including often meager daily diets and regimens of hard work. There are some implied definitions of happiness involved, but they are rarely explicit. Yet they certainly add to the evidence that finding recurrent distractions from the standard patterns of daily life, in all but the most impoverished circumstances, provided important sources of satisfaction and, probably, real sources of happiness.

One final preliminary. Some of these popular pleasures, common in relatively advanced agricultural societies, have since been lost or attenuated. This introduces a complexity into evaluations of modern happiness that we will return to later on.

72 *The Agricultural Age*

Work

The greater burdens of work constituted one of the most telling features in the contrast between agricultural and hunting and gathering societies. It is important to remember that most visions of a Golden Age emphasized the absence of the need for work, and implicitly at least, images of heaven in a life to come highlighted the cessation of work obligations as well. Still, human beings are inventive when it comes to identifying sources of satisfaction, and work in agricultural societies – particularly for some key groups – developed some clearly positive features.

In the first place, for most people in both countryside and city, the most strenuous and stressful work was confined to a few periods in the year. Planting and particularly harvest time for the peasants involved long days. Coal miners faced especially high demand in December, thanks to the advent of colder weather and, at least in Europe, preparation for the holiday season. At most other times, the pace slackened. In addition, many workers mixed in what we might see as leisure during their workday – taking naps, chatting, wandering around. Some group work was also facilitated by chants and songs.

One category, though well below the upper class, found special strengths in work. Urban artisans developed skills and even a sense of artistry that fed a sense of pride and satisfaction. The emergence of this group, along with the development of cities in every civilization, was a major innovation in the experience of work. It is vital to note that artisans were a minority in the population as a whole even in the most advanced agricultural societies: most workers were peasants, and even in the cities large groups of unskilled, sometimes transient workers outnumbered the craftsmen. But artisans were important, and their opportunities may have supported a sense of pleasure. Furthermore, their attributes blossomed in a wide range of regions: artisans in Japan, for example, were at least as proud and privileged as those in Europe, and there are similar manifestations in the Middle East and among skilled metalworkers in Africa.

To be sure, attaining a high skill level was no small chore. Apprentices spent years getting ready, often forced to menial tasks and subject to frequent beatings – even when their master-artisan supervisors were family relatives. But this might make the ultimate achievement all the sweeter. After training, people had to produce a "masterpiece" to show that they were qualified, but once that was done there was considerable freedom to display creativity in work (always subject to the whims of wealthy customers), along with enjoying a sense of fellowship with neighboring craftsmen. (In many cities, craft specialties clustered together, with neighborhoods of leatherworkers or metalsmiths.) Many artisans also enjoyed a period of wandering from town to town before settling down – this was a cherished privilege in pre-modern Japan – which provided other opportunities for enjoyment.

Popular Pleasures 73

In several regions, the pleasures of artisanal work were enhanced by membership in a guild. Craft guilds offered a number of protections, to workers and consumers alike, as they sought to limit damaging competition or unsettling changes in techniques. Both in Japan and in Western Europe, guilds were often linked to religious symbols and shrines. More prosaically, they sponsored an array of group activities – parades, banquets, ceremonial competitions with other guilds – that displayed the pride of the craft and provided warm fellowship. Artisanal work might involve some tension between a desire to demonstrate personal prowess and the emphasis on group solidarity, but it was often the combination that provided the deepest satisfaction. Note that while the most visible strengths of artisanal work were primarily centered on men, some female crafts flourished as well, at least during some periods of time.

The leading sources of popular pleasure taken up in this chapter emphasize non-work activities that provided clear contrasts to the daily routine. But some form of happiness in work itself, associated with achievement and pride, must be considered as well.

Sex

We do not know much about popular sexual pleasures. It is widely assumed that many people were constrained by hard physical labor and, often, somewhat limited diets in ways that would affect their sexual interest. Many couples, faced with the need to try to avoid having too many children and the absence of reliable birth control devices, needed to abstain from too much activity, particularly by the time they reached their 30s. Interestingly some couples deliberately sought a final child later in their thirties, hoping for someone to help in their later age; but this was more a coping strategy than a positive expression of happiness. Assumptions of male superiority could also play a role in sexual behavior, potentially affecting female response. And, as we have seen, religions might advise against too much sexual interest – or even vaunt celibacy as spiritually preferable.

Still, many signs point to the pursuit of sexual pleasure, though particularly for the upper classes; for urbanites; and for men. Prostitution developed early; it is listed in the first Mesopotamian chart of existing professions, in 2,400 BCE. All major cities had houses of prostitution – sometimes, revealingly, called houses of pleasure, not infrequently located near churches or mosques. Between the 16th and 18th centuries CE, Japanese cities developed a network of pleasure houses, in which prostitutes were licensed. Some of these evolved into larger entertainment centers, where talented women performed without necessarily offering sex; this was the geisha tradition that began to be solidified in the 18th century.

We have seen that in many societies, upper-class men regularly took on concubines primarily for sexual pleasure. Artistic representations frequently featured sexual themes, though these did decline somewhat under

74   *The Agricultural Age*

the influence of the major religions. All societies also generated sexual manuals, some of which circulated widely and advised on the means of increasing pleasure. During the Arab Golden Age, in the 11th and 12th centuries, a number of stories, like the *1101 Nights* and *The Perfumed Garden*, highlighted sexual pleasure in ways that did not strictly adhere to Islamic principle. Even earlier, in 828, a Bedouin poet, asked what love is, replied: "To look at each other constantly and to kiss each other repeatedly, this is already paradise." In Europe, a pamphlet amusingly called "Aristotle's handbook" advised on the best sexual positions. And while birth control was a real issue, many societies, from ancient Egypt onward, experimented with devices, including animal bladders used as condom, that might at least reduce the risk of unwanted pregnancies, allowing some explicitly recreational sex even within marriage. Finally, though premarital sex was actively discouraged, it did sometimes occur. In Europe, once a couple was engaged they often had sex, with a resultant first child born about seven months after the wedding.

Sexual activity and interest, in other words, could factor into available pleasure, though there were, unquestionably, a number of constraints, including abundant community shaming for activities deemed inappropriate.

Children's Play

Childhood could also offer unexpected opportunities for pleasure, some of which might even factor into adult experience at least to some extent.

Historians have debated many aspects of childhood in agricultural societies, including the alarmingly high infant death rates and the extent to which parents, partly because of the fear of loss, may have limited their attachment. Physical discipline was not uncommon (though Europeans seem to have been particularly prone, a habit that shocked native Americans during the decades of colonization). Work obligations started early and contributed to parental insistence on obedience and respect. Notably, as we have seen with the philosophers, there was no active concept of a happy childhood; to the extent that adults mused about their early years, they never viewed them as highlights, often mentioning the sternness of their fathers and softening only in noting their more affectionate mothers. The modern idea of childhood as the happiest time of life – to be taken up in a later chapter – was simply absent. This does not mean that adults wanted their offspring unhappy, but it is quite clear that an explicitly positive linkage did not exist. To the extent that adults commented on childhood in general, they stressed their preference for adult-like qualities, not childish ones. Only deep expressions of grief at the loss of a favored child, though not too common, modify this picture. Childhood and happiness did not easily mix.

However, there is one vital exception, which may provide an unexpected glimpse of happiness that might at least occasionally carry over

Popular Pleasures 75

into adulthood: Children played a lot and were frequently left to their own devices. The great historical claim here first emerged several decades ago, in the study of play by Johann Huizinga, a medievalist, who pointed to the huge gap between traditional play and the more adult-controlled, school-oriented activities that passed for play in more modern societies. But the findings have been confirmed by other historians, and also by anthropologists working on contemporary agricultural societies. Rural villages, particularly, though offering generalized group oversight over children, left young people to their own devices for long stretches of time during which there was no pressing work. Clusters of children were able to pursue a variety of games and activities and – the core of the argument – could have a great deal of fun in the process.

Play, as Huizinga pointed out, is a natural attribute, displayed by many animals as well as humans. It contrasts with ordinary activities, providing a sense of release but also opportunities for experimentation that are less possible in daily routines. All human cultures develop special words for play, some of them focused on children's play but extending into other meanings – such as games in general or sexual activities. The Chinese, for example, featured a main word that described children's games but other activities as well, along with two other words, for contests of various sorts and for organized contests in particular. Arabic words highlighted play but also mocking and teasing.

Unquestionably, childhood, again across cultures, offered special opportunities for play, and also a need for play that would contribute to social and skill development. What was noteworthy about children's play in agricultural societies was its immunity from extensive adult control and its spontaneity. To be sure, games were passed from one generation to the next – tag, for example; and in some cases a few toys or balls were involved. But children could also innovate as they filled part of their days in their small groups. Not infrequently, the separation from adult supervision caused accidents; falling through the ice in winter play was a common problem, and there could be other injuries. Occasionally authorities tried to intervene against some of the more violent games, such as rough forms of football, but they were not always successful.

In rural villages, play offered particular opportunities to interact with nature, but even in the cities children managed to engage in street games and other activities that highlighted play. Most historians also emphasize that play opportunities became available to a wide range of social groups – even including enslaved children to a degree; indeed, wealthy youngsters might be more confined in play by the manners of their class and the need for some formal schooling than poorer children were.

Some of the more inventive children's games might explicitly seek to create enjoyment out of disaster. The English game "ring around the rosie", for example, originated from the recurrent bubonic plagues that burdened Europe from the 14th through the 17th centuries. "Rosie" referred to the

76 *The Agricultural Age*

marks plague victims developed on their skin, with a "ring" around the rose-colored sore. "Ashes, ashes we all fall down" initially derived from the extensive cremation of the multitudes of dead bodies. And the posies, finally, referred to nosegays wealthy folk would carry to counter the stench of death. Here, arguably, was a revealing balancing act in agricultural societies: the exposure to problems like epidemic disease might be compensated, in small part, by translation into children's play.

Hide and seek and blind man's bluff were other games devised by children that continued to appeal for many centuries. Children also played with simple equipment, like stilts and see-saws, that they could construct relatively easily by themselves.

A vital aspect of children's play before modern times featured interactions among various age groups, from fairly young children to people who today would be regarded as young adults. Agricultural societies were not rigidly age-graded, and adulthood occurred gradually, depending on work and marital status. Play, in other words, was not centered on smaller children alone.

This age range helps explain why, in the view of scholars like Huizinga, play activities spilled over into the enjoyments available for adults as well. In the first place, adults could gain pleasure in watching children's play or even participating directly. Beyond this, they could incorporate play principles into their own activities as well. Huizinga stresses that behaviors in war – before the advent of today's fearsome weaponry – could involve a play element, and indeed some societies developed warlike games that were nothing more than play at their base. In Western Europe, as feudal warfare declined by the 13th and 14th centuries, knights began to compete in jousting tournaments that were themselves a form of play, and also provided entertainment for crowds of spectators. The fact that they involved some danger to participants was part of the play element.

Fun

Spilling over from play, agricultural societies developed a number of forms of fun, and these often became more elaborate as the societies gained greater wealth and structure. Typically, they were far more widely available in cities than in the countryside, which helps explain why, despite inferior health conditions, migration to the cities continued to be attractive to many people even as the bulk of the population remained rural. The upper classes, in this category, enjoyed opportunities not widely available, employing jesters or sponsoring more organized activities like plays and concerts. In China and later in Europe, royal households even developed private zoos that displayed exotic animals, a privilege not opened to a wider public until the 18th century or beyond. These special opportunities aside, it is not always clear how generally available some types of entertainment became.

Popular Pleasures 77

However, even in offering a brief sampling of opportunities for fun in agricultural societies, several points are clear. First, people have been very imaginative in inventing diversions, which suggests both need and opportunity – beyond levels available in hunting and gathering communities. Second, some entertainment forms emerged in agricultural societies that remain characteristic of key regions today, as in Chinese opera or Western popular drama. And third, many forms were widely copied, even in the agricultural age; indeed, borrowing forms of entertainment – as in the spread of Chinese playing cards to the West during a heightened period of contact – was one of the chief results of interregional trade. It is no exaggeration to suggest a real thirst for additional opportunities for fun. All this leads to a fourth point: while some popular entertainments developed early on, they tended to become more diverse and elaborate during the same centuries that the great religions were gaining ground. They interacted with the religions but also contrasted with them, suggesting a need for alternate forms of release.

Professional entertainers were still widely regarded as low in status, even when they performed for royalty. That some of their work was religiously suspect hardly helped their standing; religious concerns explain why, in Europe, it was not permissible for women to act, with female roles taken on by young men. But entertainers were highly valued in fact, though rarely wealthy, because of the diversion they provided.

At the same time, many opportunities for fun did not depend on entertainers at all, but facilitated a wide popular participation. In a society where most people remained illiterate, and when books were rare in any event, oral performance played an important role in providing diversion. Storytellers emerged quite widely, often providing opportunities for older people to display their wisdom and long memories. Listening to various kinds of recitation – for adults as well as children – was a much more important form of entertainment than would be the case when literacy spread and printing made books more widely available.

While storytelling traditions emerged everywhere, they were particularly strong in many parts of sub-Saharan Africa. Storytellers, called *griots* in parts of West Africa, might entertain and advise kings, but they also enjoyed considerable local prestige. In villages, drums often announced a story session after an evening meal. Griots talked about the doings of the gods; about natural phenomena, like why chickens can't fly (they were once the king of birds, but arrogant behavior caused the gods to strip them of effective wings); great attention was also paid to stories of the family lineage, providing deep knowledge of kinship ties.

In the Middle East, a tradition of poetry recitals was particularly distinctive, and it gained ground after about 600 CE. Poetry recitals entertained royal courts, but they also featured in market squares. Poets offered praise and criticism of figures of the day (mostly praise, when they performed for royalty). They often discussed love, particularly unhappy love; and they

78   The Agricultural Age

sometimes offered graphic sexuality. Wine poetry was another popular theme, despite or perhaps because of disapproval by Muslim clerics. One poet, Abi Nuwwas, in the 9th century, offered this hymn to wine: "Sing to me and give me some wine to drink, serve me a goblet to distract me from the call to prayer."

Many societies invented games, and while some were particularly available to the upper classes, others had wider appeal. In many European villages, for example, a village square created opportunities for bowling games. The Chinese invented card games during the Tang dynasty. Chess originated in northern India, around the 6th century CE, and then spread through Persia and the Middle East, from which it would later make its way to Europe. Characteristically, no elaborate equipment was necessary for most games; only the military-like jousting competitions constituted an exception.

Popular sports often invited wide participation, as well as entertainment for spectators. Village soccer games flourished in England (using inflated animal bladders or leather contraptions), sometimes with violent results. Wrestling and tugs-of-war were also popular. During the Song dynasty, the Chinese introduced a form of golf, with two teams of about ten men each hitting a ball with a stick to see which side could get it into a hole most often; the Chinese also had a version of soccer. Kite flying was invented early in China but initially for military signaling only; it became a popular form of entertainment and competition during the Tang dynasty. In Central America, the Toltecs developed what might be called a form of basketball, where teams competed in front of spectators to get a ball through a hole at the side of the court, often with dire consequences for the losing side; fortunately, the hole was small enough that it may have been hard to win or lose.

Many cities featured casual forms of entertainment, particularly on market days. Bear baiting was popular in Europe, along with sword swallowing or fire eating. In China, though the institution had developed earlier, touring circuses became more common and elaborate. China also pioneered in fireworks as an entertainment form. Even during the Han dynasty, many people burned sticks of bamboo to create loud sounds, and then later explosive powder was added for further effect. Fireworks themselves were invented during the Song dynasty; ordinary people could buy them from street vendors, though there were also far more elaborate, occasional displays to entertain royalty. The addition of color to fireworks was added in the 14th century. From China, fireworks came to the Middle East, where they were known as "Chinese flowers."

Street musicians offered entertainment in many cities, and music was also available in some villages. African storytelling, for example, often had a musical element. Drumming was an important activity in places like Africa and China, serving practical purposes of communication as well as entertainment.

Popular Pleasures 79

In Europe by the 16th century, popular theater offered another option for diversion in the cities – and while special seats were reserved for the high and mighty, ordinary people had access as well, frequently watching plays while eating and drinking and greeting actors, loudly, with cheers and catcalls. By the 16th century, lots of ordinary people, many illiterate, were filling the "cheap seats" in theaters in London, where they watched plays by Shakespeare and others, or coming to the opera in Naples. The shows were in the afternoon – there was no safe lighting available for indoor entertainment at night – and they were marked by trumpets signaling that a performance was about to begin; there was as yet no need for precise entertainment timetables. Theatrical props and costumes remained minimal; words or music alone were meant to be sufficient. The audience chatted continuously during the performance, with far less sense of a need for restraint than most modern audiences have developed. Quite possibly, in addition to the quality of the material, this impromptu byplay added to the fun.

The basic point is clear: even ordinary people had periodic access to a number of forms of diversion and were creative in their development. Some of the entertainments devised by agricultural societies remain popular today, others have faded from view and a few (like marketplace poetry readings) would probably not appeal to modern tastes. Formal performances and wide popular participation combined; emphasis on pure spectatorship was less pronounced than that it would become later on. The impressive list of options should not obscure the fact that most normal days did not feature much opportunity for distraction, particularly in the countryside. And again, there is little explicit evidence about the levels of enjoyment involved, about how much all this created a distinct sense of happiness or how it related to the more urgent religious approach to happiness during the same centuries. The fact, however, that many entertainments became somewhat more elaborate over time certainly suggests their positive role.

The Festival

It was the periodic festival that really constituted the most distinctive contribution to potential happiness in agricultural societies, by creating experiences and memories that were rather different from the patterns that would emerge in more modern times, as the festival tradition diminished. Indeed the special features of the festival, along with religious consolation and exultation, would anchor any argument that agricultural societies in fact figured out how to be just as happy as hunters-gatherers had been, despite the various new burdens agricultural conditions imposed. More prosaically, festivals frequently offered opportunities for different social classes and age groups, as well as both genders, to participate in a common experience of pleasure and community solidarity.

80   *The Agricultural Age*

The nature of specific festivals varied immensely by region; indeed, one of the charms of the festival tradition was expressing and reinforcing a sense of particular local identity. Certainly there were a number of common features: many areas celebrated the summer solstice, and versions of planting and harvest festivals were widespread. But local history; variants on one of the major religions; and other factors complicate any sweeping generalization about when festivals occurred or precisely how many there were – not to mention their celebratory trappings.

Nevertheless, many basic features were widely shared. First, there were a great number of festivals, lasting from a day to five days or more (like the Hindu Diwali, or festival of lights; and many common celebrations of the many days of Christmas). It has been estimated that a significant festival occurred at least once a month in Western Europe, and there were still more in the Eastern Orthodox tradition. Hinduism offered a bewildering variety of festivals, depending on the particular region in India. Festivals marked religious occasions above all, including some standards like Easter or Diwali, but also local patron saints or gods, as well as commemorations of locally significant historical events like a major military victory in the past. In southern Italy, for example, an annual festival celebrated a defeat of Muslim invaders that had occurred several centuries before. Itinerant market fairs provided another opportunity for celebration, and in some cultures occasional weddings or wakes took on a festival atmosphere as well. For people who did not have much daily access to entertainment – particularly, the rural majority – the sheer frequency of festivals was a vital break from the grind of work.

It was what happened during the festival that really mattered, of course, particularly in terms of the experience of happiness and the contrast with normal routines. Feasting was always an important component. For many people who had little or no daily access to meat, festivals often provided a cherished indulgence. The slaughter of a lamb or goat was a vital feature of many celebrations in the Middle East and southern Europe. In many cultures, unusual drinking was also part of the celebration, offering a break from normal abstinence and/or a chance to get drunk. But it was not just the nature and quantity of the provisions that were striking, but also the care lavished (by women) on their preparation, for this was not a matter that received much attention on a daily basis. In Europe, it was revealing that when cookbooks began to circulate, particularly after the introduction of printing, they concentrated entirely on community celebrations; attention to cooking for the family only emerged in the 18th century, when some aspects of the festival tradition were already in decline. Festivals were not only a time when one ate well – that was hardly surprising – but for many people the only time one ate well.

Colorful clothing was another festival component (often, for both genders), again stressing the theme of providing contrast with the ordinary. In cities, festivals provided guild members with opportunities to wear

Popular Pleasures 81

emblems of their craft. Individual display was discouraged, for festival dress emphasized common membership in the group.

A crucial feature was the wide variety of entertainment available, much of it participatory. Some festivals obviously offered religious ceremonies of various sorts, some rather somber, but there were other activities as well. And some festivals, like Guy Fawkes Day in England, celebrated from the early 17th century onward, had no religious content at all.

For wealthy villages, or festivals in the cities, some professional entertainment might be imported. For example, a circus tradition began to develop in Europe in the 17th century, quite separate from the much older Chinese pattern, and small troupes might be attracted to a major village gathering. But amateur activity, by members of the community itself, was far more common, providing the bulk of what was offered to local festival audiences.

Fire and light were important components, a source of delight for people who, on ordinary nights, had little illumination. Strings of lights provided the centerpiece of the Diwali celebration. Many European festivals, including Guy Fawkes, featured large bonfires. In European communities affected by Norse traditions, not only in Scandinavia proper but also parts of France, a summer solstice celebration involved burning a large tree, meant to express devotion to the sun. Many festival activities in fact maintained old pagan traditions of this sort, sometimes (as with coloring eggs for Easter) blending them with the religious calendar.

Again depending on local custom, animal performances played a role. Many European villages featured bear- and bull-baiting as well as cock fights. Only in the later 18th century, in places like England, did some groups begin to protest these blood sports, armed with new ideas about cruelty. Cockfights, embellished by various rituals as well as eager betting by onlookers, were core elements of celebrations in many parts of southeast Asia.

Sports events loomed large. Again in Europe, various ball games, wrestling matches, and competition in stone throwing were familiar features, stressing rivalries within the community. While festival sports did not approach the intensity of the old Olympic games, a man who made a name for himself in an activity like wrestling could move up in the local prestige rankings.

Dance performances played a great role in many regional festival customs, usually involving drums and sometimes other musical accompaniment. In China, festivals called forth special versions of the lion dance or other processional dances, with colorful homemade costumes. Morris dancing was a staple in England, usually featuring only male performers. This was a dance imported from Europe that began to be performed for royalty in the 15th century, and then migrated to the countryside by the 1600s, with many peasants joining in. The term "Morris" presumably derived from "Moor", reflecting a feeling that the dance seemed exotic, from

82   *The Agricultural Age*

the colorful costumes to the stylized movements. The spread of Morris dancing reflected the expansion of popular entertainment options over time, and the capacity to adopt new traditions that offered challenges to performers and enhanced the sense of spectacle for onlookers.

India developed an unusually rich array of popular dance styles, often reflecting old regional traditions; here, women characteristically played the leading role, though one regional genre, the *Kathakali*, featured men in rather military-like routines. Indian dances usually involved musical accompaniment, with instruments made locally, and, typically, very bright costumes. The festival tradition in India also featured large masses of flowers.

Dance activities in many festival traditions emphasized participation over spectatorship, allowing people to share in the pleasures of rhythmic motion and the sense of solidarity with the group – what one historian calls "muscular bonding". These were collective, not individual, displays. In this sense, they offer particularly vivid illustration of the communal qualities of happiness festivals were meant to provide.

Underlying the various specifics of festivals and their regional variety were several characteristics that deserve emphasis. First, festivals were designed to express and strengthen community ties. Outsiders were usually not invited – and that could include the marginal poor in some villages, who were not regarded as really belonging. (This obviously contrasts with festival remnants or revivals today, where outside tourists often serve as primary audience.) Community solidarity could cut across other social lines, however, grouping villagers who varied in property holdings; and local gentry often joined in as well, expressing their solidarity. Presumably, the sense of belonging, as well as the specific entertainments, added to the pleasure festivals provided.

Many festivals directly blended religious devotions, for Christian saints or gods in the Hindu pantheon, with feasting and other earthy pleasures. Here too, the combination might enhance satisfaction, reconciling some of the different definitions of the components of happiness available to ordinary people in a religious age.

Festivals could also, quite deliberately, serve as safety valves for some common community tensions. Sporting events in European villages, such as tugs-of-war, often pitted young married men against bachelors, groups that might otherwise resent each other. Young people in their teens and early twenties, though not part of the village power structure, often had special license in festival times. European tradition maintained several festivals, called Feast of Fools or Feast of the Ass, which allowed parodies of religious and political authorities and placed some subordinates in positions of power for a day. Bands of youth could be allowed, on these occasions, to commit pranks and even minor acts of vandalism, presumably letting off steam to compensate for the obedience and drudgery required of them in the normal routine. Some of these festivals periodically veered into levels

Popular Pleasures 83

of violence, drunkenness, and sexuality, which could lead to official efforts to suppress. At their best, however, by briefly turning normal patterns upside down, they made the normal more acceptable at other times.

Many students of the festival tradition, finally, emphasize the distinctive sense of the timing of pleasure that the festival calendar implied: occasions of particularly vivid delight that stood out precisely because they were not usually available. For populations not far from the edge of subsistence, unable to afford or even imagine more regular outlets, the intensity of the experience would feed memories and anticipations that could carry people through the long stretches of time that intervened.

★★★

Several reactions might respond to the short description of the various ways pre-industrial people seem to have tried to have fun, even aside from the distinctive regional specifics. One reaction might emphasize how familiar this seems, certainly compared to the rather different sources of happiness attributed to hunting and gathering societies. After all, modern people seek many similar diversions, building on precedents set by the agricultural civilizations, though we benefit from being able to combine a number of different regional patterns – fireworks as well as Shakespeare – thanks to the unfolding of greater global contacts. And if we enjoy many of these opportunities today, seeing them as part of our happiness, maybe the evaluation can be extended back in time.

Yet important differences should stand out as well, complicating the effort to assess the level of happiness among our agricultural ancestors. We will explore many of these distinctions more fully later on, but some markers now may be useful. First, it is not clear whether the notion of "having fun" can be applied to these societies, save perhaps as part of children's play. Certainly, particularly in the countryside, most people had no daily access to the main sources of fun. Enjoyment was periodic, governed by a fairly traditional calendar, not something to splice into the normal day. This may have made the opportunities all the more meaningful – this was the great strength of the festival tradition, which modern people have diluted in their insistence on more frequent fun. But the sporadic quality makes evaluation of daily happiness more difficult. Furthermore, fun was community-centered, not focused on individual or even family – as the cookbooks of the time suggested. This may or may not have made happiness richer than is the case today, but it was certainly different.

The question of disparity in access looms large, though it is still an issue today to some degree. To be sure, wide participation in many activities – rather than reliance on a few professionals for performances – was a striking feature of the festival tradition. On the other hand, the differences between the urban and rural experience could be huge, in terms of the

84 *The Agricultural Age*

diversions available. Social class distinctions were immense, even in the cities, affecting the range, the frequency, and the quality of entertainment. Gender also loomed large, though it was somewhat less salient in the festival tradition or in children's play. Men could, quite simply, attend activities that were unavailable to women (though women could go to Shakespeare's plays, just not act in them); disparities in sexual enjoyment and even in access to alcohol were also quite real.

Family life surely provided happiness for women, and some cultures, as with Hinduism in India, made a particular point of delighting in a child's birth and lavishing praise on the mother. But overall, family life did not feature as prominently in discussions of happiness as might be imagined (except in the desirability of having children as a mark of success) – and this raises some additional questions about the status of happiness for women. The elderly were a final category that did not figure prominently in popular diversions, save presumably as spectators, with the important exception of the story-telling role.

The emphasis on group activities in many of the principal diversions also had a flip side: it was hard for an individual to step aside, to indulge more purely personal tastes. Festivals compelled attendance for those involved. In France for example, if a head of household refused to contribute straw for a bonfire honoring the local saint, he would be widely shamed, with many villagers claiming that he was likely to break a leg or suffer some other misfortune in retribution.

Then there was the issue, for both genders, of how entertainment and play related to religion, or even philosophy – a question that lingers today, but less urgently. Periodically, the clash in standards of propriety and in definitions of "true" happiness complicated popular life considerably. In the Middle East, the narrowing of interests to a greater emphasis on religion alone, after the Arab "Golden Age" retreated by the 13th century, reduced some of the outlets that had previously flourished – like the public praises to earthly delights in marketplace poetry. In China, authorities periodically clamped down on signs of consumer indulgence among the urban middle classes, even putting some offenders to death. Similar sumptuary laws, seeking to regulate material life according to status, cropped up periodically in Europe. In Europe as well, the rise of Protestantism led to another set of clashes with popular taste, particularly among groups converted to Calvinism. To be sure, Protestant leaders encouraged a rather positive evaluation of the pleasures of married life. And Puritans have been given an unjustly bad press: they were quite capable of commenting on the joys of alcohol or marital sex. But they could also be grim. They disliked colorful clothing. They disapproved of some of the plays that had long delighted the people of London, shutting some of them down entirely. They disliked many of the trappings of traditional festivals, and Protestant disavowal of saints dramatically reduced the number of holy days for festivals in any event, by as much as 50%.

Popular Pleasures 85

Disputes over happiness, and whether it should be sought in this life at all, complicate any effort to figure out what happiness was like, and how it was interpreted, just a few centuries back. Certainly, while opportunities for entertainment did expand at several points in the millennium after 600 CE, there was no systematic change in the most authoritative definitions of happiness itself. Fun was available, though hardly predominant, but it could provoke doubts as well as satisfactions.

Further Reading

On pre-industrial work:

Crossick, Geoffrey. *The Artisan and the European Town, 1500–1900*. (Aldershot: Scolar Press, 1997).

Farr, James Richard. *Artisans in Europe, 1300–1914* (Cambridge: Cambridge University Press, 2000).

Holcombe, Charles. *The Genesis of East Asia, 221 B.C.–A.D. 907* (Honolulu: Association for Asian Studies and University of Hawai'i Press, 2001).

Laslett, Peter. *The World We Have Lost* (New York: Scribner, 1966).

Rosser, Gervase. *The Art of Solidarity in the Middle Ages: Guilds in England 1250–1550* (Oxford: Oxford University Press, 2015).

On sexuality:

Phillips, Kim M., and Barry Reay. *Sex before Sexuality: A Premodern History* (Cambridge, MA: Polity, 2011).

Stearns, Peter N. *Sexuality in World History*, 2nd ed. (New York: Routledge, 2017).

Weeks, Jeffrey. *What Is Sexual History?* (Cambridge, MA: Polity, 2016).

On play:

Chudacoff, Howard P. *Children at Play an American History* (New York: New York University Press, 2007).

Frost, Joe L. *A History of Children's Play and Play Environments Toward a Contemporary Child-Saving Movement* (Abingdon: Routledge, 2010).

Huizinga, Johan. *Homo Ludens: A Study of the Play-Element in Culture*. (Boston, MA: Beacon Press, 1955).

On fun:

Bowsher, Julian, and Pat Miller. *The Rose and the Globe: Playhouses of Shakespeare's Bankside, Southwark: Excavations 1988–1991* (London: Museum of London Archaeology, 2009).

Crego, Robert. *Sports and Games of the 18th and 19th Centuries* (Westport, CT: Greenwood Press, 2003).

Crowther, Nigel B. *Sport in Ancient Times* (Westport, CT: Praeger Publishers, 2007).

Eales, Richard. *Chess the History of the Game* (Reprint, Mountain View, CA: Ishi Press, 2019).

Hawkes, Terence. *Meaning by Shakespeare* (London: Routledge, 1992).

Kennedy, Phillip. *The Wine Song in Classical Arabic Poetry: Abū Nuwās and the Literary Tradition* (Oxford: Clarendon Press, 2002).

Plimpton, George. *Fireworks: A History and Celebration* (New York: Doubleday Books, 1984).

86   *The Agricultural Age*

On the festival tradition:

Falassi, Alessandro. *Time Out of Time: Essays on the Festival*, 1st ed. (Albuquerque: University of New Mexico Press, 1987).

Gerson, Ruth. *Traditional Festivals in Thailand* (Kuala Lumpur: Oxford University Press, 1996).

Hecht, Jennifer. *The Happiness Myth: Why What We Think Is Right Is Wrong* (New York: Harper, 2007) – an important study in several respects.

Malcolmson, Robert. *Popular Recreations in English Society 1700–1850*, New ed. (Cambridge: Cambridge University Press, 2010).

On dance as part of the festival tradition:

McNeill, William Hardy. *Keeping Together in Time: Dance and Drill in Human History* (Cambridge, MA: Harvard University Press, 1995).

Singha, Rina, and Reginald Massey. *Indian Dances: Their History and Growth* (New York: Braziller, 1967).

On misrule:

Davis, Natalie Zemon. *Society and Culture in Early Modern France: Eight Essays* (Stanford, CA: Stanford University Press, 1976).

Harris, Max. *Sacred Folly: a New History of the Feast of Fools* (Ithaca, NY: Cornell University Press, 2016).

Part II

The Happiness Revolution, 1700–1900

In the 17th/18th centuries in Western Europe and much of North America, a dramatically new approach to happiness emerged, which would alter how happiness was defined and how many people began to reframe their own expectations. This formative period for the new ideas of happiness would extend through the 19th century, thus cutting across the long Agricultural Age and embracing the beginnings of the industrial society.

This new period was primarily defined by the unprecedented debates over what happiness was all about and by efforts to implement the new ideas. Though "revolution" is not an inaccurate term, it took time for various groups to come to terms with novel expectations. The adjustment was further complicated by various impacts of the industrial revolution, as it gradually reshaped living standards, recreational outlets, and even family life. The global context presents another set of complications that extend through the whole period: the "revolution" was at this point a Western development, and its global impact would long be limited. The power that Europe projected in these centuries, through imperialism and economic influence, may indeed have inhibited a global reassessment of happiness.

7 The Happiness Revolution in the West

It is not hard to define the revolution in ideas about happiness that occurred in Western Europe and much of North America in the 18th century. Increasing numbers of intellectuals argued that human beings could control their own destinies – they were not victims of chance or divine judgment – and that pleasure and comfort on this earth were acceptable, even desirable, goals. In principle, these same intellectuals contended that earthly happiness should be available to everyone; and properly ordered societies should steadily expand opportunities for mental and material satisfactions. Older ideas of happiness through perfection in virtue or through the blessings of an afterlife were not abandoned, but they were increasingly subordinated to the new enthusiasms for earthly joys. Savoring the here and now and seeking worldly success did not detract from real happiness, they defined its essence; and some commentators added, there was no merit whatsoever in pain or deprivation.

While charting the unprecedented arguments of Enlightenment writers offers the most direct evidence of the revolution in definition and expectation, other manifestations also demonstrated considerable popular participation in this fundamental change – and these new features may have been even more important. Smiling became more fashionable. People were increasingly urged to be cheerful, and to expect those around them to be cheerful in turn: a "cheerful revolution" was arguably as significant as the unprecedented concepts of happiness, for it created new standards for acceptable emotional behavior. A novel kind of consumerism suggested that many people were taking greater pleasure in the acquisition of things.

A change this profound inevitably included a number of complexities. While there really are solid indications that the revolution extended beyond intellectuals alone, it is impossible to chart the extent of the popular resonance: surely, the literate more than the illiterate, for example, and the urban and middle class more than the rural and working class. Not surprisingly, resistance also swelled. A traditionalist religious minority objected to the movement away from sin and damnation. Other conservatives, influenced by classical values, found the new happiness goals shallow. And it is vital to remember that the revolution was, at this point, Western alone, without much influence on the rest of the world – a global issue to which we must return.

The Happiness Revolution in the West 89

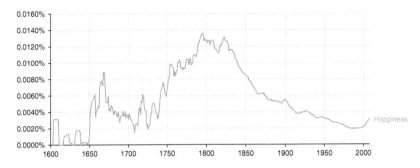

Figure 7.1 Frequency of the word "happiness" in English, 1600–2008, Google Ngram Viewer, accessed July 13th, 2020.

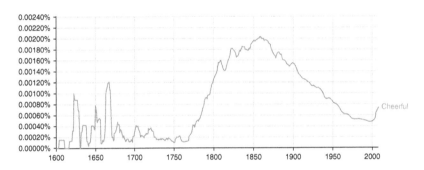

Figure 7.2 Frequency of the word "cheerful" in English, 1600–2008, Google Ngram Viewer, accessed July 13th, 2020.

Still, complexity should not obscure the fact that a fundamental shift was underway, one that continues to influence conditions of happiness even today. Two Google Ngrams, which chart the frequency with which a word was used compared to all other words in English-language writing, highlight the shift dramatically. References to happiness, rare in the early 17th century, began to soar; and roughly the same trajectory applied to the adjective "cheerful". A fundamental reconsideration was underway (Figures 7.1 and 7.2).

The Backdrop

In retrospect we can see that several developments in Europe and the North American colonies in the 16th and early 17th centuries prefigured the revolution, but at the same time it would have been very hard to predict the revolution even in 1700, when many Western societies were continuing to emphasize the importance of sober restraint.

90   *The Happiness Revolution, 1700–1900*

Here were some of the preparatory developments:

- Protestantism might have created a new sense of opportunities for happiness for some. As noted in Chapter 4, both Luther and Calvin spoke about their belief that God intended people to be happy. Protestant faiths also encouraged a greater sense of possibilities for individual contact with God, without the intermediary of priests; and it attacked monastic practices of self-denial and celibacy as irrelevant to salvation. One study of English Protestant intellectuals argues that, by the 17th century, they were encouraging people to turn away from a sense that happiness was a matter of luck and accept "worldly felicity" as part of self-improvement. On the other hand, many Protestant leaders clearly discouraged an array of popular entertainments as frivolous, along with colorful clothing and other embellishments; they did not emphasize joy in their long and somber church services, and they could fill people with dread about the omnipresence of sin.
- The scientific discoveries of the 17th century, many of which won considerable popular attention, could promote a greater belief in the powers of human reason and the possibility of improving over past knowledge and superstition. Here was an important building block for the future. At the end of the century, philosopher John Locke applied this new sense of confidence to an attack on the idea of original sin, arguing that people are born with a blank slate, neither good nor evil, which could be turned positive through education. On the other hand, the scientific burst created measurable anxiety among many religious groups. It also began to undermine traditional beliefs in magic, which many had found comforting.
- New kinds of consumerism began to gain ground, not to be sure for the very poor but for many groups beyond the aristocracy, reaching even the ranks of skilled artisans. Imported products like sugar, coffee, tea, chocolate, and tobacco may have – literally – added spice to life. They also encouraged interest in related products like porcelain serving sets, as family meals began to become more elaborate; other outlets, like coffee houses, provided opportunities for fellowship for men. Beds began to become more comfortable. How much this added to a positive sense of happiness at this point is hard to gauge, but there may have been at least modest change.
- Radical protesters, for example among extreme groups like the Diggers and Levelers during the English civil wars, began to wonder if dramatic social and political changes could not produce new levels of happiness, through greater equality. "Why may we not have heaven here, and heaven hereafter too" – a theme that would become much more important later on.
- It is possible that the first signs of a greater interest in happy endings began to emerge in the 17th century, though the great surge would

The Happiness Revolution in the West 91

await the 19th and 20th centuries. One minor dramatist thus rewrote Shakespeare's great tragedy, *King Lear,* to provide a happy ending, and it would be performed that way for another 150 years before the original was reinstated. In Naples a new opera based on Virgil's *Aeneid* retooled the story to end happily, rather than in suicide.

• Some new words began to enter the English language, which were relevant to a new interest in happiness. Notably, the word "fun" began to be employed – derived from earlier medieval terms for jesters or fools. It was first used as a verb in 1680, a noun in 1700. "Fun" continued to be associated with tricks or hoaxes until about 1730, when it began to refer to amusements pure and simple.

These examples are straws in the wind, and they should not be exaggerated. Older ideas about the limitations of happiness clearly persisted. John Locke, for example, also wrote about human folly, reflecting both classical and Christian emphasis on human frailty, "We are seldom at ease, and free enough from the solicitation of our natural or adopted desires"; "in this imperfect state, we are not likely to be ever free from (uneasiness) in this world." A book on the *Art of Contentment* by an English conservative, in 1675, placed even greater emphasis on the elusiveness of happiness. "Though every man would have happiness," the greater majority lose themselves in "blind pursuits". Happiness is in fact available to all, if they would only seize it, through recognizing the "grand and ultimate happiness" of the next life; this could allow an "intermedial" happiness now if people would only defer to authority and accept their present circumstances. There was no revolution in traditional voices like this.

Before the Big Change

Generalizing about a public mood is always risky, as so many differences exist among individuals and groups, but a few speculations are possible before turning to the arrival of more fundamental change.

First, while the 17th century did see a number of positive changes in the human condition, as with new consumerism, some clear setbacks resonated as well. Diseases, including periodic plagues, continued to run rampant. In 1665, the last great bout of bubonic plague occurred in England, quickly killing up to a quarter of the population of London. Major wars could be deadly as well. The Thirty Years War caused enough disease and destruction to carry off at least a quarter of the population in Germany, where it would take decades to recover. Frequent conflicts, though less bloody than the struggle in Germany, continued later in the century, particularly around the ambitions and destructive strategies of France's absolute monarch, Louis XIV. Here is another case where events and culture could combine in generating a common, and hesitant, approach to happiness.

92 *The Happiness Revolution, 1700–1900*

On the more purely cultural side, smiling was not encouraged in the 16th and 17th centuries, at least the kind of wide, spontaneous smile that would show a lot of teeth. In the first place, thanks to sugar and tobacco and a lack of dental care beyond the painful removal of rot, many people simply lacked any teeth to show, and clearly sought to control smiling as a result. France's "Sun King" Louis XIV, for example, had no teeth; it has been speculated that the most famous smile of the earlier Italian Renaissance, the Mona Lisa smile, was mysterious mainly because she was working hard not to show her discolored or absent teeth.

Beyond the dental challenge, broad smiles and open laughter were often actively criticized, seen as reflecting a distressing lack of emotional control. Upper-class manners insisted that a boisterous laugh was a sign of poor breeding, really no better than a yawn or a fart. A French Catholic writer argued, in 1703, "God would not have given humans lips if He had wanted the teeth to be on open display." Children might smile, to be sure, but an adult should have learned to know better.

In France again, reactions to theatrical comedies were often deliberately restrained. The great comic dramatist of the period, Molière, did win royal patronage, but he often ran into trouble: first, his plays frequently made fun of topics that were off limits, like church or aristocracy, and were simply banned. But second, the fashionable audiences that were vital for patronage insisted that laughing aloud was a behavior one would expect only from the "cheap seats". Openly enjoying too much fun, in other words, was vulgar, and Molière insisted that his purpose was not so much to entertain – though he did that – but to "correct the faults of men".

Restraint might be even more widely recommended in Protestant regions like Britain or the Atlantic colonies of North America. Several historians have noted a preference for slight melancholy in the moods of these regions, as people, conscious of their sins, sought to "walk humbly" in the sight of God. Many diary writers took solace in portraying themselves as "doleful". A head of household berates himself after punishing a servant: "and hence I am induced to bewayle my sinffull life, for my failings in the presence of God Allnighty." Another commented that in his view, God "allowed of no joy or pleasure, but of a kind of melancholy demeanor and austerity." Still another noted that severe melancholy, though distressing, was far better than sin. This was the atmosphere in which many also expressed regret for even a whiff of lightheartedness with friends or relatives, as they "grievously" reflected on their "Levity" at an evening gathering. This does not suggest that experiences of joy were absent, but they seemed to occasion genuine personal concern, and there might be real hesitation about seeking them out. It was no accident that one of the striking medical texts of the 17th century, Richard Burton's lengthy *Anatomy of Melancholy*, while suggesting ways to modify extremes, also noted that "no man living is free" from "melancholic dispositions."

The Happiness Revolution in the West 93

None of this is meant to argue that there was no interest in widespread happiness before the 18th century, except for a hope for a better world in the life to come. The signs of change should not be forgotten. The same upper-class belief that laughter was vulgar suggests that lots of ordinary people welcomed opportunities for fun, in popular theater and beyond, as had long been the case. Emphasis on melancholy may itself have been a dubious privilege of the literate, where the combination of religious anxiety and the reigning code of manners might be particularly fierce. It is important to remember after all that many preachers still urged the possibility of happiness simply through trying to be good and please God, and there were many claims that accepting one's lot in life could be a source of cheer. Traditional wisdom could still count for something. The evidence does point, however, to continued limitations on any embrace of happiness, before a more dramatic set of ideas and practices burst forth, mainly after about 1730, that would change the scene decisively.

New Concepts of Happiness

A new idea of happiness, and perhaps an even newer idea of its accessibility, was a basic feature of Enlightenment thought in the 18th century, on both sides of the North Atlantic. Earthly pleasures – dancing, food, singing, the company of friends – were no defiance of God's will, but a life as nature intended. The British poet Alexander Pope put it this way in his 1734 *Essay on Man*: "Oh happiness, our being's end and aim! Good, pleasure, ease, content! Whate'er thy name." A Scottish philosopher, Francis Hutchison, became one of the first writers to discuss the importance of a social commitment to happiness, implying that politics might have to be recast toward this goal. People deserved to be happy; by mid-century French writers were even talking about a "right to happiness".

Discussions of how to attain happiness spread in intellectual and ruling circles across the continent. In Poland, the College of Nobles organized a lecture series on "Man's Happiness Here Below", while the ruler of Russia organized a celebration featuring the "goddess felicity" and a massive "Temple of Happiness". By the end of the century the subject had become commonplace, which could obscure the extent to which this was a truly unprecedented outpouring of hope and expectation.

Christian writers themselves picked up the theme, writing pamphlets with titles like *I Want to Be Happy* or *The School of Happiness*. Of course they noted that full happiness could be found only in the afterlife, with God, but most of their attention centered on good feelings in the here and now. One historian has argued that the Enlightenment in fact began to change the old Christian question, how can I be saved? into a new one: how can I be happy? And while the new philosophers certainly referred to classic Greek and Roman writers as they discussed the pursuit of felicity,

94   *The Happiness Revolution, 1700–1900*

their approach was really quite different, in centering on pleasure itself and not some greater goal.

The new interest informed the development of what would come to be known as the social sciences, another fundamental Enlightenment contribution. Early psychology was not fully involved, but nascent sociologists, political scientists, and economists were deeply interested; their goal was both to elaborate on the definition of happiness and to suggest how society could be organized to maximize its attainment.

Thus in Britain what became known as the utilitarian school, initially guided by Jeremy Bentham, insisted that the purpose of government, or indeed any public action, was the "greatest good of the greatest number" – and by good, he meant happiness. This extended the ideas suggested earlier by Francis Hutcheson. "It is the greatest happiness of the greatest number that is the measure of right and wrong," Bentham wrote in 1776. Some budding social scientists argued that it was possible to build mathematical models bent on maximizing happiness. A number of scholars working in this vein acknowledged that people in the past had been unable to maximize happiness, but that science could now cut through outdated thinking and demonstrate a clear path.

The enthusiasm was European-wide (with some eager North American participants as well), with contributions from Italy and Germany as well as Western Europe. Legal scholars and budding criminologists chimed in. The pioneering jurist Cesare Beccaria based his ideas for the massive reform of criminal punishments on the importance of limiting suffering and unhappiness and imposing only those penalties effective in correcting behavior: his guiding principle, by now familiar enough, were policies that worked toward "the greatest happiness of the greatest number of individuals." Economists like Adam Smith, seeking the best arrangements for economic growth, assumed that greater prosperity would bring greater happiness, which in turn was mankind's proper goal. As another scholar put it – the French writer Chastellux, who wrote what he said was the world's first history of happiness: "are there any more beautiful, more worthy of our attention than those which have for their object the happiness of humanity?" The focus itself, plus the implicitly democratic belief that happiness could and should be open to all people, plus the conviction that societies could be changed and improved in ways that would promote happiness – this was a quietly revolutionary combination.

Some interesting disagreements surfaced amid all this discussion. A few writers, particularly in France, veered off into discussions of sheer sensuality, and in some cases actively experimented with pleasure-seeking in this domain; thus the famous lover Casanova wrote about the transcendence of "immediate sensual enjoyment." The sensualists prompted other Enlightenment authorities quickly to criticize their "dissolute" habits. A few writers admitted that a certain amount of illusion, or wishful thinking, was essential in the quest for happiness: there were lots of problems

The Happiness Revolution in the West 95

in life that had to be overlooked in the notion that happiness was readily available. Christianity remained a concern. There was wide agreement that old-style Christianity had missed the mark: mankind was not sinful, monastic-style denial of pleasure was truly misguided. But while a few ventured into agnosticism, more tended to argue that there was a God who in fact supported the human quest for happiness. This was the view, for example, of Benjamin Franklin across the Atlantic.

An important debate arose about the role of civilization in happiness. Most Enlightenment advocates were urbanites, interested in a variety of sophisticated pleasures including the joy of learning and rational inquiry. But another strain, most vigorously advocated by Jean-Jacques Rousseau, argued that real happiness was to be found in simpler pleasures, that people needed to return to a more "natural" existence. And this approach struck a real chord. The 18th century featured a proliferation of "pleasure gardens", in which city dwellers could enjoy the beauties of nature, and there was even a movement, popularized by people like France's ill-fated queen Marie Antoinette, to reconstruct farming cottages and water mills to indulge tastes for a simpler life. But while writers like Rousseau were deeply critical of many Enlightenment ideas of pleasure, Rousseau himself reinforced the central message: people "must be happy." "That is the first desire which nature has impressed upon us, and the only one which never leaves us."

The centrality of the Enlightenment to the new commitment to happiness, amid some variations on the theme, is undeniable. This was one of the basic ways this intellectual revolution transformed Western culture, well beyond the reaches of philosophy alone. For the Enlightenment thinkers were also ardent popularizers. They wrote deliberately for a wide public: the French thinker Voltaire, for example, was one of the first intellectuals to make a good living simply selling books, not relying on aristocratic patronage for his support. They issued unprecedented summaries of knowledge to help spread the word, while a variety of pamphleteers offered a host of vigorous summaries. Their ideas were taken up not only in the fashionable salons, organized for the well-to-do, but in the growing network of coffee shops, where public discussions might reach an audience beyond those who purchased books and pamphlets directly. The question of how many people were touched by the new ideas of happiness is not easy to answer, but this was not a movement of elites alone.

One sign of this was an increasing tendency for people to celebrate the advent of a new year with specific anticipations of the happiness to come. Thus an almanac heralding the year 1766: "May the New Year and those that follow bring happiness and peace to the hearts of all men." New knowledge had brought measurable progress during the year past, and there was more to come. The common phrase "happy new year," however, would enter common usage only in the 19th century. Here too, the 18th-century revolution in happiness launched a set of habits and vocabulary that would become more elaborate over time.

96 *The Happiness Revolution, 1700–1900*

Causation

Specifying the causes of this cultural revolution is something of a challenge. It is much easier to lay out the new concepts themselves than to explain their provenance and popularity. Basic changes do not however spring up unaided, by the musings of intellectuals alone, and they certainly do not gain an audience without a larger context. At various points in human history, ideas about happiness – both positive and negative – have been shaped by a combination of ideas and material circumstances. This formula certainly applies to the transformation of happiness in the 18th century.

Three major factors intertwined. First, on the ideas side, Enlightenment beliefs about happiness clearly extended the achievements of the scientific revolution of the previous century – a familiar point. The demonstration that human reason and experiment could explain many of the workings of nature – like the principles of gravity – and unseat many older errors promoted wider ideas of progress and improvement, and tended also to draw attention to the workings of this world rather than the next. The celebration of reason also undermined earlier beliefs about human sin, raising questions about other traditional religious ideas where the human potential for happiness was concerned. The translation of scientific discovery into revolutionary concepts of happiness was not inevitable, just as the extension of science into social science required a certain leap of faith. But the connections were clear enough.

Connection was facilitated by the second factor, again not brand new but cresting by the middle of the 18th century: a steady improvement in material standards of living for many people – not everyone, to be sure, but a growing number. There was greater access, for example, to more colorful, and more easily washable, clothing, thanks particularly to the rapid expansion of the cotton industry. By the middle of the century lots of people began using umbrellas, vital particularly in Europe's climate. To be sure, a few English writers complained about a weakening of character: a real Englishman should be able to withstand the rain, but in general the innovation was welcomed. Home heating devices improved. Growing use of whale oil lamps even cut into darkness at night (though this also allowed more sweatshop work in the burgeoning factories). Chair design improved, and chairs became more widely available. It is also true that more people also gained access to watches and clocks, though whether a greater ability to tell the time contributes to happiness or not remains an open question. That aside, new standards of comfort had wide impact. The complex relationship between consumerism and happiness, beginning to take shape at this point, launched a recurrent theme in modern history. People were buying things in part to show off – this was a motive behind buying fancy watches – but also because the "things" gave them direct pleasure. It is also true that improving standards could also promote

The Happiness Revolution in the West   97

greater aspiration, where frustrations could complicate the picture. But there can be little question that a better material life facilitated belief in new possibilities for happiness. Indeed, it is precisely at the point when living standards begin to advance that consumerism has its most positive impact – as would be true in other societies later on. Here was additional motivation for the new preachers of happiness, and for those who heard them.

Finally – the third factor – a bit of serendipity. For reasons that are not entirely clear, Europe became essentially plague-free for a number of decades from about 1730 onward. Endemic diseases continued to take their toll, but recurrent catastrophes largely disappeared. This made natural disasters that did occur, like a great earthquake in Lisbon, more noticeable and lamentable, but there was a real relaxation in normal anxiety. And while wars did not vanish, they were not particularly bloody, nor, outside of central Europe, did they affect large sectors of the population. The greatest conflict, the Seven Years War that began in 1756, only killed 20,000 Britons, and even the French did not suffer too badly – just to note two countries that were particularly involved in the happiness surge. Intellectuals were aware of the new atmosphere, particularly the easing of plagues, and it gave them hope for the future; and the change helped create the favorable audience as well. To be sure, epidemics and deadly wars would return, but by that time the contours of the happiness revolution were already set.

A combination of factors is almost always involved in any major human change, and this certainly applies to happiness. European living standards, for example, were not necessarily better than the Chinese in the mid-18th century, but the Chinese did not at this point have a scientific revolution to build on. The Russian upper class had access to the scientific revolution, and they did evince interest in the ideas of happiness; but Russia did not yet experience a wider change in physical comfort – hence a different outcome. It is less easy to assess the impact of the interruption of the plague cycle – though in the early 2020s, beset by the coronavirus pandemic, we can imagine what a relief it may have been. But Enlightenment optimism may have owed as much to this factor as to the other two.

Happiness Plus: A Ripple Effect

Enlightenment ideas about happiness were connected to several other developments, some of which would play an ongoing role in the progress of happiness itself. Without venturing too far from the basic topic, it is important to discuss a few durable extensions.

Many Enlightenment thinkers were famously optimistic. They believed that the world was improving around them but also that, as people gained in education and old institutions were reformed, further progress

98   *The Happiness Revolution, 1700–1900*

in the future was assured. The most sweeping declaration of progress was offered by the French writer Nicolas de Condorcet, who published his *Sketch for a Historical Picture of the Progress of the Human Mind* in 1795, offering formulas for the "perfectibility of society". Ironically Condorcet wrote the book while he was trying to escape arrest by French revolutionary radicals, and indeed the book appeared the year after Condorcet was jailed and died in prison. Here was dramatic testimony to Enlightenment faith, but it also illustrates one of the key corollaries of Enlightenment thought: the encouragement to hope, and to hope not for a better life in heaven but a better life just around the corner in the here and now. The new kind of hope could connect to happiness for individuals, as they planned what they thought of as their own better future; or it could provide hope to larger clusters of people as they pinned their happiness on the better society that would result from a social movement or even a new technology.

The Enlightenment, and several other developments in 18th-century popular culture, placed new emphasis on the individual, rather than the importance of ties to a group. Scholars debate the question of when individualism began to characterize Western culture, but there is little question that it received a massive boost at this point. A humble example: it was in the later 18th century that popular naming practices began to change. A penchant for using the names of ancestors or religious figures gave way to an interest in choosing more novel names for one's offspring – to emphasize their special qualities. And an old habit of reusing the name of a child who had died ceased entirely; every individual must be cherished, and that included those who had previously passed away. At the political level, huge emphasis began to be placed on individual rights, including freedom of religious choice. In marriage formation, individual preferences began to gain greater weight, over traditional reliance on parental arrangements. The shift had many facets, prompting changes from personal life to revolutionary aspirations.

In turn, the new ideas of happiness were intricately connected to the surge in attention to the individual: it was on an individual basis that happiness should be most commonly sought and evaluated. It was the individual who had the right to pursue the goal of happiness. We have seen already that the intimate connection between individualism and happiness continues to mark Western culture, as distinct for example from the Japanese approach, yielding very different answers to contemporary questions about whether one is happy or not. It was in the 18th century, on the Western side, that the formula began to take shape.

Finally – though this is a less familiar link – the novel ideas of happiness were associated with new thinking and new practices concerning death, facilitated of course by the interruption of the plague cycle. Enlightenment faith in science and overall optimism encouraged a belief that, with progress, human beings should be able to prolong life, that the specter of

The Happiness Revolution in the West 99

death would recede. At the same time, new ideas about contagion – not the germ theory yet, but an antecedent – prompted widespread efforts to relocate cemeteries, to move them farther away from daily interactions. All of this raises the possibility that the new ideas of happiness connected to a growing distaste for death; and indeed, the relative frequency of published references to death began to decline rapidly, a trend that would continue into the 21st century. Actual death rates long remained fairly high; it was only in the past century that a fuller separation between happiness and death became possible. But the seed was planted earlier, and it continues to generate questions about whether modern ideas of happiness, in the Enlightenment tradition, fail to take adequate account of death's inescapability. We will see, in Chapter 14, that some non-western societies are currently raising this issue directly, as debate about the nature of happiness becomes more global.

Keep Smiling

The most important extension of the new thinking about happiness into other aspects of daily life came with the concurrent emphasis on the importance of cheerfulness. Here was a change that is less easy to pin down than happiness itself – it did not lend itself to sweeping intellectual formulas – but it may have been at least as significant.

Enlightenment philosophers did offer some contributions in this area. Francis Hutcheson, for example, wrote extensively on the value of laughter. He disputed older ideas that people only laughed at others' misfortune, or that laughter was a sign of poor breeding. On the contrary, laughter helped build bonds between people, contributing to a more humane society.

The main interest, however, centered on a growing interest in cheerfulness, outside the domain of formal philosophy. Cheer was not a new word in the English language. Initially referring to facial expression, it had begun to take on positive connotations in the 15th century. But references began to increase rapidly by the later 17th century. It was in the 18th century that more familiar uses and associations began to emerge, like the idea of Christmas cheer or shouts of cheer to express group emotions (such shouts presumably began first in the British navy). Most revealingly, a brand new phrase, "cheer up", first appeared in 1670. Its relative frequency began to increase only in the later 18th century, but from that point on would gain ground steadily into the 20th century (though, interestingly, more precipitously in American English than in English more generally). The phrase revealed a new belief that people should be able to generate a more cheerful demeanor and that it was appropriate to tell them to do so.

Unsurprisingly, as cheer went up, references to melancholy went down quite steadily, until by the later 19th century it had become a virtual linguistic relic (Figure 7.3).

100 The Happiness Revolution, 1700–1900

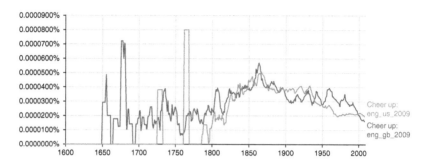

Figure 7.3 Frequency of the phrase "cheer up" in American English, 1600–2008, and British English, 1600–2008, Google Ngram Viewer, accessed July 13th, 2020.

For the new idea was that not only people should be happy, but that they had a responsibility to appear happy, yielding something of a new cheerfulness imperative. The result showed both in written advice and, even more strikingly, in a new willingness to smile broadly, and to expect smiles in return. Good manners began to be redefined toward emphasizing the positive.

The notion of a new responsibility to appear cheerful began to crop up in commentary, including private diary entries, from about 1730 onward, both in Britain and in the Atlantic colonies. It may have reflected not only the increasing emphasis on happiness but also the extent to which more and more urbanites were involved in commercial dealings with strangers, which inevitably promoted a need to embrace the most effective methods of self-presentation – sometimes with a religious reference added in as well. Thus one John Byrom wrote in 1728, "It was the best thing one could do to be always cheerful … and not suffer any sullenness … a cheerful disposition and frame of mind being the best way of showing our thankfulness to God." A Boston writer in 1758 went further in suggesting the desirability of having cheerful people around – even across class lines: "The cheerful labourer shall sing over his daily Task … a general satisfaction shall run through all Ranks of Men." People also began urging a quick recovery of good cheer even after a disaster, as in a brutal yellow fever epidemic in Philadelphia in 1792. For oneself and others, it was important to put on a good face.

This was where the new interest in broad smiles came in, a sign of approval for, and even insistence on, more open emotional expression. Out with tight-lipped self-control and a kind of grimace-like smile, in with greater spontaneity. Novels – a new genre in their own right – began to describe women with "enchanting" or "sweet" smiles, a clear new signal. New types of dentists emerged in urban areas on both sides of the Atlantic

The Happiness Revolution in the West 101

by the mid-18th century, eager to take care of teeth rather than pull them. A host of innovative products, including toothpicks and brushes, were introduced to maintain the smiles, and artificial aids like lipstick were designed to highlight the whiteness of teeth. Smiling gave evidence that a person was keeping up with the latest consumer products, as well as displaying the right kind of emotion. Smiling for several decades seemed to be a particularly French or Parisian specialty; a Scottish traveler to Paris in the 1760s complained about how Parisians seemed to be smiling all the time – a reminder of how culturally specific modern smiling is, and how it can actually seem annoying to others. Parisian smiling may have taken a hit with the French Revolution, when skulls became associated with the ravages of the Terror and the showing teeth seemed less appropriate. But smiles would recover in France, and certainly more open smiling became current elsewhere during the happiness revolution. Thus for several decades in the 18th century, Americans who had their portraits painted deliberately presented themselves with smiling faces. More generally, even before 1800 a number of European travelers noted how cheerful Americans seemed to be, commenting on their "good humor" and constant "cheerfulness" expressed through a ready smile.

For men, emphasis on the importance of smiling was accompanied by an increasing effort to discourage crying – a display that had been quite common for men in the 17th century when melancholy was more in fashion. Full conversion to the idea that masculinity and tears did not mix awaited the 19th century, and it involved more than the promotion of cheerfulness. Still, a growing sense that displays of sadness signaled weakness was consistent with the notion that a cheerful demeanor was the most appropriate form of self-presentation.

It was revealing, also, that new words began to be introduced to designate individuals who were not really depressed or deeply sad but who were not keeping up with the social need to seem cheerful. "Sullen" was a word that was already available, but in the late 18th century the term "sulky" was added (probably adapted from a different German word). Sulky was initially applied to servants, an interesting indication that people were beginning to want even their inferiors to seem cheerful. Later, as we will see, the term also began to be applied to recalcitrant children, particularly adolescents, and additional neologisms would be added to highlight undesirable resistance to the displays of good spirits.

Individual Happiness: Sexuality and Consumerism

Far from the pens of philosophers and even some of the promptings toward cheerfulness, a number of groups in Western society developed new or expanded opportunities for pleasure in the later 18th century. It is not always clear whether these linked to an explicit goal of happiness, and they also provoked criticism, but they may have contributed.

102 *The Happiness Revolution, 1700–1900*

Few individuals tried to emulate the sexual antics of a Casanova, but popular sexual habits changed considerably. Growing access to money wages, even for some young people, plus rural crowding and the beginnings of greater urbanization weakened community and even parental controls over sexual behavior, particularly for elements of what can broadly be called the working classes (in the countryside as well as cities). Sexual activity before marriage became more common, as evidenced by a rising rate of illegitimate births. Even within some marriages, sexual activity may have increased. These developments are hard to interpret, and they often put women at a disadvantage. But what one historian has called the first modern sexual revolution was certainly consistent with a new interest in pleasure and with growing secularism – at least for some.

The relevance of growing material comfort to the happiness revolution has already been noted, as has the link between consumerism and smiling. As consumerism advanced in the later 18th century, it tightened the connections with happiness, while raising a number of questions that would persist well beyond this point.

None of the philosophical proponents of happiness argued that happiness rested primarily on the acquisition of things. Cultivation of the mind, enjoyment of freedom, connections with nature – these were vital sources as well. In the British colonies of America the notion of happiness was particularly connected to independent land holdings, though material prosperity entered in as well. The fact was, however, that interest in the acquisition of consumer goods continued to advance on both sides of the Atlantic, and for many people served as one path to happiness. Further, both the philosophers and many ambitious individuals now agreed that seeking wealth was an acceptable means of promoting happiness and independence alike.

Shopkeepers and manufacturers began developing new methods to convince people that the acquisition of things, and even the act of shopping itself, could further happiness. As one French commentator noted, an increasingly commercial society made it seem like men and women could "buy and sell happiness" in various items of pleasure. Advertising began to develop, taking advantage of the advent of weekly newspapers; while there were no explicit claims yet that purchasing something would bring happiness, there were many references to comfort and keeping up with the latest trends. Shopkeepers – as their numbers proliferated – began organizing store windows to be as enticing as possible. Other gimmicks, such as pricing one item below cost to draw people into a store where they would immediately be tempted to buy more, proliferated – indeed most of the apparatus of modern consumerism developed at this point at least in embryo. For their part, manufacturers worked hard to test popular taste, quickly ramping up production of designs that proved particularly attractive. The strategy reflected a new awareness that popular pleasure could be identified and used to promote further sales.

The Happiness Revolution in the West 103

There is not a lot of direct evidence from the 18th century on the emotional experience of the people who were participating in the new consumerism, beyond the obvious fact that they were clearly drawn to the process. Consumerism was beginning to be attached to courtship and romantic love. This was a key reason for the growing interest in more stylish clothing. In 1797, an enterprising London publisher even offered a book of phrases men could use to make their Valentine's greetings more romantic. Connections among consumerism, affection and (through this) happiness were clearly emerging. On another front, wills began to include specific designation of items, particularly furniture or tableware, that their owners wanted to pass on to cherished family members as a sign of their affection – another indication that happy emotions were now attached to material objects. Consumerism, in other words, was beginning to contribute to happiness and allow the expression of remembered happiness in turn. It provided one of the channels for the new individual quest to gain and express greater pleasure.

Collective Happiness – and Joy: A Political Dimension

The growing interest in happiness and earthly hopes did not apply only to individuals, however, nor was it confined solely to the more affluent social groups. One of the most significant findings in the history of popular protest is a transition from traditional goals, which emphasized returning to some real or imagined past condition, to a "proactive" approach which emphasized the right to progress – the right to conditions better than ordinary people had ever experienced before. Various groups began to imagine that they could achieve new levels of happiness, collectively, if only they could gain economic or political reforms. Here was one way that new hopes attached to the "pursuit of happiness" could translate into collective action.

This new search for happiness broke through clearly during the French revolution, where many ordinary people gained opportunities for political voice. Thus a rural village lawyer in France, Joseph-Marie Lequinio, from humble beginnings, gained a small role during the revolution's radical phase, through which he could express his visions for the collective happiness that was just around the corner. "All, in a word, whoever we are – big or small, strong or weak, young or old – we all dream of happiness, we want only to be happy, we think only of becoming so." Thanks to the revolution, further, Lequinio could make it clear that the quest for happiness had nothing to do with waiting for an afterlife – this was only a trick that had deluded ordinary people for too long. Nor, however, did happiness center on personal wealth or individual pleasure. The real secret of happiness lay in working for progress for the masses, in "the love of others" or "public felicity". And, hinting at the new force of popular nationalism that was taking shape in France, Lequinio also attached this new vision of collective devotion to the "love of *patrie*" – the love of the fatherland.

104 *The Happiness Revolution, 1700–1900*

Official documents from the French revolution referred to a similar notion of a "happiness for all": thus, the 1793 constitution stated directly, "The goal of society is common happiness". For people like Lequinio, happiness centered on the destruction of tyranny, the end to religious hypocrisy, the advancement of the common man.

This kind of vision – a belief that greater happiness lay just around the corner under the spur of popular protest – would pop up recurrently, from this point onward. It would motivate a variety of revolutionary agitators in Western Europe – radical and nationalist alike – through the risings of 1848. It would spur the more visionary trade union movements, including British Chartism. It would inspire socialist and communist leaders in many countries. This was an ambition for collective happiness that could sustain some of the most devoted adherents of the variety of new protest movements that cropped up from the late 18th century onward.

More than expectation could be involved. Shared enthusiasm and fellowship could provide happiness for many ordinary people even during the struggle itself, as they met, sometimes in secret, to plan their next moves and express their devotion to the cause. Songs, chants, fraternal embrace could reinforce the sense of comradeship involved, a kind of shared happiness that was possible even before the goals were realized.

Occasionally, at least when victory seemed within grasp, this sense of collective happiness could generate feelings of real joy. Take, for example, the night of August 4, 1789, when the French revolutionary assembly managed to meet together for the first time as the old regime was toppling. The mood was magical, "We wept with joy and emotion", one participant wrote. All the representatives, across social ranks, "treated each other with fraternal friendship", and the assembly would go on to pass motion after motion designed to create a better society. Moments like these, of contagious happiness founded on shared visions for the future, were not common, but they would crop up recurrently in modern history to show the new power of high hopes.

Assessing the Happiness Revolution: A First Cut

A genuine revolution in the definitions and expectations associated with happiness occurred in the 18th century, in much of the Western world. It was obviously complicated by different particular approaches, and especially the sometimes clashing options presented by the emphases on individual versus collective fulfillment. Praise for sensual indulgence jostled against the idea of happiness through self-sacrifice for the public good or even individual happiness through consumerism or education. The shared ideas of realization in this world and hope for future progress might be obscured by competing specific goals. The same applies to the disputes Rousseau and his followers provoked, about the tensions between modern civilization and a more natural happiness.

The Happiness Revolution in the West 105

Predictably also, the new ideas of happiness, of whatever stripe, encountered many critics. The crusty Samuel Johnson, in England, when asked whether a person can be happy in the moment answered simply, "only when he is drunk." Johnson, a rather traditional Christian (who also loved his wine), wrote scathingly about the "vanity of human wishes". Only faith in an afterlife could provide glimpses of happiness on this earth.

Enlightenment writers themselves sometimes faltered, admitting moments of sadness, even despair. Greater knowledge might actually increase human misery. A number of leaders worried that happiness was being distorted by the emphasis on personal pleasure – an old concern, which the newer trends could heighten. Thus, Immanuel Kant lamented the fact that "the principle of one's own happiness" might actually undermine morality, obliterating the difference between virtue and vice. "Making a man happy is quite different from making him good."

Criticism and doubt legitimately complicate appraisal of the scope of the happiness revolution by 1800. Many traditional Christians, from opponents of the French revolution to Protestants still deeply attached to belief in original sin, clearly stood apart, even if they did not always become active opponents of the new beliefs. Large numbers of people, particularly amid the illiterate minority or in the countryside, probably were simply unaware of the new ideas. Even some of the participants in new behaviors, the eager consumerists or those involved in premarital sex, may have had no real sense that they were expressing new values. It is impossible to determine the extent of conversion, even to new expectations for the future, particularly in societies where death rates remained high and many people continued to suffer serious deprivation.

For the new approach to happiness involved deep cultural change, and this usually takes time. As the following chapter suggests, it was in the 19th century that many of the basic new ideas about happiness began to be translated into more concrete beliefs and practices – and even then there were ongoing limitations. But the foundations were clearly established. Growing numbers of people were coming to believe that they should be able to find happiness in their lives and, equally important, that they should present a happy face to the world around them.

Further Reading

Two basic works on the transformation are:
Kotchemidova, Christina. "From Good Cheer to 'Drive-by Smiling': A Social History of Cheerfulness." *Journal of Social History* 39, no. 1 (2005): 5–37.
McMahon, Darrin M. *Happiness: A History*, 1st ed. (New York: Atlantic Monthly Press, 2006). This book is a pioneering guide to the intellectual history of happiness, with particular attention to the 18th-century revolution.
See also:
Boddice, Rob. *A History of Feelings* (London: Reaktion Books, 2019).

106　*The Happiness Revolution, 1700–1900*

Greene, Jack. *Pursuits of Happiness: The Social Development of Early Modern British Colonies and the Formation of American Culture* (Chapel Hill: University of North Carolina Press, 1988).

McMahon, Darrin M. "Finding Joy in the History of Emotions." In Susan Matt and Peter Stearns (Eds.), *Doing Emotions History* (Urbana: University of Illinois Press, 2013).

Slack, Paul. *The Invention of Improvement: Information and Material Progress in Seventeenth-Century England*, 1st ed. (Oxford: Oxford University Press, 2015).

Wootton, David. *Power, Pleasure and Profit: Insatiable Appetites from Machiavelli to Madison* (Cambridge, MA: Harvard University Press, 2018).

On the ways Enlightenment ideas were popularized:

Darnton, Robert. *The Business of Enlightenment Publishing History of the Encyclopedie, 1775–1800* (S.l: Belknap Press, 1987).

On melancholy:

MacDonald, Michael. *Mystical Bedlam: Madness, Anxiety, and Healing in Seventeenth-Century England*, 1st pbk. ed. (Cambridge [Cambridgeshire]: Cambridge University Press, 1983).

Stearns, Carol Zisowitz. "'Lord Help Me Walk Humbly': Anger and Sadness in England and America, 1570–1750." In Peter N. Stearns and Carol Z. Stearns (Eds.), *Emotion and Social Change: Toward a New Psychohistory*, 39–68. (New York: Holmes & Meier, 1988).

Watkins, Owen C. *The Puritan Experience: Studies in Spiritual Autobiography* (New York: Schocken Books, 1972).

On smiling, both before and after the big change:

Jones, Colin. *The Smile Revolution: In Eighteenth Century Paris* (Oxford: Oxford University Press, 2014).

See also:

Braddick, Michael J., Joanna Innes, and Paul Slack. *Suffering and Happiness in England 1550–1850: Narratives and Representations: A Collection to Honour Paul Slack*, 1st ed. (Oxford: Oxford University Press, 2017).

Stearns, Peter N. *Satisfaction Not Guaranteed Dilemmas of Progress in Modern Society* (New York: New York University Press, 2012).

Vincent-Buffault, Anne. *The History of Tears: Sensibility and Sentimentality in France* (New York: St. Martin's Press, 1991).

On comfort:

Crowley, John E. *The Invention of Comfort: Sensibilities and Design in Early Modern Britain and Early America* (Baltimore, MD: Johns Hopkins University Press, 2001).

DeJean, Joan. *The Age of Comfort When Paris Discovered Casual—and the Modern Home Began* (New York: Bloomsbury USA, 2010).

On consumerism:

Roche, Daniel. *A History of Everyday Things: The Birth of Consumption in France, 1600–1800* (Cambridge: Cambridge University Press, 2000).

Stearns, Peter N. *Consumerism in World History: The Global Transformation of Desire*, 2nd ed. (New York: Routledge, 2006).

On sexuality:

D'Emilio, John, and Estelle B. Freedman. *Intimate Matters: A History of Sexuality in America*, 2nd ed. (Chicago, IL: University of Chicago Press, 1998).

The Happiness Revolution in the West 107

Shorter, Edward. "Illegitimacy, Sexual Revolution, and Social Change in Modern Europe." *The Journal of Interdisciplinary History* 2, no. 2 (October 1, 1971): 237–272.

On individualism:

Taylor, Charles. *Sources of the Self: The Making of the Modern Identity* (Cambridge, MA: Harvard University Press, 1989).

Wahrman, Dror. *The Making of the Modern Self Identity and Culture in Eighteenth-Century England* (New Haven, CT: Yale University Press, 2004).

On changing attitudes toward death:

McManners, John. *Death and the Enlightenment: Changing Attitudes to Death among Christians and Unbelievers in Eighteenth-Century France* (Oxford: Oxford University Press, 1985).

Stearns, Peter N., ed., *Routledge History of Death Since 1800* (London: Routledge, 2020).

See also:

Pape, Walter. "Happy Endings in a World of Misery: A Literary Convention between Social Constraints and Utopia in Children's and Adult Literature." *Poetics Today* 13, no. 1 (1992): 179–196.

Shackleton, Robert. "The Greatest Happiness of the Greatest Number: The History of Bentham's Phrase." In Theodore Besterman ed., *Studies on Voltaire and the Eighteenth Century* (Oxford: Voltaire Foundation, 1972).

8 The Expansion of Happiness? The New Expectations Encounter Industrial Society

In 1904, a producer in the new movie industry, G.W. Bitzer, filmed a "Cake Walk" dance at the popular New York beach, Coney Island. The film featured male-female pairs of dancers, smiling broadly and often mugging for the camera, improvising more and more elaborate dance routines, while spectators cheered and often joined in. Americans were increasingly expressing themselves through novel forms of leisure, creating what some at the time and since have called a new "play ethic". Were modern people, at least in the West, finally learning how to have fun? Were they smiling more often because they were happier than ever before? Or was the situation, in historical perspective, more complicated?

The 19th century unquestionably saw the translation of many of the basic guidelines of the happiness revolution into a variety of new practices, some of them experimental but a number increasingly adopted among many groups in the Western world. Somewhat ironically, happiness now generated less explicit political interest than it had during the revolutionary decades of the 18th century, but the real action lay elsewhere. Some new ideas about happiness emerged as well, but the emphasis really shifted to various aspects of popular culture. The notion that people should be able to find happiness and appear happy showed up in a number of new expectations, practices, and behaviors.

The century also witnessed the industrial revolution, launched slightly earlier in Britain but now really beginning to reshape society both in Western Europe and the United States. This massive process challenged happiness in many ways, but it also generated new needs and new expressions. It is vital to remember that industrialization did not create modern Western ideas about happiness: these were already part of the cultural context. The 19th century formed the period in which the implications of industrialization for happiness first played out; but this was also the point at which specifically Western concepts of happiness helped shape the popular response.

The challenge was clear enough: in a situation where many groups were predisposed to seek happiness and even to expect people around them to be cheerful, how could these principles be translated into the emerging forms of industrial society? And what new complications emerged? The partial merger of the happiness imperative and Western industrial society became clearer in the second half of the 19th century, as the industrialization process outgrew its initial birth pains, but some important trends emerged early on.

The Cultural Framework

Philosophy and Science

Happiness remained a vital theme in Western intellectual life during the 19th century. Enlightenment emphases persisted, with some new twists; but alternative approaches developed as well – some of them supporting the belief in happiness, others raising new perspectives. Several schools of thought had direct impact on the actual experience of happiness but, overall, there was no systematic revolution to match what the Enlightenment had already produced.

A progressive approach. A number of writers built directly on the 18th-century legacy. Most liberal economists and political theorists continued to argue that happiness was the chief human goal and that greater freedom would steadily expand opportunities for its achievement. For John Stuart Mill, for example, happiness was the "test of all rules of conduct" and the true goal of life. Devoted to liberty, Mill granted that in principle people should have the right to make unhappy choices, so long as these did not unfairly impinge on others, but overall he confirmed the Enlightenment approach. Most liberals remained optimistic that prospects for happiness were improving, thanks to industrial progress and political reform; indeed, what now seems a rather simplistic view of history developed, rather in the spirit of Condorcet, that saw contemporary society as the pinnacle of human happiness to date, with even better things to come.

Liberal nationalists added the importance of the nation-state to the liberal vision. Particularly in Italy and Germany advocates promoted the idea that achieving national unity (with a constitutional and parliamentary political order to follow) would provide a vital spur to progress. The individual would be enhanced by belonging to a common national community. To be sure, leaders like Giuseppe Mazzini worried that the notion of happiness, itself, placed too much emphasis on the individual, and urged the importance of duty; this was a tension that would become more important later, under more conservative versions of nationalism.

Though bitterly opposed to liberal economics, Karl Marx and his followers also built on Enlightenment ideas. Marxists condemned the capitalist system around them, which was clearly making most people more and more unhappy, indeed alienating them from society. Only revolution could correct this misery. But revolution would come, and Marx massively spurred the kind of hope for a happier future that popular protest movements had already begun to generate. Once the capitalist order had been

110 *The Happiness Revolution, 1700–1900*

overturned and the proletariat was victorious, true happiness on earth would at last be possible. As Friedrich Engels put it, "there exist certain irrefutable basic principles which being the result of the whole of historical development, require no proof": these were that "every individual strives to be happy" and that the "happiness of the individual is inseparable from the happiness of all." The Marxist vision would in fact provide comfort to many participants in the rising labor movement and would help shape a major approach to happiness in the 20th century.

A Romantic approach. Early in the 19th century, a growing Romantic movement drew a wide array of thinkers and artists on both sides of the Atlantic, with some offshoots that continued even after 1850. Romantics contested the Enlightenment in many ways. Notably, they objected to the undue insistence on reason, seeking more passion and wild beauty than the 18th century had emphasized. In some cases this led to direct disputes with the emphasis on happiness itself. Romantic intellectuals might be attracted to more traditional Christianity. They might savor darker visions, and even delight in scenes of melancholy and sadness. From this strand of Romanticism came the earliest version of the suffering artist, misunderstood by his time but resolute in his unhappy condition.

This was not however the only Romantic approach. Romantics also talked about joy (more commonly than happiness). Thus the English poet Percy Shelley: "All art is dedicated to joy, and there is no higher or more serious undertaking than to make men happy." From this Romantic impulse would come a wealth of poetry and fiction, along with visual arts, often highlighting scenes of nature or the charming simplicity of peasant life, that were expressly designed to bring pleasure to their viewers. It was from this same impulse, and a poem by the writer Friedrich Schiller, that Ludwig van Beethoven would write the fourth movement of his ninth symphony, the "Ode to Joy", undoubtedly the most influential musical tribute to happiness ever composed.

Impacts: utopianism and variety. In combination, the progressive and the romantic impulses combined to generate other contributions to happiness in the 19th century.

The first was a fascinating series of efforts to create special communities where social organization would introduce maximum happiness here and now. Utopians criticized the industrial world taking shape around them, but they believed that alternatives were possible, without revolution, that would solve all the problems of greed and inequality. Largely conceived in Europe, actual utopian experiments spread particularly on the more abundant land available in the United States.

Charles Fourier, for example, envisaged a community in which different kinds of work would be freely contributed, with the results equally distributed among members. "Universal happiness and gaiety will reign. A unity of interest and views will arise, crime and violence will disappear... Elegance and luxury will be had by everyone." Some utopian communities

New Expectations Encounter Industrial Society   111

also sought to maximize sexual pleasure. And, while all the communities ultimately failed, some of the aspirations involved might provide hope even to people unable to participate in such dramatic experiments.

More important in the long run was the extent to which Enlightenment and Romantic legacies might combine in producing greater diversity in the novels and works of art and music available to growing audiences. Greater, though still incomplete, freedom of the press plus improvements in printing technology and literacy supported a wider range of opportunities than had been available in the 18th century. For several decades, large numbers of people were attracted to public lectures, often in the progressive spirit. Romantic writers contributed a host of novels and short stories, some highlighting sorrow, others (like *Young Frankenstein*) indulging in fear and horror, still others featuring fulfillments of young love. On the whole, the most popular work tended to offer happy endings – the budding writer Louisa May Alcott was told by her publisher that her stories must have an upbeat ending in which the principal couple successfully marries – but the variety itself was impressive. Accommodation to different tastes – including, now, those who took pleasure in being artificially frightened – was not an unprecedented cultural feature, but it unquestionably extended in the 19th century.

Science and doubt. A third general intellectual current took shape particularly after 1850, and without displacing progressive or neo-romantic themes it raised some new doubts about happiness. Charles Darwin, though himself a happy man convinced on the whole that people in general could seek happiness, famously linked humankind with the animal world in his groundbreaking *Origin of Species* in 1859. Darwin noted that many animals displayed an interest in pleasure, but his findings might cast doubt on any special or higher human quality to happiness. Most human emotion, after all, could now be linked to analogues in the animal world, and happiness was no different.

A few decades later Sigmund Freud raised another set of complications from the standpoint of psychiatry. Much human action is determined by an unconscious, and while the unconscious might seek pleasure it was also burdened by a host of fears and repressions that could severely compromise mental health, not to mention happiness. Freud hardly denied the possibility of happiness, but he unquestionably made it seem more complicated, more likely to encounter frustration or be undermined by darker impulses.

Partly because of the new scientific emphases, partly because of a certain Romantic legacy, a segment of European high culture at the end of the 19th century became fashionably pessimistic. The *fin de siècle* mood highlighted a sense of cynicism and decadence, a feeling that bourgeois civilization was drowning in materialism, that a crisis was imminent. For some – for example, those who turned to militarism or virulent anti-Semitism – happiness, either now or in future, was almost irrelevant.

112 *The Happiness Revolution, 1700–1900*

These were, on the whole, still minor themes, and even the more complex findings of the biologists and psychologists did not necessarily have much impact on popular views of happiness. It was revealing that the many newspaper commentaries that looked back on the recent past and anticipated the future, as a new century came into view in 1900, strongly emphasized the positive. This had been a great century, full of progress from the abolition of slavery to the advent of universal education, and the new century would be even brighter, with even greater possibilities for human happiness. Still, it is probably fair to say that the intellectual climate around happiness had become somewhat more complicated.

Popular Culture: Signs of Good Cheer

Dominant popular ideas about happiness built more clearly on the themes of the 18th century than was true for the world of intellectuals and artists, though there was important overlap. Before turning to the principal interactions between expectations and advancing industrialization – which is where the main 19th-century history of happiness centers – we can consider a few leading cases of continuity and enhancement.

The interest in cheerfulness continued to mount. Early in the nineteenth century, childrearing manuals in the United States began to emphasize the importance of "cheerful obedience" in children. Obedience was an old interest, but the notion that it should be accompanied by cheerfulness was a really new (and potentially demanding) idea. The theme would persist into the 1860s, when obedience began to drop away in favor of cheerfulness all by itself. During the mid-century decade, the word sulky was particularly directed at children who failed to follow through on the new emotional requirement.

Early self-help manuals, while paying primary attention to the importance of frugality and hard work, sometimes noted how important it was to be cheerful on the job. Thus the British guru Samuel Smiles proclaimed – his name was purely coincidental – "Cheerfulness is also an excellent wearing quality. It has been called the bright weather of the heart."

Southern planters began to emphasize the importance of cheerfulness among their slaves, highlighting instances of singing and dancing and claiming frequent smiling. This was a claim that had not figured in slave descriptions in the previous century. A new ulterior motive was unquestionably in play: the myth of the happy slave was concocted in part to counter the rising abolitionist sentiment. But the idea that a good planter patriarch had happy slaves around him as testimony to his beneficent rule may have comforted Southern whites themselves. It fit in with the increasing hope for a cheerful social environment, as well as allaying fears of revolt.

Cheerfulness began to feature in etiquette manuals. Thus Walter Houghton, a popular later 19th century expert in the United States, while

New Expectations Encounter Industrial Society 113

stressing the importance of avoiding boisterous laughter or the horrible habit of making puns, urged a positive approach in conversations with others. "No one has a right to go into society unless he can be animating as well as animated. Society demands cheerfulness – and it is the duty of everyone to help make it and sustain it."

Records of smiling in the 19th century are complicated by the fact that the growing popularity of photography involved a time-lapse technology that made sustaining a smile very difficult; 1900 was a turning point here. But continued innovations in the English language suggests the mounting effort to enforce the appearance of good cheer. Thus, along with sulky, cranky came into use. Originally derived from German to describe people who were sick, the meaning shifted around 1800 to mean "crabby and irritable". Crabby itself was an additional label, increasingly common. Grumpy was yet another term that grew steadily in usage from the very late 18th century.

Then in the 1890s, apparently first among college fraternities in the United States, the words "grouch" and "grouchy" took on their modern meaning, again denoting someone who was not meeting the current social standard. For a time, to "have a grouch on" was a common slang expression. A story in 1902 amplified the meaning.

> The Grouch, on the other Hand, gave a correct imitation of a Bear with a Sore Toe. He carried a Facial Expression that frightened little Children in Street Cars and took all the Starch out of sentimental young ladies. He seemed perpetually to carry the Hoof-Marks of a terrible nightmare.

The barrage of new or redefined terms was unprecedented, constituting a revealing campaign to encourage adherence to the new norm and to reproach nonconformists. Had it not been increasingly important to cajole people into cheerfulness or to make them feel bad when they did not measure up, such novel words would have been unnecessary.

The 19th century was also the seat, chronologically, of the idea of a merry Christmas, with appropriate family ceremonies attached. The first known use of the term (from a British navy admiral, wishing well to his crew), occurred in 1699, which was also the date of the carol, "We wish you a Merry Christmas". But it was in the 19th century that the term came into its own, again translating the "happiness revolution" into compelling ritual.

The idea of celebrating Christmas was not new. This had long been a festival that gave rise to feasting and, often, a good bit of rowdiness, including efforts by poor people to intimidate wealthier passers-by into small gifts. The idea of happiness was not explicitly attached. Indeed, the rowdy quality so often got out of hand that Puritan authorities, both in England and what became the United States, banned the practice. Though it was restored fairly quickly as a holiday in Britain, it long remained rather

114   *The Happiness Revolution, 1700–1900*

disreputable. In parts of Western Europe as well, Christmas was also associated with fright, with St. Nicholas or a companion striking fear particularly among children, or administering punishment for bad behavior.

It was only in the 1820s that an effort to revive a more sedate and positive Christmas began to take shape, with an indelible association with the idea of happiness. A story by the American writer Washington Irving, in 1822, highlighted the kind of cheerful celebration that he had experienced among Anglicans in Britain. Also in that year, Clement Moore wrote the famous poem that came to be called *The Night Before Christmas*, with its rich evocation of children's excitement, a resolutely jolly Santa Claus, and family gift-giving.

In Britain itself the crucial turning point came in 1843 with Charles Dickens' story, the *Christmas Carol*. It was this story that really began to popularize the phrase: "Merry Christmas", and to enhance the association with family pleasure, feasting, and a charitable spirit. The story also provided yet another term, "Scrooge", to characterize people who were not measuring up to the requisite happiness and generosity. It was also in 1843 that the first Christmas card was made available commercially, again spreading the notion that this was a vital time for happiness.

Actual celebrations expanded accordingly. In 1856 the American poet Longfellow commented, "The old puritan feeling prevents it from being a cheerful, hearty holiday, though every year makes it more so." By 1860 many American states had made Christmas a legal holiday, and on both sides of the Atlantic the German custom of setting up Christmas trees became a standard part of the celebration. Gift-giving to family and friends became steadily more elaborate. Here was a crucial illustration of the steadily increasing commitment to happiness – though it would also pose a challenge to non-Christian minorities in Western society.

Divisions of Industrial Life

Clear extensions of 18th-century ideas about happiness and cheer also began to combine with the sweeping effects of industrialization. Happiness began to connect, or at least to be recommended, for a number of the basic categories of industrial existence.

For growing numbers of people, the rhythm of ordinary life began to change. Preindustrial society had been marked by the intermixture of family, work, and relaxation time, spiced by the periodic festivals. A normal day involved alternations between labor and breaks, including chatting and napping, all in a family context.

Industrial life was different, though this became fully clear only in the later 19th century. Family and work were increasingly separated. Then, as hours of work shortened, normal days were divided between time on the job and a period (in addition to sleep) set aside for leisure and family. Increasingly, the weekend was also expanded. Experiments with granting

New Expectations Encounter Industrial Society   115

Saturday, or part of Saturday, off began in Britain in the 1840s; the first English-language reference to the "weekend" occurred in 1879, and soon workers in countries like France also began demanding what they called the "English week". Here was another earmarked time for family and leisure, plus any religious activity.

These new time divisions also described the categories in which specific ideas of happiness and cheer began to be applied to the normal pattern of industrial life. For many, family time was partially redefined in terms of emotional satisfaction; the leisure component of happiness expanded noticeably; the work category raised several vital issues. For people at least partially predisposed to an expectation of happiness, accommodating to the new rhythms of industrial life offered a mixture of opportunity and challenge.

Happy Families

From a late 19th-century letter sent by an American to the woman he was courting:

> Dear Darling Sarah! How I love you, how happy I have been! You are the joy of my life…. I cannot tell you how much happiness you give me, nor how constantly it is in all my thoughts….My darling, how I long for the time when I shall see you.

In many Western countries, the 19th century was the heyday of the romantic letter, filled with the association of love and happiness.

The history of the family is a huge subject, and a challenging one. The Western family changed frequently over time, but assessment must always be combined with a recognition that some families, regardless of the time period, must have experienced some standard emotions – including recurrent happiness and a hope for more. We have seen that Protestantism may have helped enhance the positive emotional experience of family life in key parts of the Western world. In point of fact, however, it was only in the late 18th century that the words "happy" and "family" began to be commonly associated. Applying the growing anticipation of happiness to family life was a crucial development at a time when, regardless of emotional content, the family was undergoing a daunting set of challenges. This was one of the arenas where the happiness theme interacted most urgently with the structural changes brought by mounting industrialization.

The big changes – and they would occur whether a new happiness theme was involved or not – centered on the reduction of the traditional economic functions of the family. For, with the industrial revolution, production moved out of the home – a transition that often occurred literally within a few decades. In many families, men became the chief "breadwinners"; women worked only until marriage, if at all, and at most informally

116 *The Happiness Revolution, 1700–1900*

thereafter. Soon, children also lost their economic importance in many cases. More complicated production equipment reduced the tasks that younger children could perform, at least within a few decades, while new expectations of schooling drew many children away as well. Increasingly, children became an expense, rather than an asset, and not surprisingly the birth rate began to drop.

These changes were compounded by other challenges, some of which had emerged already in the 18th century. Most obviously, arranged marriages declined as parental authority diminished. When young people moved to the city – and rapid urbanization was a vital component of early industrialization – parental control was directly reduced.

Of course family functions remained. Even as it declined as a production unit, families could help adults cope with the difficult combination of work and the other necessities of life: preparing food, maintaining some kind of home, and caring for the children even with their reduced numbers.

But families were also being sought for emotional support, and this was where the expanding notions of love and happiness came in. Increasingly, many observers, and many family members themselves, argued that amid the confusing changes of an industrial, urban society, the family provided vital refuge – as one put it, a "haven in the heartless world." A happy, peaceful family would be able to raise children properly and would offer adults themselves tranquility and satisfaction.

The family itself would presumably be launched by a romantic courtship, free from direct parental interference but not usually in conflict with parental wishes. Through courtship, a couple would develop the kind of love that would offer true happiness – the kind of love suggested in the many letters courting couples actually exchanged.

Short of classic courtship, many single adults began to advertise for a suitable mate in the local newspaper – a sign that traditional family arrangements were often no longer possible. This recourse began first in London, in the 1790s, but would spread widely on the continent and in the United States, and later beyond. This want-ad section expanded steadily. Some ads stressed a desire for financial security, but a growing number simply sought an emotionally fulfilling partnership, the basis for a happy marriage. Thus one ad expressed the hope of finding someone "with *brains* and *heart* (the latter especially)", while another, from a woman, wanted "love and affection". Men often claimed that they had found success in other aspects of life, but needed the loving partner to complete real happiness.

The image of the happy family, described in many advice books and magazine articles through the century, would of course be completed with children, who would be loved and loving in turn (and presumably cheerful), plus, increasingly, the novelty of a family pet. When the happy family could gather around the piano – another consumer innovation of the 19th century, but widely adopted in the middle class and beyond – the picture might seem complete (Figure 8.1).

New Expectations Encounter Industrial Society 117

Figure 8.1 Frequency of the phrase "happy family" in English, 1700–2008, Google Ngram Viewer, accessed May 27th, 2020.

This was powerful stuff, promoted by a variety of print materials and, insofar as can be judged, truly sought by many people in their own right. Without claiming that the fact of a happy family was brand new, there is little question that it was more explicitly noted, and more widely sought as a goal in itself, than ever before in Western society. The term "happy-family" emerged powerfully, and for the first time, in published material in English right at the end of the 18th century, and then crested periodically in the decades that followed.

The combination raised two questions: the obvious one – of how many people actually sought, much less found, this emotional experience in family life, will be discussed at the end of this chapter. For now, we can simply note that the same value system that touted the happy, loving family also gave rise to a mounting divorce rate; for if a family was not happy, could a partner not freely seek to pursue happiness some other way?

The second question is more subtle, but it has been much discussed: was this particular combination, either in principle or in fact, aimed at the happiness of both husband and wife, or slanted disproportionately toward the former?

The issue of gender and happiness has come up before – back with Aristotle, for example, or with some of the sources of pleasure available in premodern cities – and it is an important one. The notion of a loving courtship implied that emotional satisfaction of both partners was involved, and letters and diaries suggest this was often the case. Women as well as men could find happiness as they fell in love. In practice, however, and particularly in industrial settings where men alone were bringing down a wage, the relationship could turn markedly unequal, with men calling the shots without much attention to the impact on a wife's happiness. Further, even in the imagery, women were seen as disproportionately responsible for the family's emotional well-being, called upon to maintain a happy disposition for husband and children alike. Male virtues

118   *The Happiness Revolution, 1700–1900*

and male work should be matched by the particularly affectionate qualities of good women.

There is no reason to be too cynical about gender disparities. Wives and mothers did have more latitude in the home than ever before, and the responsibility for promoting happiness might truly be compatible with happiness itself. But there could be some new tension.

The Happy Child

Children were a vital part of the happy family model, a component that may have first been expressed in the idea that they should be expected to contribute cheerfulness in response to loving parenting. But the idea gradually emerged that they should be happy themselves. Google Ngrams suggest that the combination "happy childhood" was rarely used in English-language writings before 1830, but once introduced its relative frequency rose quite rapidly.

For the idea of the happy child was a major innovation, one of the really important extensions of the growing interest in happiness in general. We have seen that traditionally, children and happiness were not normally associated. They might have been happy, in fact; their opportunities for play were truly important. But they were not *expected* to be happy, nor was there any overall parental obligation in that regard. Childhood was too precarious, the duties of work too pressing for childhood to seem a particularly happy stage of life. This was why, in memoirs, childhood had almost never been recalled with much pleasure.

This now began to change. Raising happy children was not simply part of the new family imagery, but an increasingly explicit goal in itself. Parents began to seek active ways to make their offspring happy. This was the principal reason, for example, behind the emergence of newspaper comic strips, which began, revealingly, to be called "funnies" in the later 19th century. Pioneering work here was done in Germany and Switzerland, but the genre flourished particularly in the United States. By 1905, American papers were regularly offering the Sunday funnies, a section that was long shared by parents and children alike as a source of mutual amusement.

Nothing indicated the shift toward cherishing the happy child more than the rise of the birthday party – a genuine 19th-century innovation on both sides of the Atlantic. Before this time, birthday celebrations had been limited to upper-class adults. Rulers had publicly proclaimed birthdays, going back to the Egyptian pharaohs; here was a chance to evoke the adulation of faithful subjects. Christmas, of course, highlighted a birthday, but this also was a special case. Aristocratic adult males may have celebrated birthdays in the Roman period, and they began to do so again in Western Europe in the 18th century. But ordinary people, no; and children of any class, not at all.

New Expectations Encounter Industrial Society   119

The first child's birthday party in North America involved the daughter of a wealthy family in Boston, in 1772. It provided a chance for the family to display its wealth, and teach the child the importance of gratitude. Gradually, in the first half of the 19th century, the practice spread – aided by new equipment that allowed commercial bakers to concoct and sell fancier cakes – and it became more clearly associated with honoring the child and creating a happy occasion. Various books and articles began to discuss the birthday and what its purposes were; women's magazines made this a regular feature during the second half of the century. One of the great institutions intended to symbolize the modern importance of happiness was being born. By mid-century, popular birthday books began to guide people in what to do.

Parties were still, by standards today, fairly low-key. Family and a few friends; cake and often fruit (which was a more infrequent treat a century and a half ago); modest gifts. Children were expected to be grateful, and sometimes in the upper classes they gave some goodies to servants, as an expression of charity. Religious overtones were common as well.

But the main focus was the child and its happiness, with a bit of consumerism thrown in. An early birthday manual told children that properly done, "your birthdays will be happy ones". Another commented, "poor little things, they need all the fun they can get." Yet another more grandiosely suggested that a child's birthday should be a "rejoicing jubilee" – after all a full year was "a glorious thing". An American authority put the birthday in the larger context of the happy family, seeing it as the expression of "domestic felicity".

The expanding practice did prompt a bit of revealing criticism from social conservatives. Some already worried about consumer excess: the term "selfish indulgence" was bandied about. Others argued that children should be giving thanks to parents and to God, rather than getting so much attention themselves. But the greatest concern – reflecting the way children themselves were connecting to happiness – was the fact that children were increasingly expecting birthday parties and gifts as a matter of course, giving them an inappropriate hold over their parents; "the presents were regarded (by both children and their parents) as the discharge of a debt."

But the birthday, and the explicit association with a child's happiness and expectations, was irrepressible. More and more groups participated, so that by 1900 it was clearly a commonplace. To be sure, another 26 years would pass before the classic hymn "happy birthday" would see the light of day, confirming and spreading the emotional standard still further; but in fact it was already a done deal. Attention now shifted to providing birthday celebrations for adults themselves.

To be sure, children in birthday-honoring families were not always happy; the celebrations themselves could misfire. But the idea that children should be happy; that parents had responsibility for this; that childhood

120   *The Happiness Revolution, 1700–1900*

should be looked back upon as a happy time; and that finally, an unhappy childhood was something to deplore – these major changes were well established by 1900, and would only develop further thereafter.

Along with merry Christmases, happy birthdays represented an unprecedented effort to institutionalize happiness in Western society, both occasions representing ways that 19th-century families strove to translate the earlier happiness revolution into an annual cycle.

Work

In contrast to the changing family ideals, the relationship between work and happiness during the 19th century was far more problematic. The subject was front and center: work was the scene of dramatic changes during the industrial revolution. And there was unquestionably an impulse to apply the happiness formula to this experience as well. But the connections were more difficult; a number of unpleasant realities intruded. Indeed, the idea that work and happiness might be rather separate subjects– expressed today in the otherwise odd formula that urges attention to "work/life balance", as if work was not a part of life –began to emerge at this point, if only implicitly. After all, one of the reasons to emphasize the importance of happy families was a recognition that other aspects of modern life might be rather grim. At the least, the happiness/work equation was a complicated one in the industrial context.

Work had long maintained a rather uncomfortable position in visions of happiness, as earlier chapters have discussed. The industrial revolution added to the burdens in many ways, though because the types of work available expanded considerably, generalizations are difficult. Certainly, the kinds of satisfactions enjoyed by artisans in preindustrial economies were progressively stripped away; they even lost ground in the craft areas that survived. Skill levels were reduced in the interest of faster, more uniform production. Autonomy on the job decreased: more and more people worked, lifelong, under the supervision of others. Early in the industrial revolution, many workers made their displeasure quite clear, by frequent labor protests and, often, returning to rural jobs whenever conditions permitted. Most dramatic were Luddite efforts to destroy industrial machinery directly, in hopes of returning to an idealized artisanal economy. None of these efforts really succeeded, though they may have given some participants a bit of release, but they vividly indicated new tensions over what work was all about – and the great gulf between many daily routines and happiness.

In the long run, even when workers became more accustomed to novel settings like the factory, several liabilities persisted. It was difficult to maintain any sense of personal control, when foremen or other supervisors monitored the shop floor and rigid rules sought to make routines as uniform as possible. Many workers had little sense of their final product,

New Expectations Encounter Industrial Society   121

working as they did on only one segment of the manufacturing process; critics like Karl Marx correctly indicated how this could generate deep alienation. Most challenging was the sheer pace of work, which intensified steadily with each new generation of machinery. By the end of the 19th century many workers were complaining of nervous exhaustion, and a series of new terms – from what was called neurasthenia to, later, nervous breakdowns or stress, translated this pressure into diagnosable disorders.

All this could increase the distance between modern work and happiness. It was revealing that in the 19th century, no rich literature on workplace happiness emerged – in marked contrast to the attention lavished on the family. This would change later on, but for now the void was noticeable.

Most telling was the absence of explicit reference to happiness in the most widely publicized discussions of the importance and function of work. Beginning in the later 18th century and reaching full flower around 1850, a number of authorities laid out what can be called a new, middle-class work ethic, and their views were shared by many actual employers. Here was the formula: hard work was the anchor of success. Putting in long hours, avoiding distractions, learning how to work rapidly and efficiently – these were the keys to a good life. People who did not succeed, including the poor, had only themselves to blame, for they clearly did not work hard enough. This was a powerful formula, preached in all the industrializing countries by people like Ben Franklin, Samuel Smiles, or Horatio Alger. What was missing – aside from occasional recommendations about cheerfulness, from people like Smiles – was any clear connection to happiness.

For their part, many workers, aware that this work ethic served the interests of the business class, tried to pursue a different set of values, putting in their time but also making it clear that they were reluctant to work too hard, since the profits from their labor went to others. Many employers complained that, thanks to chatting or wandering around the shop floor, most workers contributed about 60% of the effort the owners claimed to expect. The limitations of the work ethic were real, but the alternative – working a bit more slowly – did not really feature happiness any more clearly.

In many ways, industrialization simply deepened the old belief that work and happiness did not mix, that whatever happiness might be available in life must be found off the job.

Many workers, of various sorts, did truly feel trapped, and profoundly alienated. A German coal miner named Max Lotz, at the end of the century, wrote of his hatred of his job, the extent to which it exhausted him mentally and physically, leaving him even unable to sleep properly. While his anguish was unusually articulate, many workers surely shared it to some extent.

122 *The Happiness Revolution, 1700–1900*

The picture of alienation, however, needs to be modified in several ways, complicating any overall judgment of work and happiness in this phase of the industrial revolution.

1 People varied in their responses to situations, and many struggled hard to find some meaning in what they did. And jobs differed. Locomotive engineers, by the middle of the century, often commented on the pride they felt in driving their mechanical monsters through the countryside. Puddlers, a new and dangerous occupation in the growing steel industry, took pleasure in their skill.

2 Members of the middle class, working in business or the growing modern professions, might buy into the work ethic quite directly, finding that devotion to the job really did bring a kind of happiness even though they rarely used the word explicitly. Factory owners struggling for success, doctors enjoying the growing prestige and expanding knowledge available in medicine, could easily become obsessed with their jobs, even finding it difficult to enjoy time off. They would have been hard-pressed to come up with a different definition of happiness.

Another tricky category took shape toward the end of the 19th century, in the growing array of white-collar workers – a "lower middle class" – that served as secretaries, department store clerks, primary school teachers. Many of these people did not have intrinsically interesting jobs, but they often absorbed the middle-class work ethic and found satisfaction in toeing the line – proud, among other things, that they were clearly superior to blue-collar factory hands.

3 Many members of the middle and lower middle classes, and in their own way many workers, came up with a newer means of connecting work and happiness: they modified much hope of deeply enjoying the job itself but valued it for the support it provided for life off the job.

Segments of the working class came up with this option most explicitly, beginning around the middle of the century. British printers in the 1850s began bargaining with their employers around the following formula: they would accept new machinery, higher speeds, less rewarding conditions in the job in return for higher wages that they could enjoy off the job. Work became, not a source, but an *instrument* of happiness. Happiness, in turn, would be found in the pleasure one could take in providing for the family (connecting to the happy imagery around family life, and the real pride and love that successful breadwinning could express). And it might be found, as well, in higher levels of consumerism. Many middle-class personnel, similarly, particularly as business bureaucracies began to supplant individual entrepreneurship, developed a somewhat comparable calculation, finding that somewhat disappointing work could be balanced by the other aspects of life that salaries supported. Instrumentalism might connect

New Expectations Encounter Industrial Society   123

work and happiness at least indirectly, so long as real earnings were increasing.

4   Finally, and even more directly connected to the work ethic, there was the lure of social mobility, another notion that began to win explicit attention from the late 18th century onward. What if the job, whatever its current limitations, served as the basis for rising higher in society? Here was a potential link between happiness and a very specific kind of hope, that could prove quite compelling.

Mobility was not new: from Confucian China to medieval Europe individuals had periodically managed to rise out of the peasantry thanks to education or initiative or some combination thereof. But mobility was never officially valued or promoted by any preindustrial culture: it was far more important to urge contentment with one's current position in life. This now began to change, and from Prussia to the United States school systems and popular articles began to promote the idea of getting ahead. This sat at the base of the new work ethic: hard work would propel one forward, make one, in Benjamin Franklin's terms, "healthy, wealthy and wise." Happiness, here, centered on how work would connect to the future.

Not everyone found this relevant or possible. The impulse to remain in place, to do what one's parents did, was still strong. But there is no question that the mobility theme became a powerful one. Particularly in the United States, in a culture that boasted about individualism and equality of opportunity, what people at the time and since have called the "American Dream" rested strongly on the notion that a person, or a person's children, could rise in life, and that success through mobility was in turn the essence of happiness. As a German immigrant put it around 1850: only in the United States could "the talents, energy and perseverance of a person" have full "opportunity to display" and, presumably, seal success and happiness in the future.

Links between work and happiness remained elusive in the first century of industrialization. At the same time, the thrust of the "happiness revolution", plus sheer human adaptability, made it impossible to abandon happiness in work entirely. In the process, however, much of the connection depended on satisfactions off the job, or on fervent hope for mobility.

Leisure

Without question, the most dramatic innovations involving happiness in the 19th-century Western society centered on innovations in consumerism and leisure. They were not necessarily more important than the new commitment to the happy family, and indeed the two facets often connected. But they steadily changed the nature of life off the job, even the structure of the day and week, and clearly sought to serve a growing taste for happiness.

124   *The Happiness Revolution, 1700–1900*

Challenges to leisure were considerable in the new industrial context. In the first place, there were strong remnants of older suspicions about having fun, inherited from religious conventions or upper-class snobbery about popular tastes. Second, industrial work itself simply took up a great deal of time, and while this began to be modified by somewhat shorter hours – factory days of 12, even 10 instead of 14 – the process of change was slow. Third, as we have seen, the kind of instrumentalism that arose in the workplace assumed that life off the job should become steadily more entertaining: that was the modern happiness bargain, but it assumed that leisure opportunities would respond accordingly.

And finally, novel leisure forms emerged in the aftermath of a substantial destruction of the old festival tradition that had served as such an important source of happiness, particularly for the masses of people, in preindustrial life. As cities grew, festivals were hard to maintain amid groups of relative strangers; they had depended on relatively stable communities. New police forces were suspicious of festivals, because they were so often rowdy and might, in urban contexts, lead to collective protest. Industrial employers disliked festivals because they took too much time away from work and often left workers lethargic and hungover for days after the festival itself. Here was a powerful combination of factors, often supplemented by more traditional religious disapproval, that gradually dismantled the festival tradition, leaving only remnants or, with Christmas, confining them to a largely familial context. For several decades in the early 19th century, there is simply no question that popular leisure deteriorated, focusing largely on increased drinking and modest family outings.

Modern leisure, then, had to provide compensation for work and either duplicate or replace the older values of the festivals. It is not clear that the innovations entirely did the trick – that's a judgment for later – but there was no question about the effort involved, particularly as work hours shortened somewhat and more people gained some resources beyond subsistence.

Three new or expanding outlets deserve attention: a second phase of modern consumerism; the dramatic expansion of entertainment outlets; and the striking ascent of modern spectator sports.

Consumerism. The notion of using things and the process of acquisition itself to provide happiness had already accelerated as part of the revolution in happiness that took shape in the 18th century. Now, however, the process visibly expanded. Beginning in the 1830s a new institution, the department store, became the urban consumer mecca, offering unprecedented arrays of goods, alluringly displayed, to tempt and beguile shoppers. In the United States, mail order catalogs offered similar opportunities to anticipate and enjoy a variety of goods, even in the countryside.

The goods themselves became more elaborate and enticing, thanks to factory production and rising imports. Middle-class homes filled with imported "oriental" carpets and lamps. Urbanites enjoyed an increasingly

New Expectations Encounter Industrial Society 125

sensationalist mass press, bent on conveying excitement and variety even more than news. In the final decades of the century, the bicycle provided a vital innovation. Useful to get to work, it was also a trigger for periodic escapes. Bicycle trips ushered in a new road network. Courting couples could use bicycles to get farther away from adult supervision, while women's clothing had to become looser, less cumbersome to accommodate the new machines.

Arguably, consumer opportunities, including the new pleasures of shopping, were expanding rapidly enough to satisfy the needs generated by the pressures of work while often, as well, embellishing family life. Yet questions about the real contribution to happiness became more complicated as well. Were people buying things that really made them happy, or were they simply being dazzled by department store displays? More sophisticated advertising added to the conundrum: the first professional agencies emerged in the United States in the 1870s, while improved printing techniques and vivid language made posters and magazine pages more enticing. Gone were ads that mainly touted the value and quality of the item; in was material that directly connected items to a notion of happiness. Thus by 1900 silk stockings were being presented not in terms of practicality and durability, but because they were "bewitching", "alluring" – "to feel young again, buy our silk." At an extreme, a new problem with kleptomania, mainly by middle-class women in a frenzy to buy, suggested that consumerism could express more compulsion than happiness.

Entertainment. More than ever before, people began to buy entertainment, rather than relying on occasional offerings or festival occasions. Correspondingly, the prestige of leading professional entertainers began to rise steadily – a clear sign of their new importance. Actors were no longer relegated to the lowest rungs of society.

For some, periodic opportunities to travel – for pleasure, not for religious purposes – formed part of the new entertainment package. Upper-middle-class families increasingly took advantage of the railway network to take a few weeks in the country during the summer – often with the husband staying back at work and only joining on weekends. Networks of resort hotels sprang up in mountain and seaside locations near major cities. Thomas Cook's travel company emerged in the 1840s in Britain to help travel novices organize regional and, soon, continental European trips. By the end of the century, working-class families were taking weekend train trips to beaches and seaside resorts.

The rise of the amusement park was an American contribution to the growing interest in pleasure and entertainment, as the label suggested. It also built on the opportunities industrial technology presented to provide new thrills, with Ferris wheels and other devices, and an abundance of electric lighting. The park maintained some of the earlier entertainments associated with commercial fairs and pleasure gardens in Europe, but now added more regular opportunities for excitement – beginning with the

126   *The Happiness Revolution, 1700–1900*

rides built for the 1893 Columbian Exposition in Chicago. Traveling carnival shows began to embellish rural county fairs and other occasions even outside the amusement parks themselves.

In the long run, however, nothing was more indicative of the new "fun ethic" than the expansion of popular theater, both in Europe and the United States, during the final decades of the 19th century. What was called music hall in Britain, vaudeville in the United States drew growing audiences to mixtures of comedy, dance, and music. Electric lighting allowed several shows a night (which meant that audiences now had to keep track of time, another leisure innovation), while urban streetcars and subways carried crowds from various parts of the city.

Most popular theater had working-class origins, but it increasingly drew middle- and upper-class crowds eager to escape the moralism or stiffness of some of the more fashionable entertainments such as lectures or orchestral concerts. The blending was fascinating. For their part, entertainers toned down the language and sexuality of the performances to meet their new clientele halfway. By 1900, this kind of popular entertainment, and the professionals involved, would begin to populate the new movie industry – expanding opportunities even further. In addition to new technical effects, movie theaters also developed a new culture of silence: mass entertainment no longer was supposed to include incessant conversation, though this conversion would take some time.

Clearly, for audiences drawn from several social classes, for men and women alike, for various age groups though disproportionately younger adults, the question of what to do to have fun was increasingly easy to answer, and this undoubtedly contributed, as least periodically, to a sense of excitement and happiness. To be sure, the experience was largely passive: spectatorship was reaching new levels. On the plus side, the exposure to skilled professionals, rather than a largely amateur diet, may have counted for something.

Sports. The unprecedented rise of sports, both participant and spectator, provided the final main component of industrial-style leisure, again particularly during the second half of the 19th century, in all parts of the Western world (and soon beyond). Many sports derived from older games – the phenomenon was not new – but the range and involvement, and the level of emotion involved, were unprecedented.

Interest in sports rose steadily from the 1840s onward. Soccer football drew the greatest attention in Europe, baseball in the United States; but boxing and horseracing were extremely popular. American college football developed from the 1870s; the great Wimbledon tennis tournament began in 1877; the modern Olympic games launched in 1896. Professional teams in baseball and soccer football steadily grew in popularity. Sports had long played a role in recreation, but there is no question that the kind of interest they were drawing by the second half of the 19th century was truly novel. The emergence of sportswriting reflected but also promoted

New Expectations Encounter Industrial Society 127

increasingly passionate interest. The first magazine dedicated to sports appeared in England in 1792; regular newspaper columns emerged in the 1850s, aided by the ability to send news of distant games by telegraph. While some debate continues over its derivation, the word "fan", first applied to baseball and horseracing enthusiasts in the United States, appropriately captured the fanatic interest that many people now applied to sports: playing them, watching them, and reading about them in the new sports sections of the popular press.

A host of plausible explanations have been offered for the rise of modern sports. The fields on which some of them were played contrasted with the overbuilt urban environment. They allowed adult spectators to recall games they played as children. Their speed and precision – particularly, as standardized rules and record-keeping were developed – meshed with the industrial age. They helped create communities, but also allowed people to vent anger, even hatred, of other groups. They provided catharsis amid the increasingly regulated, sometimes boring routines of modern life.

Sports also made people happy, which is why they must figure prominently in any account of the 19th-century effort to merge the interest in happiness with the new structures of industrial society. Actual participation, aside from physical benefits, contributed to more positive feelings generally, sometimes enhanced by fellowship with teammates. Spectatorship could be a mixed bag; teams lost, and many fans reported the strain they felt in the home stretch of a competition. But they also expressed joy – "I'm the happiest guy in the world" was a common exaggeration – when their teams came through. The steady expansion of interest in sports testified to their emotional role.

Happiness and a New Emotional Context

It is not farfetched to argue that for many people at least, the interaction of cultural expectations of happiness and the formation of industrial society generated a new aspirational model for happiness in real life. Family came high on the list, now not primarily in terms of economic stability or procreation (indeed, the numbers of children now must be more carefully limited than ever before): the key was positive emotional interaction among the family members. The new range of leisure activities was a second pillar, providing unprecedented opportunities for fun. In between, with some question marks attached, was successful work: essential for economic survival, possibly providing some intrinsic satisfactions, but also embellished by hopes for growing prosperity and advancement.

The formula created a new set of ties between happiness and several other emotions. The linkage with romantic love was fundamental: never before had this connection been so strongly emphasized. As we have seen, many people found it hard to imagine happiness without a loving family.

128 *The Happiness Revolution, 1700–1900*

Envy was reevaluated. Long held to be a sin, a variety of advice literature, even from some of the churches, now began to contend that envy was a positive quality, because it motivated people to dress better and consume more abundantly. Happiness should not be obscured by envy, for in a consumer society a bit of envy was now a good thing, providing a spur to happiness.

Most striking was a new preoccupation with boredom. The word itself was new – suggested at the end of the 18th century but becoming commonplace only after 1850. The neologism was revealing: without a clear word for the experience, it is possible that people previously had endured periods of dullness more passively and patiently than seemed possible in industrial society. For now, particularly with the rise of new leisure interests; happiness became increasingly associated with frequent rather than recurrent entertainment. Injunctions of cheerfulness made it clear that it was more important than ever not to *be* boring or to be forced to tolerate dullness in others. The "fun" aspect of happiness needed frequent feeding – which ironically might make it easier, when expectations were not met, to feel impatient and unhappy. The new emotional connections for happiness could be demanding.

Complexities

The links between happiness and more specific targets in family, work, and leisure life in the 19th century raise a number of issues. Differences in social class and, to a degree, gender, present some important red flags. Areas of repression, or attempted repression, inhibited the pursuit of pleasure, while death posed a greater burden than Enlightenment optimists had anticipated. Finally, there was the obvious potential problem of disappointment: new expectations were clear, but they could be frustrated. All three of these categories must be considered in any assessment of happiness in 19th-century life.

Class Divides

Evaluation of happiness is always complicated by huge social inequalities, from the advent of agricultural society onward, and the problem persisted in the industrial age. Middle and upper classes had opportunities workers lacked, while the rural/urban divide became more important than ever before.

Gaps were particularly acute in the first half of the century. The quality of working-class life in early industrialization has been debated, but it posed huge challenges for happiness. Harsh and unfamiliar working conditions combined with new limitations on popular leisure and few opportunities for consumer indulgence.

Even when conditions eased, workers continued to reflect a different approach to happiness from their middle-class counterparts. Less likely to

New Expectations Encounter Industrial Society 129

indulge in romantic definitions of family life, instead they formed families that might help provide some assistance in finding jobs or offering support during economic recessions. Work was less likely to be leavened, or complicated, by hopes for mobility; workers might be more realistic here than their white-collar counterparts. On the other hand, while workers had fewer recreational opportunities than their middle-class or white-collar counterparts, there was some convergence around a new leisure ethic. Indeed, as we have seen, middle-class types often learned how to loosen up by participating in popular entertainments. While sports interests first surfaced among the upper classes, by 1900 they embraced workers as well, as fans and, sometimes, aspiring professionals where they notoriously played games more vigorously, with less restraint, than elite amateurs.

Class divisions might involve more, however, than differential access or distinctive ideas. In societies where ideas spread increasingly readily, groups that were unable to attain the dominant happiness standards might also feel a new resentment, one that might not be fully satisfied through hopes for a better society at some future point.

Sex and Death

Even for the middle classes, an interest in happiness was complicated by several common concerns. Criticism of popular rowdiness and irresponsibility continued, in a class that valued respectability. Emphasis on fairly formal manners, in social situations, did not necessarily run counter to an interest in pleasure, but it imposed some rigidity. Massive debates occurred over the subject of drinking, where popular habits seemed particularly suspect. Active temperance movements sought, with some success, to limit access to this form of pleasure, at least by restricting drinking hours in bars and pubs. (Late in the century, a new concern about opiates emerged as well.) The middle classes were not uniformly abstemious, but there was tension.

Sexuality, however, was the most obvious concern. Middle-class codes insisted on the importance of preventing premarital sex, and even advised against too much sexual ardor within marriage; respectable women, in particular, were not supposed to have much sexual desire. More than respectability was involved here: middle-class life depended on reducing the birth rate and, absent reliable and available birth control devices, this forced reliance on periods of abstention. Unusual efforts to repress masturbation was one sign of the new anxiety about sex, and this too could affect adult behavior. Only toward the end of the 19th century did this prudish aspect of middle-class morality begin to relax a bit, most notably permitting greater interest in sexual pleasure within marriage. But sexual sticking points would continue to affect the "fun ethic" well into the 20th century.

130   *The Happiness Revolution, 1700–1900*

Death was an acute challenge as well. The interest in happiness argued for limiting the impact of death – this had already been clear during the Enlightenment – but death rates remained fairly high until about 1880. Several characteristic reactions reflected the tension. A growing movement, on both sides of the Atlantic, sought to remove cemeteries from city centers and to make them more park-like, to ease the encounter with death. Later in the century, interest in embalming revived, as a new breed of professionals vied to make dead bodies as life-like as possible, and the actual preparation of the body for burial shifted from home to funeral parlor. There was an effort, in other words, to reduce the interaction with death. But the 19th century also emphasized elaborate expressions of grief and mourning; arguably, in a culture that normally valued good cheer, death was now provoking even more sorrow than before. Here, certainly, was a substantial complication in a search for happiness.

Great Expectations

A final complexity in any evaluation of 19th-century happiness involves recognition that several of the key adjustments to industrial life involved aspiration and risk. This was least obvious in the vital leisure category: of course, one or more of the new recreational outlets might prove disappointing, but there was a growing range of choice to compensate. Rising sports interests were perhaps the most vulnerable: passionate spectator attachments were routinely disappointed when the team lost. The intensity of fan involvement could make this a real emotional blow. On the other hand, other aspects of the spectator experience could provide some recompense, and teams did sometimes win. Research has shown that, happily, people remember team victories more clearly than defeats.

Family aspirations were another matter. The happy family ideal was real, but it was undoubtedly cherished more often in principle than realized in fact. Many a loving couple began with every hope of maintaining a happy relationship, only to encounter growing stress when, for example, a man's work interests began pulling him away or the woman's responsibility for bearing and raising children bogged her down; love and gender inequality did not always mix well. At an extreme, the vulnerability of the happy family showed in the rising divorce rate; but even aside from this, excessive aspiration often invited disappointment.

The same was definitely true for the role of hope in cushioning the experience of work. Mobility dreams were great, but they could easily be frustrated. Business failures dotted the 19th century, and they often brought public disgrace; a new industry developed around keeping credit scores, and many people were found wanting. Aside from failure, the rise of big business thwarted many middle-class hopes to set up shop on one's own; even lawyers were increasingly forced into large, impersonal offices.

New Expectations Encounter Industrial Society   131

Americans, deeply wedded to beliefs in rags-to-riches stories, may have been particularly vulnerable to the gap between hope and reality.

Finally, even the interest in cheerfulness might provoke unexpected resistance. The need to invent the series of new terms for grumpiness or grouchiness suggested that some people simply resisted the new standards. Christmas celebrations were splendid, but there were Scrooges around. The attachment to symbols of happiness surely helped shame or prompt people into some compliance, but here too there might be gaps between aspiration and performance. The glum faces that stare out from 19th-century photographs reflected the state of technology, but perhaps a bit more.

★★★

Unlike the 18th century, where the Enlightenment crafted the basic framework for reconsidering happiness, the 19th century offered no overall orchestration. Leading developments occurred at the level of popularizers – like the people who wrote manuals for parents – and the various sponsors of new kinds of entertainment. Specific social experiments were interesting, like the utopian communities, but the real action centered on finding ways to implement the interest in happiness and cheerfulness amid the emerging patterns of industrial life.

Industrialization itself arguably created new opportunities for happiness, by the end of the century, particularly through greater leisure time, a wider range of consumer products and, though it had not yet fully registered, improving health conditions. Yet new challenges emerged as well, in the workplace and the new social and gender divisions. Efforts to promote happiness and pressures to appear cheerful could create tensions of their own – even for children. A key question – would industrial society advance human happiness? – had yet to be answered.

Whatever doubts we may have in retrospect, there is no question about the confidence felt in some quarters at the turn of the century. Greeting the new century, the *New York Times* thundered, with an enthusiasm that Condorcet would have recognized: "We may therefore say without fear of dispute that men are freer at the end of the Nineteenth Century than at its beginning. Are they for that reason happier? Demonstrably, and beyond the possibility of doubt." And again:

We renew the expression of our belief that the sum of human happiness has been largely augmented in the last hundred years by the transfer of the control over the destinies of nations from the hands of Princes to the hands of the people.

And there was more to come, with further advances in medicine, "national wealth", and knowledge.

132 *The Happiness Revolution, 1700–1900*

Further Reading

On relevant ideas about happiness,

Quennell, Peter. *The Pursuit of Happiness* (Oxford: Oxford University Press, 1990).

Taylor, Charles. *Sources of the Self: The Making of the Modern Identity* (Cambridge, MA: Harvard University Press, 1989).

von Eckardt, Ursala. *The Pursuit of Happiness in the Democratic Creed: An Analysis of Political Ethics* (New York: Praeger, 1959).

On utopianism,

Beecher, Jonathan. *Charles Fourier: The Visionary and His World* (Berkeley: University of California Press, 1986).

Taylor, Keith. *The Political Ideas of the Utopian Socialists* (London: Cass, 1982).

On Christmas and birthdays,

Baselice, Vyta, Dante Burrichter, and Peter Stearns. "Debating the Birthday: Innovation and Resistance in Celebrating Children." *Journal of the History of Childhood and Youth* 12, no. 2 (April 1, 2019): 262–284.

Restad, Penne L. *Christmas in America: A History* (New York: Oxford University Press, 1995).

Waits, William Burnell. *The Modern Christmas in America: A Cultural History of Gift Giving* (New York: New York University Press, 1993).

On the family and romantic love,

Coontz, Stephanie. *Marriage, a History: How Love Conquered Marriage* (New York: Penguin Books, 2006).

Lystra, Karen. *Searching the Heart: Women, Men, and Romantic Love in Nineteenth-Century America* (New York: Oxford University Press, 1989).

On pets,

Grier, Katherine C. *Pets in America: A History* (Chapel Hill: University of North Carolina Press, 2006).

On children,

Fass, Paula S. *The End of American Childhood: A History of Parenting from Life on the Frontier to the Managed Child* (Princeton, NJ: Princeton University Press, 2016).

Mintz, Steven. *Huck's Raft: A History of American Childhood* (Cambridge, MA: Belknap Press of Harvard University Press, 2004).

Olsen, Stephanie. *Juvenile Nation: Youth, Emotions and the Making of the Modern British Citizen, 1880–1914* (London: Bloomsbury Academic, 2014).

On work,

Berlanstein, Lenard R. *The Industrial Revolution and Work in Nineteenth-Century Europe* (London: Routledge, 1992).

Rodgers, Daniel T. *The Work Ethic in Industrial America, 1850–1920,* 2nd ed. (Chicago, IL: The University of Chicago Press, 2014).

Stearns, Peter N. *From Alienation to Addiction: Modern American Work in Global Historical Perspective* (Boulder, CO: Paradigm Publishers, 2008).

Thompson, E. P. (Edward Palmer). *The Making of the English Working Class,* 1st Vintage ed. (New York: Vintage Books, 1966).

On the new leisure,

Adams-Volpe, Judith. *The American Amusement Park Industry: A History of Technology and Thrills* (Boston, MA: Twayne Publishers, 1991).

Bailey, Peter. *Music Hall: The Business of Pleasure* (Philadelphia, PA: Open University Press, 1986).

New Expectations Encounter Industrial Society   133

Gleason, William A. *The Leisure Ethic: Work and Play in American Literature, 1840–1940* (Stanford, CA: Stanford University Press, 1999).

Jackson, Lee. *Palaces of Pleasure: From Music Halls to the Seaside to Football, How the Victorians Invented Mass Entertainment* (New Haven, CT: Yale University Press, 2019).

Levine, Lawrence W. *Highbrow/lowbrow: The Emergence of Cultural Hierarchy in America*, 1st pbk. ed. (Cambridge, MA: Harvard University Press, 1990).

On the rise of sports,

Anderson, Nancy F. *The Sporting Life: Victorian Sports and Games* (Santa Barbara, CA: Praeger, 2010).

Crego, Robert, and Gale Group. *Sports and Games of the 18th and 19th Centuries* (Westport, CT: Greenwood Press, 2003).

Guttmann, Allen. *Sports Spectators* (New York: Columbia University Press, 2012).

Steen, Rob. *Floodlights and Touchlines: A History of Spectator Sport* (London: Bloomsbury, 2014).

On envy and boredom,

Fernandez, Luke, and Susan J. Matt. *Bored, Lonely, Angry, Stupid: Changing Feelings about Technology, from the Telegraph to Twitter* (Cambridge, MA: Harvard University Press, 2019).

Matt, Susan J. *Keeping up with the Joneses: Envy in American Consumer Society, 1890–1930* (Philadelphia: University of Pennsylvania Press, 2003).

On various complexities,

D'Emilio, John, and Estelle B. Freedman. *Intimate Matters: A History of Sexuality in America*, 3rd ed. (Chicago, IL: The University of Chicago Press, 2012).

Sandage, Scott A. *Born Losers: A History of Failure in America* (Cambridge, MA: Harvard University Press, 2005).

On death,

Farrell, James. *Inventing the American Way of Death, 1830–1920* (Philadelphia, PA: Temple University Press, 1980).

Stearns, Peter, ed., *Routledge History of Death Since 1800* (London: Routledge, 2020).

On the issue of modern inequality and happiness,

Ahmed, Sara. *The Promise of Happiness* (Durham, NC: Duke University Press, 2010).

9 Global Developments in the 18th and 19th Centuries

No overarching or worldwide pattern of change emerged in attitudes and experiences involving happiness during the centuries in which Western standards were shifting so rapidly. The new Western ideas about happiness did not yet exercise a clear global influence, nor – with a few exceptions – did they even provoke any explicit reaction. Regional religious traditions, or in parts of East Asia the Confucian legacy, had more to do with shaping happiness than did any new cultural influence; continuity was more obvious than change. To be sure, a few religious innovations are worth noting, such as the rise of the strict Wahabi or Salafi version of Islam in what is now Saudi Arabia, which ushered in new restrictions on secular activities; but the impact was long confined to that particular region.

Nevertheless, the increasing global reach of the West – through the familiar combination of military conquest, imperialism, and economic exploitation – surely had potential implications for happiness. During both the 18th and 19th centuries, but particularly once industrialization took hold in the West, the economic gap between the West and other parts of the world expanded considerably. Western societies became richer, though the results were not evenly distributed; but more to the point other societies actually saw their living standards deteriorate. Growing Western pressure to produce cheap foods and raw materials often drove wages down; in some cases, rapid regional population growth contributed to poverty as well. Further, the century also experienced serious cycles of epidemic disease, particularly in a recurrent pattern of cholera outbreaks. The combination of new problems and old introduced important constraints on happiness in many regions, generating some deep popular grievances.

Even as it deployed new economic and military power, the West made no particular effort to export its revolutionary ideas about happiness. To the extent that Western countries worked to extend a new cultural influence, sometimes with references to a "civilizing mission", the targets centered on certain local customs viewed as immoral or unproductive, or in some cases on reforming educational systems, rather than any particular concepts of happiness. Somewhat ironically, given the challenges to religion in the West itself, missionary activity guided much of the

Developments in the 18th and 19th Centuries   135

West's wider outreach aside from outright imperialism and economic pressure. None of this was irrelevant to happiness, but the relationship was at best indirect.

Yet the combination of growing Western influence and regional political and economic change could promote some novel debates about what happiness was all about. The result never generated a fully Western model, but there were some new combinations – most obviously, in Russia and Japan and possibly in Latin America. Any world "happiness map", as of 1900, would be unusually complicated.

The problem of evidence looms large in any assessment of global patterns in the age of imperialism – partly because of the absence of any systematic cultural change, partly because the subject of happiness has not won a lot of research attention from historians of this period outside the West. At a guess, if there was any large global trend it would center on a deterioration of happiness, mainly because of economic and political decline and Western interference. But even this is speculative, and may not take adequate account of the new ideas that were also gaining ground or the power of existing regional traditions.

This chapter will proceed in three sections. The first briefly sketches some key developments in China and the Ottoman Empire, two of the large states that avoided outright Western control; both suffered growing instability in the 19th century that had some implications for happiness. The second section centers on the relevant impact of Western imperialism, as it affected some traditional outlets for pleasure and promoted religious change. Finally, turning more specifically to the later 19th century, we will consider some additional reactions, around the introduction of new forms of consumerism and the rise of non-Western nationalism in several key societies.

The Chinese and Ottoman Empires

In China, established Confucian ideas about happiness were not systematically displaced. A host of relevant traditions largely persisted. For example, emphasis on parentally arranged marriages, with betrothal gifts from the groom's family and a dowry from that of the bride, continued. These were largely economic arrangements with little concern for emotional factors, though of course it was assumed that a family was vital to happiness. The double happiness symbol in Chinese calligraphy was attached to the wedding ceremony; on the other hand, it was common for brides to display, and often to feel, considerable sadness because they were being detached from their parents. The implications were complex, but they were not fundamentally novel in light of established traditions.

However, the 19th century brought numerous challenges to Chinese society overall, and these could be highly relevant to happiness. Economic dislocations mounted, partly because of growing Western interference but also thanks to growing population pressure. British insistence on

136   *The Happiness Revolution, 1700–1900*

importing opium led to widespread drug problems, and when the government tried to resist it was forced to back down.

This mounting instability was the context for an extraordinary new religious movement, which ultimately provoked an exceptionally bloody civil war, that lasted from 1850 to 1864. What is often called the Taiping rebellion was led by Hong Xiuquan, who translated some training under an American Baptist missionary into a hybrid doctrine that, he claimed, would purify China and establish a "heavenly kingdom" on earth – with Hong himself as king. Private property was to be abolished, the sexes were to be equal but largely kept separate, and a strict moral code was imposed. Some of the rhetoric of the Taiping version of Christianity and its idea of a heavenly mandate framed the importance of absolute obedience to the movement in terms of happiness: "One portion of disobedience to heaven will be met with one portion of weeping/And one portion of reverence will be met by one portion of happiness." The idea of happiness through collective loyalty was a theme that would recur, in China and elsewhere, even though the Taiping movement itself was ultimately brutally crushed. It had picked up, though arguably distorted, some earlier Chinese values as well as a version of Christian millenarianism, but it probably also reflected the growing difficulty of finding happiness in the increasingly grim environment of late-19th-century China.

Although the Ottoman Empire suffered some of the same challenges as China in the 19th century, including growing Western interference and political instability, some new references to happiness were less idiosyncratic.

The big focus of the middle decades of the century rested with massive reform efforts, the Tanzimat reforms, undertaken by the central government. Most of these reforms were not explicitly directed at happiness – again, happiness was at most a minor political or religious theme in many regions during the 19th century. The reforms aimed at improving legal structures, creating a more efficient state, attempting to spur industrial growth. Reform-minded sultans were indeed interested in Western models. They began to import Western art and sponsor translations of Western literature, and they were certainly eager to incorporate Western science. However, the Western preoccupation with happiness did not figure explicitly on this cultural agenda.

Yet references did occasionally creep in, and even a limited association of reform and happiness might have been something of a precedent for the future. Thus, an article in 1862, touting the importance of expanding education, offered a convoluted reference to happiness as part of the rationale:

> The only way to glorify the state is to expand general education. Both female and male students should attend schools. A woman that makes her family happy should be decent in both secular and spiritual practices. Education of girls is the duty of their parents.

Developments in the 18th and 19th Centuries   137

The argument that education of women was important mainly for family improvement was a common one in the 19th century, even in the West, but the notion that family happiness was a criterion was an interesting extension of the argument in the late Ottoman period.

Other linkages between happiness and what might be regarded as modernization were more straightforward. Thus in 1904 – after the reform period itself had ended in failure –an appeal for support for a railroad development project in Hejaz province assumed an obvious connection: "Everyone should help in an initiative that will bring happiness to 300 million people." Again, there is no basis for contending that standards of happiness were shifting significantly in the Middle East at this point, but the fact that the term was displayed in order to justify change was something of an innovation.

Imperialism and Happiness

Imperialism and happiness are not commonly associated terms, and with good reason. European imperialism arguably brought some benefits on occasion: the initial, robust railway network in India, the efforts to end formal slavery in Africa. But imperialism also brought new economic controls aimed at benefiting the home country: thus, in India, the British long sought to discourage manufacturing in favor of reliance on British imports, while in many regions of Africa European agents pressed local populations into low-wage labor in mines or on sugar plantations. Political controls might be slightly more ambivalent, benefiting certain groups and providing some new kinds of training; but always the top slots, and the policymaking, were reserved for European officials.

Even the widely proclaimed notion of a European responsibility to bring civilization to the barbarians was not usually framed in terms of happiness, quite apart from its obviously demeaning vocabulary. The "white man's burden" emphasized promoting good order and improving education, but also correcting moral deficiencies and, often, encouraging missionary activity. Europeans might have claimed, if pressed, that all this would improve happiness, but they did not make the connection directly. And many subject people would have been unlikely to see happiness even remotely involved, and historians of the colonial experience would largely agree. Most African historians, for example, would argue that the Enlightenment ideal of a happy, self-determining individual had little influence on their continent, in any formal sense.

Not surprisingly, when happiness did occasionally show up explicitly in imperialist rhetoric, it seemed to apply to the conquerors, not the conquered. Thus an American apologist, Senator A.J. Beveridge, writing in 1900 on the heels of amid United States expansion in the Caribbean and Pacific, pointed to his nation's "divine mission" in bringing progress to the "savage and senile" peoples of the world – a mission that "holds for us

138 *The Happiness Revolution, 1700–1900*

all the profit, all the glory, all the happiness possible to man. We are the trustees of the world's progress, guardians of its righteous peace."

Still, without pretending great detail for a subject that has not received much explicit attention, a few connections between colonialism or imperialism and happiness might be suggested – often toward addressing some probable deteriorations depending somewhat on the group involved.

Latin America. Spanish and Portuguese colonization of Latin America brought huge hardships beyond the experience of defeat in combat. Disease carried away over 80% of the population. Established rulers and upper classes were shunted aside. New labor systems imposed harsh burdens on many indigenous workers, for example on sugar estates or the Andean silver mines. It is hard to imagine that unhappiness, and active awareness of unhappiness, did not increase at least for a considerable period of time.

The slender direct evidence on the subject comes mainly from Catholic clergy, eager to convert native populations to Christianity. The conversion process itself was not always as harsh as might be imagined, as many traditional beliefs and even some local leaders were able to blend their views and activities with those of the Church. But the Catholic viewpoint dominated commentary on emotion and, perhaps combined with the native experience, tended to emphasize sadness and melancholy over happiness.

In colonial Mexico, for example, faithful Catholics, focused on the joy that might await them in heaven, found it natural to think of a life in this world filled with sorrow. Undue despair was not acceptable, for it would call God's mercy into question; but excessive happiness was not normal either. Images of a suffering Christ or a sorrowing, tearful Mary – a *Mater dolorosa* – were widespread in the colonial Church. Images of the Virgin Mary with flowing tears were common. Religious ceremonies and processionals highlighted grief as well. This emphasis might well have corresponded to the many hardships of life during the colonial period. Many individuals, seeking religious solace, reported strong feelings of melancholy.

Most direct evidence about emotional standards and experiences during this period comes from European colonists, who had brought Catholicism with them; we know less about indigenous people. But the colonists routinely described indigenous communities in terms of melancholy, and this may have been an accurate reading, as conversion to Catholicism combined with the real challenges of life under Spanish rule. Thus, one speech to upper-class indigenous women stressed:

> Oh, my daughter, in this world, it is a place of weeping, and afflictions, and unhappiness... Listen carefully my child. The earth is not a good place. It is not a place of joy. It is not a place of contentment.

Similar sentiments about sadness and tears, and the need for humility, were conveyed to young men as well. The Virgin of Guadalupe, which

Developments in the 18th and 19th Centuries 139

became the most famous Catholic symbol in Mexico, was represented as a consoler for the miseries of this life: as a Nahua account put it in 1649, she would "listen to their weeping and sorrows".

By the 17th century, some European visitors contended that the emotional tone of Mexican life had become measurably different from the standards common in Europe itself, and the emphasis on sadness was the key point.

Glimpses of happiness do emerge. Religion itself was a source of consolation that might at least lighten the load in anticipation of salvation later on. One source also noted the rewards of reproduction, "with which we multiply in this world. All of this gives us some contentment to life, so that we do not suffer with continuous weeping and sorrow." Ardent Catholics also talked of the happiness that could come from the contemplation of God. Indeed, some ordinary Mexicans were sometimes described as "drunk on God", as they experienced what was often profound joy from mystical experiences in their relations with the divine.

More prosaically, the colonial experience also offered an array of amusements, which formed the most common sources of happiness outside of religion itself. There is abundant evidence of Mexicans' ardent pursuit of pleasure, or what was often described as "delight", through various diversions. Some of the distractions were personal, as individuals, for example, took pleasure in studying astrology. But many communities also held celebrations, often combining a religious occasion with parades and feasting. Carnivals and dances occasioned a great deal of laughter. Popular culture managed to rescue a number of older traditions, including colorful clothing, while also creating new styles that blended native, European and often African elements. Sheer joy in sociability was part of this same popular tradition. Occasionally the Church would try to intervene against too much earthly pleasure – there was a great deal of suspicion about excessive local sexuality – but there was a good bit of de facto tolerance as well.

Officially, and possibly in real life, this experience of happiness was seen as transitory, not a normal or steady condition. This is where sorrow predominated. But the popular experience may have provided real precedent for expectations of happiness later in Latin American history.

What does *not* seem to have happened in the 18th century – the last century of colonial rule – was the kind of happiness revolution that was occurring in Western Europe and the Atlantic colonies at that point. Enlightenment thinking did have some impact, but amid limited literacy and restricted printing facilities its range remained narrow. There is some evidence that the upper classes in Mexico (European in origin) were beginning to think of excessive melancholy as a medical disorder that warranted treatment, not a normal emotional state. But the full apparatus for a larger redefinition of happiness was not present. Among other things, there were no sweeping changes in consumerism or levels of material comfort. And while the worst ravages of imported diseases had passed by this point, health conditions remained precarious as well.

140   *The Happiness Revolution, 1700–1900*

Another component would be added in the early 19th century, however. Leaders of the wars for independence, like Simon Bolivar, had been thoroughly steeped in Enlightenment thought, including of course the thinking that had gone into the United States' Declaration of Independence. Bolivar was particularly influenced by British utilitarianism, and wrote and spoke frequently about the "greatest happiness of the greatest number". "The most perfect system of government is that which results in the greatest possible measure of happiness and the maximum of social security and political stability." He argued that Latin Americans were rising on behalf of liberty and freedom "out of that universal human instinct to aspire to the greatest possible happiness, which is found to follow in civil societies founded on the principles of justice, liberty and equality." An ardent nationalist, he also spoke of the happiness associated with national independence and "*la patria*".

This kind of thinking would persist in 19th-century Latin American history and beyond, providing a consistent liberal current that had much in common with its counterparts elsewhere in the Atlantic world. But this liberal strand encountered more opposition in Latin America than in Western Europe or the United States, among other things from an entrenched Catholic Church that maintained its rather different ideas about happiness. And, suffering still from severe economic disparities with the industrial West, Latin America did not engender the standards of living associated with evolving Western ideas about happiness. The result is something of a conundrum: a genuine link with the happiness revolution, but also a measurable distance.

One other 19th-century development warrants attention: a growing interest in marital love, and the importance of this kind of bond for happiness. Already in the colonial period, the notion of a "bad life", or *mala vida*, had been associated with domestic discord and, sometimes, outright domestic violence. By the 19th century, this evolved into a fuller definition of the role of a solid marriage in a happy life – along with the awareness that bad marriages were still common, and damaging. The new aspirations for marriage differed from the ideas about romantic love developing in places like Britain and the United States: mutual respect and obligation, rather than deep emotional fulfillment, seem to have been the goal. But they did contribute to some sense that happiness might be a permanent part of a good life, rather than an episodic experience amid common sorrows. Latin American ideas of happiness continued to evolve.

The result is something of a comparative challenge. Evolving Latin American concepts of happiness seem to have been somewhat distinctive, particularly when the pleasures available from popular celebrations are added in. Linked to a larger Western pattern to some extent, they developed in a different context – including less emphasis on individualism – and featured different emphases. It is tempting to suggest a connection between this early Latin American interest in happiness and the distinctive

Developments in the 18th and 19th Centuries 141

regional levels suggested in contemporary happiness polls, but we simply do not know enough yet about this aspect of Latin American history to evaluate the relationship.

Sub-Saharan Africa. The impact of imperialism on sub-Saharan Africa came much later than was the case in the Americas; it was just beginning to take shape in the later 19th century. Quite apart from chronology, it involved much different levels of European influence. There was no sweeping depopulation of this huge subcontinent, and while European settlers moved into some areas, they never had more than a minority foothold; and in key areas, including populous West Africa, their footprint was smaller still.

Yet there was influence, and some relevant elements can be suggested even though the subject of happiness has not yet commanded much attention among historians of Africa. The most obvious changes were disruptive. Africans in many regions were pressed to work for low wages, often in unsafe conditions. Men were often pulled away from their villages, while many women stayed back, destabilizing family life. Customary economic patterns were upended in favor of producing precious metals, minerals, cotton, vegetable oil, and other items destined for the export market.

Material challenges were compounded by other innovations. Missionary activities attacked traditional beliefs and sometimes unseated village leaders. Europeans also criticized African sexual habits, using terms like "debauched" and "licentious", and they sometimes tried to introduce new regulations, particularly directed toward women. Polygamy, customary in parts of the subcontinent, was widely deplored. New laws, based on European codes, could have diverse effects; in some cases, it became easier for women to divorce; in other instances, the authority of husbands and fathers was reinforced. Overall, it seems highly probable that many Africans felt increasing strain.

On the other hand, there were some positive features, including an ability, in many rural regions, to hold on to key traditions. Emphasis on the vitality of family life and extended kin relations remained strong, despite some challenges: here, arguably, was a core element of the African definition of happiness. Zulus, in southern Africa, stressed the importance of "building the homestead", for the sake of one's happiness but also that of other living relations and even one's ancestors. Creating a large family promoted happiness by providing security. At the same time, a variety of customs, sometimes including witchcraft accusations, worked to keep any individual from overstepping community norms and accumulating too much prosperity or happiness; undue personal happiness could attract feelings of envy and misery from others, and sometimes the vocabulary used to describe happiness embraced these dangers as well.

Many Africans may have experienced a larger feeling of connectedness, to a wider community – again reflecting an idea of happiness focused on relationships rather than individualism. A new word for humanity, *ubuntu*,

142   *The Happiness Revolution, 1700–1900*

was introduced into a Bantu language in southern Arica from the middle of the 19th century, though it would gain greater importance later on. It conveyed a sense of sharing with a larger humanity, with an emphasis on kindness.

Religion could also be a source of support, despite the changes encouraged by Muslim and Christian missionaries. While conversions to Christianity deeply offended village elders, they might provide new meaning to other members of the community, such as women and young people. Various versions of Christianity developed, including some regional adaptations. On the whole, while Christian leaders might belabor sinfulness, they did not convey the kind of sorrow that had pervaded Latin American Christianity during the colonial period. In practice, they also brought educational and medical reforms, which could add to the positive message. Religion in Africa gained intense loyalties, and frequently featured an emphasis on joy and hope. Many Protestant preachers, particularly, offered "gladness" and good tidings through the promise of a personal relationship with God.

One other potential component of happiness gained new prominence in the late 19th century, though it had divisive consequences. Workers in some of the African mines made enough money to return to their villages periodically, eager for sexual or romantic conquests. They disrupted traditional, parentally arranged relationships. Often they bought enough cattle to pay for "seduction fines" or even to offer the customary bridewealth gift without their fathers' contribution or consent. In other words, they were implementing a novel and more individualistic definition of pleasure or happiness. Similar themes emerged from signs of new types of consumerism in some urban areas, at least by the early 20th century. *No Longer at Ease*, a Nigerian novel, set in Lagos during the 1920s, features a young man, who has received a Western-style education and holds a job in the colonial administration, who is so preoccupied with his consumer lifestyle that he ignores his traditional obligations to his extended family, refusing to go back to the village when a parent dies.

Obviously, in this confusing period around the turn of the 20th century, no one definition of happiness prevailed – and there were many reasons for mounting discontent. The combination of traditional or more novel sources, and the tensions among them, raised important questions for the African future.

Russia and Japan

Not surprisingly, Russian and Japanese developments involving happiness, including some explicit discussions, were rather different from those in other regions outside the West by the end of the 19th century. These were the two countries where reforms proved most extensive, compared for example to the Ottoman Empire, and where early industrialization took shape.

Developments in the 18th and 19th Centuries 143

Contacts with Western ideas plus the extent of social disruption created a distinctive context.

The two countries shared several key features. First, for both, reform was a serious business, rarely framed in terms of happiness. For better or worse, both societies launched industrialization without the prior reconsideration of happiness that had occurred in the West: there was no "happiness revolution" to help guide responses. Second, clear resistance to Western ideas of happiness emerged in both cases; debate arose in the West as well, for example, expressed in the end-of-the-century pessimism popular with some intellectuals, but the Japanese and Russian alternatives were more elaborate and more widely shared. Third, however, some important overlaps emerged with Western notions as well, including the impact of new forms of consumerism.

Russia. As Russia experienced its mixture of reform and repression from the 1860s onward, several general reactions emerged, creating a distinctive overall balance. Evidence comes largely from the literate upper and middle classes; as usual, the orientations of the masses of the population are less clear, though high rates of rural and urban protest certainly suggest considerable unhappiness.

Some groups, at least some of the time, were delighted with the changes they saw around them. Modern cities came in for particularly favorable comment, particularly as they installed street lighting, as department stores were imported from the West (the first store in Moscow was set up by a French businessman), and as consumer goods proliferated for the well-to-do. Shop windows filled with "the inventions of Western civilization" – easy chairs, silk stockings, household goods. Cities were "bright temples", filled with a "mood that is bold and full of the joy of life". The most popular novel of the early 20th century, entitled the *Keys to Happiness* (1910), featured a young woman deliberately bent on finding happiness. Urban entertainment centers, including popular theater, highlighted the "pursuit of happiness"; even advertisements for patent medicines (many imported from the West, and of dubious merit) claimed they would contribute to the "joy of life". This optimism was a new component in Russian culture, and it would build into a Marxist approach in the 20th century, particularly in its commitment to economic progress.

But a second reaction featured strong disapproval, and while similar criticisms of consumerism arose in the West itself there is little doubt that the Russian concern was stronger, particularly among the upper classes and many intellectuals. Much of this "happiness", after all, was foreign, as well as shockingly novel. Women were criticized for their new slavishness to fashion. The novelist Tolstoy lamented somewhat obscurely that "women, like queens, have forced nine-tenths of the human race to labor for them as their slaves". Morals were decaying; upper-class women, with their fancy dresses, were no better than prostitutes. Another criticism, somewhat inconsistently, blasted the new uniformities created by factory-made

144   *The Happiness Revolution, 1700–1900*

products; everyone now looked the same. Foreign influences, along with the new machines, were destroying "the former good nature, the conviviality, the appealing disorderliness and freedom" of traditional Russian life. Even peasants, that staple of Russian life, were picking up on new tastes, and some of them, buying urban clothing, were beginning to look like "dandies."

Debate between "westernizers" and conservatives in Russia went back to the early 18th century, but it picked up new intensity at this point. While conservatives rarely zeroed in directly on happiness, they certainly mounted a steady campaign against Western values. In their eyes, the Russian soul centered on religion and a deep sense of community. It was vital to preserve these traditions against the lures of individualism and innovation. Many conservatives began emphasizing the importance of a distinctive Russian nationalism, a sense of passionate group identity that could serve as an alternative to more facile ideas of happiness.

A third theme to a great extent cut across liberal and conservative lines, though it certainly resisted Western-style optimism. A sense of loneliness and despair cropped up frequently in Russian commentary, often emphasizing the word "disillusionment" and arguing against the "senselessness and purposelessness of modern life". Struggle and suffering replaced any sense of happiness; at most, this approach centered on "happiness denied". This was a dark pessimism, feeding anarchist or "nihilist" groups that saw no recourse but to engage in often random violence, often at deliberate risk to their own lives. Some anarchists, to be sure, held out hope for a better society in future, but others, including those that were frankly suicidal, simply saw chaos, with no happiness in sight.

Japan. The sweeping reforms Japanese leaders began to introduce from 1868 onward, in the so-called Meiji era, were framed in terms of stern purpose and devotion to the common good. The slogan "rich country, strong army", bent on preserving national independence and advancing national strength in face of growing Western pressure, had little to do with Western-style definitions of happiness. And, quite apart from solemn official pronouncements, the beginnings of Japanese industrialization were built on the backs of highly taxed peasants, female silk workers laboring in miserable conditions, and strict, though not always successful, efforts to repress any significant popular protest. This was a solemn nation.

There were, of course, outright Westernizers, who not infrequently brought up a happiness theme. Thus the leading educational reformer, Fukuzawa Yukichi, who studied widely in Europe and the United States, spoke directly of what he called "the greatest happiness of the greatest number". Carefully noting the many merits in Japanese traditions, which should not be completely overthrown, Fukuzawa urged the advantages of Western education and Western science, which is where he thought the West had an edge in promoting happiness. For a few years after introducing mass schooling requirements, in 1872, even the Japanese government

Developments in the 18th and 19th Centuries 145

seemed open to promoting new values, installing an American to head up its education unit. And a new interest in science and technology did prove to be durable features of modern Japanese culture.

Further, while the Japanese did not rush into avid consumerism – for quite a while, watches and clocks, along with tooth brushes, were the only Western items that drew wide popular enthusiasm – there was certainly some change. Department stores opened in Tokyo by the 1890s, though they were long associated with foreign products and had to work hard, offering music and theatrical entertainments along with consumer items, to build a clientele. Larger changes in popular fashion would await the 1920s, but some new interests emerged. The first Western-style chair was installed in a public building as early as 1871. Baseball, learned initially from American sailors, also won new attention, particularly when a Japanese team beat an American group in the 1890s.

However, the dominant official approach warned against facile definitions of happiness and undue individualism. A change of tone at the education ministry set in from 1881 onward. Group loyalty was now emphasized, as Western texts in the social studies were newly banned. School curricula filled with attacks on excessive selfishness or personal preoccupations. Consumerism also came in for rebuke. An Imperial Rescript in 1908 urged people to be "frugal in the management of their households… to abide by simplicity and avoid ostentation, and to insure themselves to arduous toil without yielding to any degree of indulgence." Japanese conservatives, including many successful business leaders, emphasized Confucian themes like obedience and a sense of duty, criticizing individualistic ideas of "self-reliance". Many leaders played up military virtues, talking of "faithfulness and righteousness", and "fulfillment of one's duty".

Arguably, in fact, Japanese officials at this point were developing something of a nationalist alternative to Western ideas of happiness, leavened by emperor worship. Devotion to a common cause, self-sacrifice, displaced more direct discussions of happiness. Group loyalty and a sense of belonging potentially provided a sense of satisfaction that was different from the Western formula, even to the point of a distinctive vocabulary.

Yet even this is not quite the whole story. Quietly, by 1900, in the throes of urbanization and industrialization, many Japanese were also finding a new interest in family life, though without all the bells and whistles of the contemporary Western version – aided in this case by advice offered by Japanese converts to Protestantism, newly permitted though not encouraged by the reform regime. Thus a home education manual in 1894 urged that the "true essence of domestic entertainment is for all in the house," with man and wife to come together for mutual enjoyment. Parents could look at a baby's "endearing face" and "smile together". This new emphasis could at least modify earlier traditions that had husbands largely seeking pleasure outside the home, or, within the home, the notion that wives should simply serve husbands (who might even eat alone). Interestingly,

146 *The Happiness Revolution, 1700–1900*

the purchase of dining tables began to become popular by 1900, suggesting joint family dining instead of gender isolation. The theme of happiness in the Meiji period generated a variety of responses, clearly different, collectively, from those in the West or indeed in Russia, but involving considerable change from purely traditional patterns.

★★★

No region adopted Western patterns of happiness during the 19th century. Some areas were simply uninterested – it is vital to remember that most people were still rural, and largely unaware of changes that disproportionately affected urbanites. Many religious leaders, as in Hinduism or Islam, simply maintained a traditional approach, urging the importance of spiritual exercises as the best chance for glimpses of happiness in this life. A number of groups were actively opposed to Western concepts, though focusing on what they saw as the downsides of individualism and consumerism more than on happiness by name; in a few cases, most notably Japan, something of an alternative was being vigorously promoted, through group loyalty and nationalism. But this was not the whole story, for a combination of economic changes and Western influence did introduce some new enthusiasms for certain forms of happiness as well. Much of this diversity – including but not confined to outright resistance – would carry over into the more elaborate global patterns that emerged during the 20th century.

Further Reading

On the Taiping rebellion,

Reilly, Thomas H. *The Taiping Heavenly Kingdom: Rebellion and the Blasphemy of Empire* (Seattle: University of Washington Press, 2004).

Yapp, Malcolm. *The Making of the Modern Near East, 1792–1923* (London: Longman, 1987).

On Latin America,

Lipsett-Rivera, Sonya, and Javier Villa-Flores. *Emotions and Daily Life in Colonial Mexico* (Albuquerque: University of New Mexico Press, 2014).

Seed, Patricia. *To Love, Honor, and Obey in Colonial Mexico: Conflicts over Marriage Choice, 1574–1821* (Stanford, CA: Stanford University Press, 1988).

On Africa,

Achebe, Chinua. *No Longer at Ease* (London: Heinemann, 1964).

Carton, Benedict. *Blood from Your Children: The Colonial Origins of Generational Conflict in South Africa* (Charlottesville: University Press of Virginia, 2000).

Eze, Michael Onyebuchi. *Intellectual History in Contemporary South Africa*, 1st ed. (New York: Palgrave Macmillan, 2010).

Therborn, Göran. *African Families in a Global Context* (Uppsala: Nordiska Afrikainstitutet, 2006).

Developments in the 18th and 19th Centuries 147

On nationalism,

Suny, Ronald Grigor. *The Revenge of the Past: Nationalism, Revolution, and the Collapse of the Soviet Union* (Stanford, CA: Stanford University Press, 1993).

On Russia,

Geifman, Anna. *Thou Shalt Kill: Revolutionary Terrorism in Russia, 1894–1917* (Princeton, NJ: Princeton University Press, 1993).

Steinberg, Mark D. *Petersburg Fin de Siècle* (New Haven, CT: Yale University Press, 2011).

Steinberg, Mark D., and Valeria Sobol. *Interpreting Emotions in Russia and Eastern Europe* (DeKalb: Northern Illinois University Press, 2011).

On Japan,

Minichiello, Sharon. *Japan's Competing Modernities: Issues in Culture and Democracy, 1900–1930* (Honolulu: University of Hawai'i Press, 1998).

Seidensticker, Edward, Donald Richie, and Paul Waley. *Tokyo from Edo to Showa 1867–1989: The Emergence of the World's Greatest City.* (Tokyo: Tuttle Pub., 2010).

Tobin, Joseph Jay. *Re-Made in Japan: Everyday Life and Consumer Taste in a Changing Society* (New Haven, CT: Yale University Press, 1992).

Part III

Happiness in Contemporary World History

By the early 21st century, when the influence of social media began to become a global phenomenon, almost anyone posing for what was now called a "selfie", anywhere in the world, was careful to smile broadly. It became more important than ever before to look happy. To be sure, some societies encouraged more smiling than others, but it is also probable that encouragements to smile became more widespread than ever before.

There was still no single global history of happiness during the past century. Many key regions maintained distinctive approaches to happiness; even family happiness continued to be variously defined. As before, variations in material standards and earlier cultural traditions combined in several different regional patterns.

Some common trends did emerge, however. The influence of consumer culture, some of it shaped by Western standards, became more widespread than ever before. As more and more societies industrialized and urbanized – developments that began to encompass most of the world's people – older ideas about happiness could be shaken. By the early 21st century, some outlines of a global, or at least multi-regional, approach to happiness could be discerned.

On the whole, the Western commitment to happiness has held on fairly well, in Western Europe, the United States, Canada, Australia, and New Zealand, though it has faced some internal challenges; in recent decades, some influences from other cultures have added to the regional approach. And limitations of the Western commitment to happiness have also become more obvious.

At the same time, the past century has seen a number of deliberate attempts to development alternatives to Western models of happiness, some reflecting updates on traditional values, others, as with communism, seeking to strike out in newer directions.

Not surprisingly, analysis of happiness during the past century must also account for some internal chronological divisions. The miseries of world war and economic depression prompted some particularly vigorous disputes over happiness in the decades after 1920. Ideological controversies were less sharp after1945 and particularly as the Cold War faded. This was

150 *Happiness in Contemporary World History*

the point at which some global dimensions to happiness began to emerge, but in complex interaction with regional trends.

Far more clearly than in the 19th century, developments in the past several decades, with most of the world generating basic features of industrial society including urbanization, begin to allow an interim assessment of the larger implications of industrialization for happiness – and a tentative comparison with the assessment applied to the advent of agriculture in Chapter 3. The conclusion takes up this challenge directly, if somewhat inconclusively.

10 Disputed Happiness, 1920–1945

This chapter highlights several dramatically different trends affecting happiness in various parts of the world during the period of the world wars and great depression. On the one hand, World War I put a serious damper on happiness in Western Europe, ushering in a period of doubt that significantly modified dominant 19th-century patterns. Yet at the same time, though particularly in the United States, earlier themes were amplified, with some important additional components. The rise of fascism in many parts of Europe during the 1920s and 1930s signaled an explicit rejection of the primacy of individual happiness, offering a starkly different definition in which the word happiness rarely figured explicitly at all. Finally, in the rising anti-colonial and nationalist movements, leaders like Gandhi and Ataturk developed yet another set of alternatives concerning happiness, informed by earlier traditions but also the needs of nation-building.

There is, deliberately, no unifying theme in all this: the only unity is the shared chronology of the troubled period between the world wars. Global patterns remained highly diverse, though none of them was static. A few patterns would leave only a modest legacy – interwar despair and fascism, as interrelated responses to military and economic disaster, would not survive intact. But the theme of diversity would continue to complicate the contemporary history of happiness.

Shock

World War I was a horrible war, the bloodiest ever fought, to that point, in such a short span of time. Death rates in the many millions were compounded by the presence of many mutilated survivors, visible reminders to themselves and those around them. The experience of brutal trench warfare and constant bombardment marked even those who were physically unscathed, in ways they felt the civilian society around them could not understand. A British poet, Wilfred Owen, himself killed in the later stages of the war, pointed to what he called "that old lie", that it was at all noble to die for one's country.

The war was all the more shocking because of the widespread optimism that had preceded it: expectations of happy progress can make realities

152 *Happiness in Contemporary World History*

seem particularly disheartening. Many troops had initially gone off to battle, in 1914, assuming that the struggle would be easy, with quick and glorious victories and back home in a few months. British recruitment posters claimed explicitly that joining the army was a path to happiness. But actual combat troops soon found out the brutal truth. More generally, Western societies had been widely exposed to the kind of confidence expressed in the glowing turn-of-the-century evaluations, which claimed that decades of progress in the 19th century would unfailingly continue in the century to come. This was now almost impossible to believe. A generation of articulate young people, whose ranks had been particularly decimated by trench warfare, would grow into adulthood confused, often despairing.

At the intellectual level, the new mood was best captured by Oswald Spengler, whose book, *The Decline of the West*, was published in 1918. Spengler argued that Western civilization was in its death throes, that an event like the war was merely an episode in an irreversible collapse. Less important than its stark claim, the book's wide popularity – it was quickly translated from the German into several other languages – suggests how it captured and furthered the public mood. New artistic styles also arose to convey confusion or despair, particularly around surrealist or Dadaist themes.

Economic dislocations greatly heightened the problem. Massive inflation affected several countries right after the war, and then the global depression seized center stage beginning in 1929. Unemployment reached unprecedented heights, causing the psychological trauma of job loss compounded by rising poverty. In the United States, suicide rates increased by about 25% during the worst years.

The ensuing decade of the 1930s was further marked by growing international instability, and with the rise of Nazi Germany and an aggressive military regime in Japan, war fears mounted. Confidence faltered, as the leadership of many Western countries seemed unable to contend with growing economic and diplomatic problems. Again in the United States, a fictional radio broadcast in 1938, about an alien invasion, caused considerable panic, a sign of the level of public anxiety.

Expectations of happiness had never been evenly distributed in Western society, and the problems of the interwar years were not uniformly shared. But it seems very likely that many people experienced substantial deterioration in their sense of satisfaction or hope. The culture of happiness was not replaced, but it was certainly challenged.

New Frontiers

These same decades, however, saw continued signs of happiness in some sectors of Western society. Not only were some of the established themes maintained, but at least two further components were added, both of which would continue after World War II.

Disputed Happiness, 1920–1945 153

Both the continuities and the enhancements showed the power of the culture that had already been established. Persistent commitments to happiness also reflected the fact that some sectors of the population, most obviously in the middle classes, were able to continue to enjoy opportunities as consumers and spectators despite the disruptions around them, intensifying earlier interests in sports and enjoying the steady expansion of the movie industry. Stiff Victorian manners relaxed, as more revealing female fashions demonstrated. The new phenomenon of "dating" began to replace more formal courtship. The picture was not uniformly bleak, even in the depression-wracked 1930s.

It is also worth noting that this was the period when public smiling became easier to record. Improved photography eliminated agonizing waits for a picture to be taken, and the popularity of presenting one's smiling face was impossible to resist. Politicians like Franklin Roosevelt, in the United States, mastered the public appeal of the wide smile. Contributing as well was a crescendo of advertisements for toothpowder and paste, claiming a shining smile as a rewarding outcome.

National factors entered in. The United States was largely free from the postwar gloom that measurably affected many in Europe. Despite some war deaths and dislocations, the country was not deeply altered by World War I; indeed, its global economic position measurably improved.

Indeed, American popular advice literature filled with more recommendations about happiness and cheerfulness than ever before. Many childrearing manuals now routinely included a chapter on "how to make your child happy" – a 20th-century innovation; and a few whole books on the topic emerged. Parents, it was now assumed, had a responsibility to make sure their children were happy, though there was some confusion over how much effort this required: were children naturally happy, so that parents simply needed to avoid messing them up, or was extra care essential? The often-discussed notion of an "unhappy childhood" reflected the importance of trying to provide the contrary and a sense of how failure would continue to reverberate into adulthood. (The phrase began to be widely mentioned for the first time in the interwar years.) The wider emphasis on the cheerful family was also maintained; a husband should be able to rely on his wife's "never-tiring" good humor, and a proper wife should "always wear a smile". In some quarters, clearly, the happiness revolution was alive and well.

American cheer. For many foreigners today, one of the easiest ways to spot an American is by a wide and frequent smile. Unusual, or at least unusually displayed, American cheerfulness wins frequent comment, particularly among Europeans. It can be very disconcerting. It can seem disrespectful, or simply fake. But it was and is certainly widely noticed, along with a European sense that Americans remained naively overoptimistic. A Finnish observer, recently asked about how to identify Americans, repeated a modification of the Russian joke: when one sees someone

154 *Happiness in Contemporary World History*

smiling broadly at strangers, the assumption is he is either insane, drunk, or American. American businesses, trying to set up shop in Europe, often try to preach smiling salesmanship; this was an issue as Walmart tried, and failed, to gain a foothold in Germany.

The question is: when did this American proclivity first emerge?

Some comments about unusual American cheerfulness go back to the early 19th century. Harriet Martineau, a British visitor, noted how her hosts not only smiled a lot but told an inordinate number of jokes to try to get her to do the same. Was this cheerful emphasis part of the democratic culture Americans were trying to build in the wake of the successful revolution? Was this being baked into "national character" at this early point?

One theory argues that societies that receive many immigrants – including but not confined to the United States – emphasize smiling because, amid different cultures and languages, positive facial expressions become vital in trying to create a constructive atmosphere. (The same theory also notes that lots of smiling does not necessarily indicate special happiness.) But this does not entirely explain the special American proclivity, compared for example with Canadians.

Conditions between the wars may have amplified disparities at least in terms of transatlantic comparisons, given the greater challenge many Europeans encountered from the burdens of World War I and ensuing tensions. Whatever the causes – and explaining comparative differences in smiling is something of an analytical challenge – what is clear in that the United States began to take the lead in some of the further innovations in the "happiness revolution", even when these quickly involved other parts of Western society as well.

Thus, it was in 1923 that the Disney Company began its fabled entertainment career, from a base in California, explicitly around the theme of "creating happiness". The company quickly became involved in redoing classic fairy stories for children, eliminating cruelty and sadness in favor of uniformly happy endings and creating new characters, like the resolutely cheerful Mickey Mouse, meant to promote delight for parents and children alike. Here was one of many instances in which an American innovation would quickly generate wider impact.

Another American innovation was revealing, the introduction of canned laughter into radio and then TV comedies (in 1946; it was first used on television in 1950) – in contrast to patterns in Europe, where home audiences were left to decide on their own whether to laugh or not. Did the American gimmick suggest greater cheerfulness, or a greater compulsion to seem cheerful – or a bit of both?

Or on another front: during or shortly after World War I that the song "Happy Birthday" first appeared in the United States; its use in a 1931 Broadway show was what sealed its popularity, by which point it began to spread to other English-speaking countries and soon appeared in a variety of translations. Here was another American contribution to a happy popular culture.

Happiness at work. Two other innovations, emerging in the United States but with active European involvement, not only illustrated but measurably intensified the continuing commitment to happiness, even in the difficult terrain of the interwar decades.

The first involved a more explicit attempt to associate happiness and work – an area that had constituted a bit of a conundrum during 19th-century industrialization when the relationship of happiness to the dominant work ethic was at best ambiguous.

Older ideas that work could be an instrument for a happier life off the job, or the basis for social mobility, persisted strongly. But now a clearer notion began to creep in that work could or should be enjoyable in itself. Two related sources contributed.

A new subdiscipline, industrial psychology, began to emerge toward the end of the 19th century. Initial practitioners were German, but the field developed definitively in the United States shortly after World War I. Industrial psychologists strove to study the workplace, and workers themselves, in order to make the production process more efficient and to reduce labor strife. Some of their innovations had little to do with happiness, but others directly sought to improve worker morale. Studies by leaders like Elton Mayo discovered, for example, that judiciously placed rest periods improved productivity; so did playing soft music for 45 minutes every hour. A great deal of attention was devoted toward training foremen and other lower-level managers to be more tactful with workers, including listening to grievances more patiently. By the 1930s, on the heels of this kind of guidance, many corporations began to establish personnel, or human resources, departments, and while these had several functions, trying to make work more enjoyable, or at least less burdensome, was a prominent goal – as is still the case today. Here was a bureaucratic innovation that soon took hold in most Western countries.

At the same time, the growth of managerial bureaucracies and professional sales forces prompted explicit attention to the importance of cheerfulness at work. Training courses emerged to "produce cheerful salespeople careful to avoid provocation of vital customers". By the 1930s, American railroad companies were introducing "smile schools" to reprogram conductors and sales clerks. Dale Carnegie, also in the 1930s, made cheerfulness the keynote of his courses for aspiring salesmen, and for his widely popular book, *How to Win Friends and Influence People*, Carnegie boasted about his ability to keep smiling even in the face of the angriest customer, arguing that this was the best way to close the deal.

None of this necessarily made work, even for white-collar personnel, a happier experience. Indeed, the emotional manipulation involved could be extremely stressful. But increasing resources were being devoted to trying to promote happiness and, even more widely, it became steadily more important for certain kinds of workers to *seem* happy. The old theme – dating back to the 18th century – of wanting people around oneself to be cheerful was gaining an additional venue.

156 *Happiness in Contemporary World History*

Grief and death. One of the great challenges to 19th-century ideals of happiness, the high death rate, was substantially redefined by the early 20th century throughout the Western world – despite the huge losses in war.

By 1920, infant death rates were down to as low as 5% of all children born – massively below the 25% or more that had still been common just 40 years before. Further, while the influenza epidemic of 1918–1919 had a major impact, the epidemic cycle thereafter was greatly modified, thanks to improved public health measures. Overall, in the advanced industrial societies, widespread death was increasingly confined to older age groups. Finally, it was also in the first half of the 20th century that death began to occur primarily in hospitals, rather than in or around the home.

All this meant that encounters with death were becoming far less common than they had ever been in the human experience. It became far easier to embellish the 19th-century impulse to smooth over this unpleasant reality, and to hope for continued progress in future. Doctors, death-fighters by training, now became the dominant figures in dealing with death, with more traditional consolers relegated to lesser roles. A key ingredient in happiness, now, might involve not having to think about death much at all.

One immediate result of this transformation, widely discussed in popular magazines in Europe and the United States in the 1920s, was a redefinition of grief from essential to undesirable. As one popular magazine intoned, "Probably nothing is sadder in life than the thought of all the hours that are spent in grieving over what is past and irretrievable." Any prolonged tearfulness suggested "something morbid, either mental or physical". Manners books shifted gears, from offering long passages about how to deal politely with a bereaved family to urging that displaying much grief was now simply discourteous, an unreasonable burden on other people. Anyone suffering from more than temporary grief was urged to get psychological counseling, and a whole category of "grief work" developed in the field simply to promote greater control. It is no exaggeration to suggest that having to deal with other people's grief, particularly outside the immediate family, now often seemed to be an unreasonable burden on happiness.

Correspondingly, mourning practices steadily diminished, on both sides of the Atlantic (modified only, in the United States, by high levels of religious devotion). Gone were elaborate draperies at the windows of a home where a death had occurred. Disappearing even were black armbands. Funeral services became shorter, and children were often kept away entirely. Death still happened, but it should be as unobtrusive as possible.

Even the preferred manner of death changed. For centuries, a good death had meant a process that might take several weeks, when an older person, suffering most commonly from a respiratory ailment, would have a chance to say goodbyes to friends and family. Now, for almost everyone, the best death was sudden and unexpected, requiring no thought or preparation at all.

Disputed Happiness, 1920–1945 157

These huge changes in the incidence and experience of death ultimately provoked an equally huge debate, about whether happiness is really best served by minimizing death – though arguments about the deleterious effects of the so-called modern "taboo" about death emerged mainly after World War II. Is modern happiness dangerously shallow because death is relegated to the background? Are people actually more fearful of death, in this sense less happy, because they encounter it with less preparation? A variety of evidence suggests that many people actually make their deaths needlessly complicated by failing to prepare appropriate arrangements in advance. For example, many avoid specifying whether they want life prolonged through "heroic" medical measures. This kind of reluctance arguably illustrates a radically redefined problem of happiness and death.

At least superficially, however, the decline of death – including the unprecedented fact that parents no longer had to expect at least one child to die, as a matter of course – contributed to a larger emotional realignment from the early 20th century onward, on both sides of the Atlantic. Increasingly, psychological experts and popularizers alike distinguished between positive and negative emotions, with the latter to be avoided as much as possible (and with parents urged to protect their children accordingly). Fear, anger, grief, shame, and even undue guilt normally were seen to serve no useful function, and while they could not be avoided entirely they should be downplayed. This left the way free, in principle, for emotions like love, joy, or possibly moderate envy – emotions that were compatible with active consumerism, and with happiness.

Pleasures. One of the striking features of the 1930s in most Western societies, though probably particularly in the United States, was the successful pursuit of pleasure amid the more obvious grimness of the Depression. Social class was a vital factor here: workers suffered more than business and professional groups, the young more than the middle-aged.

But the growing entertainment industry, headed globally now by the Hollywood studios, sought to lighten the mood whenever possible. Happy endings became a movie staple, with only elite art films daring to buck the trend. Shirley Temple became a characteristic star, with extraordinary popularity as a child actress: as Franklin Roosevelt put it, "It is a splendid thing that for just 15 cents, an American can go to a movie and look at the smiling face of a baby and forget his troubles." But there were many others – romantic sensations, comedians, dancers – to provide distraction. Professional sports and college football were booming. The popularity of "Happy Birthday" – often sung to celebrating adults via a "singing telegram" – was directly attributed to its service as antidote to Depression worries. In Britain the end of the decade even saw the first steps in the next mass distraction: television.

Relative affluence (alongside grinding poverty) and the expectation of happiness were arguably generating an unprecedented combination in the 1930s: a dismal decade combined with a widespread commitment

158 *Happiness in Contemporary World History*

to fun. World War II would continue this odd combination, particularly for American troops, with elaborate efforts to provide Hollywood-style entertainment shows in military camps (comedians and attractive female starlets preferred). The United Service Organizations (USO), formed in 1941, specialized in organizing performance tours for military facilities at home and abroad.

Fascism and Happiness

Adolf Hitler, the leader of Nazi Germany, made his position very clear: "The day of individual happiness has passed." Italy's Mussolini offered essentially the same point: "Fascism is therefore opposed to all individualistic abstractions based on eighteenth century materialism....It does not believe in the possibility of 'happiness' on earth as conceived by the economistic literature of the 18th century." Nazi and fascist leaders did not often talk about happiness directly, but they quite deliberately sought to build a different sense of human purpose from the concepts of happiness that had been building in the West for a century and a half. While the fascist attack on happiness is not often highlighted, it was actually a prominent – and extraordinary – feature of the movement. Conventional happiness, indeed, became an enemy.

Correspondingly, cheerfulness was replaced with stern faces and military bearing. As Mussolini put it, "Life, as conceived of by the fascist, is serious, austere....The Fascist disdains an 'easy' life." Discipline and authority were the new watchwords, all under the guidance of the State and its leader.

The fascist experiment was fairly short-lived, largely buried with defeat in World War II. But the experiment was an interesting effort to counter the standard expectations of happiness with a dramatically different model.

In this vision, the individual was to be subsumed through passionate loyalty to the nation – or in the Nazi case, the *Volk*, or race – and the state. Duty and devotion were the hallmarks. Huge rallies sought to create an excitement that would easily supplant more personal pleasures. Many forms of modern consumerism were discouraged, some of them dismissed as modernist decadence. As Mussolini put it,

> Fascism sees in the world not only those superficial, material aspects in which man appears as an individual, standing by himself, self-centered...urge(d) toward a life of selfish momentary pleasure, but also the nation and the country, individuals and generations bound together by a moral law, with common traditions and a mission which by suppressing the instinct closed in a brief circle of pleasure, builds up a higher life, founded on duty, in which the individual, by self-sacrifice, the renunciation of self-interest, by death itself, can achieve that purely spiritual existence in which his value as a man consists.

Disputed Happiness, 1920–1945 159

Fascism, and particularly its Nazi version, also urged the importance of a family life devoted primarily to childbearing, with women clearly subordinate to their husband.

The causes of this effort to replace what had seemed to be well-established notions of happiness in countries like Italy and Germany were complex. Disruption and disappointment from World War I, serious economic dislocation combined with forceful leadership, masterful propaganda, and intimidation through force. For many people, happiness had been declining anyway, so the appeal of a radically different model might make sense.

Fascism also sought to provide alternatives for some of the conventional trappings of modern happiness. Both Mussolini and Hitler created new, collective opportunities for leisure. In the German case, a movement interestingly called "Strength through Joy" sought to provide workers with a number of outlets, tailored for people with relatively low wages and imbued with Nazi propaganda. From 1933 until preempted by the outbreak of World War II, Strength through Joy organized films, plays, concerts, and day trips. Hiking was strongly emphasized; fascists liked to tout physical activity in preference to undue intellectualism. Ambitious annual vacations were offered through standardized mass resorts, as the movement for a time became the largest tourist operation in the world. By 1938 a large minority of Germans were taking Strength through Joy holidays. There was even some effort to recruit foreign tourists as well, in one case featuring Germany's propaganda minister uncharacteristically grinning out from a colorful poster.

The fascist effort to displace conventional happiness was also fueled by active propaganda and intimidation by a network of secret police. Youth movements promoted excited group loyalties, hoping to build a different type of personality for the future. And of course any sign of dissent was ruthlessly repressed. It is hard to evaluate the balance between acceptance and fear in this effort to create an alternative to happiness.

Nationalism Outside the West: Other Visions of Happiness

Though overshadowed by military conflicts and economic challenge, the interwar years also saw the solidification of a number of crucial nationalist movements outside the West. While the need to take a stance on happiness was hardly the leading nationalist concern, it was not uncommon to offer brief comments. No leader fully embraced the Western concept of happiness – among other things, too much individualism and consumerism could distract from the common cause. This had already been a challenge for Japanese national leaders of course, but now it applied to other regions. On the other hand, fascist bombast (Japan partially excepted) gained few adherents either.

Two emphases were attractive: one would simply emphasize the importance of duty and social obligation, since building the nation or achieving

160 *Happiness in Contemporary World History*

independence were fundamental to happiness of any sort. The other might more elaborately appeal to national cultural traditions, to emphasize a concept of happiness that was much more clearly differentiated from either the Western or the fascist approach.

Turkey. Kemal Ataturk led in the foundation of the new Turkish nation on the ruins of the Ottoman Empire, in the early 1920s, and then served as president until his death in 1938. He was an ardent modernizer and reformer, incorporating many Western values into his drive to make Turkey a leading nation. Changes ranged from requirements for wearing Western-style clothing, to utilization of the Latin alphabet, to granting women the vote. In his work, he walked something of a fine line in overseeing major changes that would not, however, impose complete Westernization; he was eager, for example, to avoid Western-style political competition.

In this vein, without attacking Western ideas of happiness directly, Ataturk was eager to emphasize an alternative vision. First, he wanted to associate happiness with nationalist success. In 1933, on the tenth anniversary of the foundation of the Turkish republic, he offered a list of the many improvements in national life over the previous decade. He claimed that Turkey was well on the way to becoming a great nation, and would soon lead the world in levels of prosperity and civilization. This meant, in turn, that happiness consisted in rejoicing at this national success: "Happy is the one who says, 'I am a Turk'". This catchy phrase was used periodically by later regimes to promote loyalty to the system, and it simply sidestepped larger questions about more personal definitions of happiness.

But Ataturk could go further, beyond the strictly nationalist emphasis, to insist that happiness consisted of working hard for national progress.

> The necessary thing for anyone to be happy and contented is working for the ones who will come after him rather than working for himself. One can reach true delight and happiness in this life only by working for the existence, honor and happiness of the future generations.

This was a slightly different, perhaps vaguer formulation than the Japanese approach in the Meiji era, but it had similar overtones. It lacked the bombast and self-sacrifice of fascist definitions. But it also clearly suggested an alternative to the more individualistic, consumer-oriented Western approach.

India. Nationalism in India under British rule had begun, fairly mildly, in the 19th century. It became much more vigorous after World War I, in part because many Indian troops had served in the war and gained fuller awareness of nationalist goals. Demands for outright independence mounted.

A number of leaders helped spearhead agitation, but without question Mohandas Gandhi was the most visible and influential among them. Gandhi's outlook was shaped by a number of influences; Hinduism was

Disputed Happiness, 1920–1945 161

the most profound, but Gandhi also read Western and Russian authors, blending a number of different ideas into his own philosophy. The result, most famously, was a deep commitment to nonviolence and, ultimately, certain reforms in India's tradition including abolition of the caste system. But a distinctive approach to happiness was another interesting feature of Gandhi's approach.

For Gandhi saw happiness not in terms of duties to the state or society, though he believed deeply in the importance of service to others; and certainly not in terms of personal pleasures on advancement. Rather, harking back to some of the thinking common among earlier religious and philosophical leaders, happiness was a matter of cultivating a proper mindset. His most famous quote on the subject went as follows: "Happiness is when what you think, what you say, and what you do are in harmony."

Some people, particularly in more recent decades, have interpreted this as a praise of what is now called positive thinking, as developing attitudes that encourage self-love. It might also be seen as an appeal to be trustworthy, to match actions with beliefs; Gandhi placed great stock in integrity and sincerity. Probably the core meaning, however, involves the emphasis on harmony, on alignment of the self and the surrounding environment; as with many earlier Hindu thinkers, the importance of truth-seeking and self-realization was fundamental to Gandhi's beliefs. These were the elements that other Hindu and Buddhist thinkers have emphasized in embellishing Gandhi's thoughts, and that helped win him a reputation as a Mahatma, or "great soul" from many Indians at the time. Further, this more spiritual approach to happiness was fully consistent with Gandhi's deep interest in peace and non-violence, as well as his lack of any particular concern for the material aspects of life. Peace within oneself was a vital component of social peace in the more conventional sense.

For all his undeniable success in galvanizing Indian nationalism, Gandhi was an atypical figure, compared to nationalists like Ataturk or even most of his colleagues in India. While passionate about independence, Gandhi did not want to see India march in the path of economic development or greater military power. He envisaged a rural and artisanal economy, deliberately different from most of the societies of the 20th century. His views on happiness are, correspondingly, unusual, however thoughtful. He does remind us, though, that traditional ideas and new movements could combine in unpredictable ways, and that earlier, religious views on happiness wielded continued influence. The role of tradition in Indian concepts of happiness – though not exactly a Gandhian formula – will gain further attention in Chapter 11.

★★★

Happiness became a disputed concept in the decades of war and depression, not just because of varied traditions but because of new levels of competition

162　*Happiness in Contemporary World History*

for people's loyalties. The results added to global diversity, though some of the statements proved short-lived. The only common denominator was a growing sense that the topic of happiness had to be explicitly addressed in modern politics, even if the resulting definitions clashed directly. This need to produce clear-cut standards for happiness would also play a considerable role in the rhetoric and policy generated by the rising communist movement, first in the Soviet Union and then more widely.

The absence of a clear global standard for happiness clearly complicates analysis for these troubled decades, and the emphasis on a largely regional approach would be modified later in the 20th century. But the interest in finding some alternative to Western concepts, even as the West added some new ingredients to the commitment to happiness, suggested an important challenge that would echo in subsequent decades as well.

Further Reading

On the growing role of governments and businesses in trying to advertise and sell happiness,

Davies, William. *The Happiness Industry: How the Government and Big Business Sold Us Well-Being* (London: Verso, 2015) – applicable to later periods as well.

On the impact of World War I,

Winter, Jay Murray. *Remembering War: The Great War between Memory and History in the Twentieth Century* (New Haven: Yale University Press, 2006).

On cheerfulness,

Kotchemidova, Christina. "From Good Cheer to 'Drive-By Smiling': A Social History of Cheerfulness." *Journal of Social History* 39, no. 1 (2005): 5–37.

Stearns, Peter N. *Satisfaction Not Guaranteed Dilemmas of Progress in Modern Society* (New York: New York University Press, 2012).

For the American mood between the wars:

Allen, Frederick Lewis. *Only Yesterday; An Informal History of the 1920s* (New York: Harper, 1931) and *Since Yesterday: The 1930s in America* (New York: Harper, 1939).

On changes at work,

Hochschild, Arlie Russell. *The Managed Heart Commercialization of Human Feeling*, Updated, with a New Preface (Berkeley: University of California Press, 2012).

On grief and death,

Ariès, Philippe. *The Hour of Our Death*, 1st American ed. (New York: Knopf, 1981).

Gorer, Geoffrey. *Death, Grief, and Mourning* (New York: Arno Press, 1977).

Stearns, Peter N. *Revolutions in Sorrow: The American Experience of Death in Global Perspective* (Boulder, CO: Paradigm Publishers, 2007).

Stearns, Peter N., ed., *Routledge Modern History of Death* (London: Routledge, 2020).

On fascism,

Paxton, Robert O. *The Anatomy of Fascism* (New York: Knopf, 2004).

Redles, David. *Hitler's Millennial Reich: Apocalyptic Belief and the Search for Salvation* (New York: NYU Press, 2005).

Disputed Happiness, 1920–1945   163

On Ataturk,

Gokalp Ziya, and Robert Devereaux. *The Principles of Turkism* (Leiden: E.J. Brill, 1968).

Hanioğlu, M. Şükrü. *Atatürk: An Intellectual Biography*, Revised Paperback Edition (Princeton, NJ: Princeton University Press, 2017).

On Gandhi,

Erikson, Erik H. *Gandhi's Truth: On the Origins of Militant Nonviolence*, 1st ed. (New York: Norton, 1969).

Gandhi, Rajmohan. *Gandhi: The Man, His People, and the Empire.* (Berkeley: University of California Press, 2008).

11 Communist Happiness

Beginning with the Soviet Union in 1917, communist societies would play a major role in world history for at least 80 years, with important echoes still today. Communist leaders faced a fascinating dilemma concerning happiness. On the one hand, happiness was a vital goal; there could be no sidestepping happiness through references to duty or an afterlife. Marxism, and communism in its wake, was in this sense fully in the tradition of the Enlightenment, even when it spread to societies outside the West.

While communists embraced happiness, they were resolutely opposed to the kind of happiness that, in their view, was being emphasized in the West itself. They saw Western-style happiness as inconsistent with their commitment to social progress toward an ultimate goal of equality and freedom. It risked in fact distracting ordinary people from the noble task of building toward this ideal future. In this sense, Western-style happiness was a bourgeois trap, a foreign lure, that had to be vigorously opposed.

So the question was how to define a definite but distinctive idea of happiness. Part of the challenge was resolved by pointing to the future, but a future here on earth: full happiness could not be achieved until the revolution had completely obliterated all traces of capitalism and its trappings. But hope was not enough. Communist leaders, eager to inspire popular loyalty – and particularly, working-class loyalty – needed to offer some happiness in the present as well.

The challenge of defining a communist approach to happiness became even more acute when Cold War competition with the United States heated up in the late 1940s. Americans made no bones about showing their consumerist version of happiness at every turn, using international fairs to tout the latest in kitchen conveniences and other consumer lures. Communists, eager to prove the superiority of their system, were torn between wanting to show they could beat Americans at their own game through growing strength and prosperity, and continuing to work on a distinctive definition of happiness.

By this point, the challenge of Marxist happiness was also being taken up by the Chinese, after the communist victory in 1949. Here was another opportunity to build an alternative version, with some explicitly Chinese values added in as well.

It is vital to remember that all the major communist societies in the 20th century were also seeking to accelerate the process of industrialization, a process that Western societies had advanced a century or more before. Early industrialization, as we have seen, places its own stresses and constraints on happiness, and this must factor into the assessment of communist alternatives as well.

The Soviet Commitment

Writing recently about Lenin, the leader of the communist victory in Russia in 1917, A.J. Polan argues that Lenin's fundamental vision resembled that of Thomas Jefferson a century and a half before. Both men wanted more than the removal of the evils of a current regime; they sought to build a new society in which people would be able to achieve a new level of happiness through a greater range of freedom. Lenin himself argued, in defending the need for revolution, that Russians faced "two roads, freedom and happiness or the grave".

To be sure, Lenin and other Russian leaders talked less frequently of happiness than Enlightenment enthusiasts had done. They also, true to Russian culture, smiled rather rarely, though Lenin apparently loved good jokes and Stalin liked to portray a happy crowd looking up at him with smiling faces. The whole Soviet project involved a complex mixture of undeniable hopes for the future, when a socialist society would have been fully constructed, and a deep interest in emphasizing measurable levels of happiness in the new Russia that was already being built. But there was no question that happiness was the ultimate goal, in contrast for example to the fascist effort to move away from a concept of happiness altogether...

To many in a Western, and particularly American, audience, discussion of Soviet happiness in any terms other than false propaganda may seem odd, even objectionable. And there was no question, particularly under Stalin in the 1930s and 1940s, of a strong element of outright indoctrination – though even with this, it was revealing that so much explicit emphasis was placed on happiness. The regime relied heavily on fear and repression, killing millions of its own citizens, especially under Stalin. But it also massively expanded education, advanced public health and reduced child mortality, and provided many opportunities for mobility. Its claims for happiness were not always entirely hollow.

It is also important to remember that Russia had established some slightly skeptical approaches to happiness before the revolution. Communists would work hard to change prior culture, including a major assault on established religion; and they certainly sought to construct a more positive attitude, explicitly attacking gloom or despair. But some of the themes developed in the tsarist days were not entirely erased.

Work. Communist leaders were even more comfortable than happiness advocates in the West in seeing work and economic life as the central

166 *Happiness in Contemporary World History*

pillar of happiness – assuming the injustices of the capitalist system had been eliminated. By the 1930s, posters of strong, hopeful workers and peasants – rarely smiling, but certainly conveying a positive air, heads held high – were becoming a staple of the government-sponsored Socialist Realist style. In 1935, what was called the Stakhanovite movement was launched, named for a coal miner, Alexy Stakhanov, who presumably produced 14 times his allotment of coal in a single shift. Heroic workers began to be identified in all sorts of industries to symbolize Soviet economic advance and the rewards of hard work. Of course the program fit the agenda of a regime pushing for rapid industrialization, but it also highlighted this aspect of happiness. As Stakhanov's daughter claimed, "He loved his job, and everything he achieved was through his hard work."

Childhood and youth. From the beginning, the Soviets placed great emphasis on the younger generation, hoping to convert it to a set of values different from those of the tsarist days. Not only schools but various young communist groups proliferated. By the 1930s, these efforts combined with a growing need, centered on Stalin's obsessive concern with loyalty, to promote the successes of a regime now two decades old: the government and communist party worked hard to convince people that progress was occurring, that happiness was steadily gaining ground – and young people formed a key audience.

"Thank you, dear comrade Stalin, for a happy childhood." This motto began to be painted over the entrances to kindergartens and nursery schools. Even orphanages filled with similar messages. Posters depicting a serious but benign Stalin in front of widely smiling young people became common – a key part of the upbeat poster campaign more generally. Children's stories filled with similar themes. The campaign featured collective happiness – the whole society was advancing – not individual fulfillment. But there was no doubt about the powerful emphasis.

Some of the literature directly addressed the idea that suffering was a basic part of Russian culture. Communist success was meant to unseat this image, with the promise of even further gains in the future. The program also highlighted what it claimed was the obvious unhappiness of capitalist society in the West: the mistreatment of workers, racism, lack of opportunities for women. And every effort was made to embed this idea of happiness deeply into personal life. The programs for children were one aspect of this, but the happiness theme also infused popular cookbooks and other materials. And, without question, many people were persuaded – including some in Russia and Eastern Europe today who look back on the communist period with deep nostalgia.

Collective programs. Soviet emphasis on happiness did not rest on propaganda alone. Stalin and other leaders were deeply conscious of a need to promote popular satisfaction, particularly in the growing working class – despite the demands of an industrializing economy. While wages remained rather low – with rewards for individual productivity – the regime worked hard to provide a number of collective outlets for popular entertainment and pleasure. The range of available performances steadily expanded, including movies as well as theater and dance productions and, particularly after World War II, a wide array of spectator sports.

State-sponsored vacations constituted the most ambitious effort, very similar to what Nazi Germany was developing in the same period. Here was a chance to provide reward for work but also an annual alternative, without the need to cater to individual tastes. Huge beach resorts were built on the Baltic and Black Sea coasts. Specialized programs catered to youth groups, while more luxurious spas rewarded higher-ranking officials with thermal baths and other amenities.

By the 1970s and 1980s, Soviet tourism became even more venturesome, encouraging vacation trips to other communist countries. By this point, about half the population was taking an annual trip of some sort. The program, despite its collective overtones, also promoted a sense of personal choice and some degree of self-expression. People began to arrange their own specific trips and, obviously, had a growing range of individual options.

The dilemma of consumerism. When it came to more routine consumerism, and its potential relation to happiness, the Soviet regime faced a more difficult problem, which it never fully resolved. There were two constraints. First, despite increasingly successful industrialization, this was not a wealthy society, and investments continued to privilege heavy industry and weapons development. Building a rich range of consumer options proved difficult. But the Soviets also worried about the individualist aspect of consumerism, which conflicted with the interest in a more collective definition of happiness and the desire to create a visible alternative to the presumably decadent values of the capitalist West.

As a result, the goods available to most Russians tended to be of low quality; by the 1960s for example, it was fairly easy to get television sets but they often did not work well. Early on the Soviets converted a previous department store to a state-run operation nicknamed GUM, with a prime location in Moscow. By the 1950s, 130,000 people were visiting the Moscow emporium daily – second only, globally, to attendance at Macy's in the United States. But again, the products on display were inconsistent at best.

Equally interesting, from the standpoint of happiness, was the lack of attention to service. GUM clerks did not even have cash registers, using abacuses instead. Waiting lines were long even for basic foods. Clerks were not encouraged to smile, or even be particularly civil. In a proletarian society it seemed more important to let clerks express themselves, despite often grumpy results, rather than try to manipulate them emotionally.

But it was impossible to avoid consumerism entirely. As early as 1934 a luxury foods store opened in Moscow, for communist party bigwigs, complete with imported delights. By the 1950s, more and more Russians

168   *Happiness in Contemporary World History*

became at least vaguely aware of consumer standards in the West; this was also the point at which the United States government began to use international fairs to brag about American appliances and the like. Even aside from this, some attention began to be devoted to clothing, which was not as uniformly drab as Western Cold Warriors liked to claim.

In 1959 the Russian premier, Nikita Khrushchev, visited the United States, where his hosts again showed off American consumer styles. He was genuinely shocked by the scanty costumes he saw on a Hollywood set – by Soviet standards, public sexual display was another sign of decadence – but he ended his visit with a revealingly ambiguous slogan: "We will bury you," in reference to the emphasis on consumer happiness in the United States. Did this mean the Soviets would triumph with a different version of happiness, or was it a boast that they could beat Americans at their own game? The tension was never resolved, and contributed to the dissatisfaction that ultimately brought the Soviet Union down at the end of the 1980s.

Communist China

As leaders like Mao Zedong worked to build a communist society in China after they won control of the government in 1949, their approach to happiness resembled that of the Soviet Union in many ways. However, some crucial differences did emerge. China was a poorer country, wracked by over a century of unrest and external invasion; building an industrial society was a more demanding process, at least for several decades. Even though Mao vigorously attacked Confucian traditions, Chinese culture may have facilitated an emphasis on collective rather than individual satisfactions.

As had occurred with the Soviets, Chinese leaders quickly began to expand education and improve public health. They had fewer resources, however, to build some of the community facilities that the Soviets highlighted, such as public resorts. Further, while pointing to the ultimate goal of a classless society, Chinese communists in some ways were attempting an even more dramatic social and cultural restructuring than had occurred in the Soviet Union. For example, they tried to reduce the hold of individual families (while pressing for a high birth rate); a widespread system of communes sought to introduce collective meals and limit separate family activities.

Mao himself had considerable experience in working to orchestrate changes in emotional patterns. During his long years of struggle against Chinese opponents and Japanese invaders, with a largely peasant following, he had emphasized the validity of anger against injustice, seeking to modify traditional Confucian deference – with some success.

The Great Leap Forward. The Maoist approach to happiness went through two somewhat distinct phases. In the first phase, extending into the 1960s, great energy was devoted to what the leader called the Great Leap Forward, seeking to promote rapid industrialization without however a strong technological infrastructure. The communist party urged mass loyalty by emphasizing, on the one hand, deep indignation against the traditional structures that had brought such misery to the people, and on the other, equally deep hope in rapid progress. Small-group meetings highlighted "enemies" of the working class, including older ways of thinking, but also emphasized what one scholar has called "euphoria" – excited hopes for an imminent brighter future. One revealing motto suggested the basic message: "Hard work for a few years, be happy for a thousand".

This approach placed little emphasis on happiness here and now. Consumer options were extremely limited, as the government tried to mobilize all available resources for investments in the future. Clothing, for example, was deliberately drab: following Mao's lead, a unisex jacket, usually in muted colors, was widely adopted. At most, inspiration from Mao himself was supposed to provide uplift "Chairman Mao said a word, Happiness dropped from the sky"; thanks to the Leader's vision, "the sound of happiness is like thunder…old people laughed till they cried." Thanks to Mao and the Communist Party, "any miracle" can be created.

This encompassing propaganda utilized some of the same apparatus that Stalinists had employed in the Soviet Union. Images of a "happy Mao" were distributed. Posters often proclaimed simply, "Chairman Mao gives us a happy life," complete with smiling crowds.

A new debate. The Great Leap Forward, however, was a gigantic failure, and by the 1960s widespread disillusionment called Mao's own position into question. Many younger Party members, particularly, began to express an interest in more material possessions and greater leisure time. The result, briefly, was an intriguing, if somewhat manipulated, discussion of what happiness was all about, now that future-oriented euphoria had become insufficient.

Here was the new wisdom: "Happiness is a Hard Day's Work". Mao and his followers began to emphasize this new message in the mid-1960s. His statement capped a yearlong, rather public debate about the nature of happiness in communist China. A number of newspapers, first in the northern region, then nationwide, began instead to suggest the need for greater satisfaction here and now. As a writer from Hainan island put it, "I do not agree with the opinion of some comrades that 'hardship is happiness'." "What is the use of the products of this kind of labor or hard labor? Do we not labor for the sake of enjoying these products and material things?" Or another: "I think that happiness means leading a peaceful and pleasant life, not a life of fighting amid hardship every day."

After some hesitation, the Party came down hard on this soft, "bourgeois" definition of happiness. Newspapers that carried the appeals soon featured explicit correctives, causing some to believe that the whole debate

170 *Happiness in Contemporary World History*

was a setup to highlight the "right" approach and to help identify enemies of the revolution who might need "special education." To be sure, progress was not going to be easy, but it must involve far more than material goods; moral qualities must be "appreciably raised": "The happiest and most satisfactory Communist society...is the result of selfless labor and arduous struggle carried out for a long time by our revolutionary forerunners and our revolutionary successors."

"Since the bourgeoisie regard personal happiness as above everything else, their idea of so-called happiness naturally consists of eating, drinking and having a good time."

> As far as the proletariat is concerned, collective happiness is above individual happiness, spiritual life is above material life....We shall not hesitate to go through thick and thin and then our whole spiritual world will be filled with a sense of pride and happiness.

This was a more extreme approach than that taken by most Soviet leaders. It argued that even after the achievement of communism, "arduous labor" would still be necessary. Devotion to the cause, fighting for the people and noble ideals, would always be the essence of "glory and happiness". The definition was arguably rather vague: what happiness was *not* was much clearer than what it was or would be. The spiritual references were left unspecified. But there was little mistaking Mao's desire to maintain the sense of struggle that had brought him to power in the first place.

Cultural revolution. The new emphasis went well beyond rhetoric, as Mao introduced what would come to be called the "cultural revolution" (officially, the "Great Proletarian Cultural Revolution") in 1966. Remnants of older institutions and ideas were brutally attacked by groups of communist youth called the Red Guards. Local communist leaders were assailed, amid the new authorization to struggle and rebel. Institutions like universities were substantially dismantled.

In this effort, many intellectuals and students were forced to go to the countryside, to engage in agricultural labor that would presumably purge them of residual "bourgeois" sentiments, deliberately disrupting their lives at the time and, as things turned out, often well into the future. Here was a concrete illustration of the notion that work for the collective cause was the essence of happiness.

The cultural revolution itself failed by the mid-1970s, and Mao himself died in 1976. China soon adopted a host of new policies that included new limitations on family size, greater encouragement for conventional economic growth and even some private initiative, and far more extensive contacts with the outside world. As with the Soviet Union ten years later, though without a formal renunciation of communism, China was launched on a new path.

Communist Happiness   171

Aftermath

The communist attempt to develop a distinctive approach to happiness was intriguing. This was hardly the first effort to attack material pleasures and entertainments for their inadequacy or to insist that happiness must be based on some higher principles. It was, however, the most extensive program that had emerged since the West's happiness revolution, the most ambitious attempt to develop alternatives within the context of an industrializing society. The program was shaped in part by the political needs of the communist parties and the leadership cults of Stalin and Mao, but it also responded to a valid underlying question about the purpose of life in an industrial age.

The effective failure of the most ambitious experiments did raise a further question, for Russia and China alike: after decades of intense propaganda and systematic attacks on what was seen as a Western approach, how would happiness now be defined? Could some other option be developed?

Answers to the question are still being developed. Considerable nostalgia for the days of Stalin or Mao – surprising, to most outside observers – reflects the power of the earlier communist message and the difficulty of defining acceptable alternatives. Both China and Russia have also seen a greater emphasis on nationalism; both have seen a partial revival of religion – though in the Chinese case particularly, carefully monitored by the state.

But both countries have also witnessed a considerable turn to more consumerist values. By the 1990s a breed of so-called "new Russians" emerged, essentially a new urban middle class, eager to take advantage of a growing array of consumer goods. A similar phenomenon occurred in China as industrial prosperity mounted; a new online shopping day for example, introduced on 11/11/2011 as "Singles' Day", quickly became the largest consumer festival in the world. Studies early in the 21st century claimed that most Chinese were now defining a good life in terms of adequate "freedom to choose" and "having the means to obtain desired resources." To be sure, this appeal to more self-expression might be leavened with a bit of traditional wisdom as well, as with a father who advised his adult son, in 2002: "Strive to be content and you will find pleasure." But the new orientation was a far cry from the days of Stalin or Mao.

In China particularly, new levels of individual ambition emerged, further suggesting a recalibration of ideas about happiness. "I struggle for a better life. It is this struggle to improve that makes life worth living." "I want to embrace and enjoy life as much as I can." "I want a challenge. Money isn't everything, but it is important these days." Or most succinctly: "Happiness is a good motive." Attitudes of this sort often focus not only on personal satisfactions and self-fulfillment, but on a commitment to creating opportunities for an even better life for one's child. Emotional commitment to

172 *Happiness in Contemporary World History*

the nuclear family, and for women particularly an intense bond with what is usually a single child, also loom large in the contemporary value system.

Both in Russia and China, experiences shared with other consumer societies form a growing part of the contemporary picture, from Shanghai's Disneyland to spectator passions for sports like soccer and basketball. A student in Shanghai explains that he likes to go to McDonalds restaurants not because the food is better, but because it gives him a sense of participating in a cultural experience with youth around the world. A Russian woman describes her first visit to McDonalds when it opened in Moscow in 1990: she was so excited that she kept the burger wrapper as a souvenir. She was particularly impressed with the smiling employees who actually wiped the table after a customer left. (The smiles reflected deliberate company policy, as against the national tradition.)

Questions remain, however, in both countries. In both cases, after all, distinctive earlier approaches to happiness leave a legacy, and the communist experiment itself, as well as its disappointments, are recent memories. While some observers find happiness levels higher in China than they were in the Maoist past, others note the nation's relatively low international ranking and some probable slippage in recent years. Russia, also, has faced a happiness problem, judging by international polls. The dislocations of rapid industrialization – and the extent to which many people, particularly in the countryside, feel left out – definitely leave a mark. Russians' widespread willingness, under Vladimir Putin's presidency, to emphasize national aspirations over consumer goals raises another set of issues. People in both these major countries may still be experimenting with post-communist options for happiness. Finally, the turn toward greater authoritarianism after 2013, particularly in China, has seen a revival of propagandistic uses of happiness reminiscent of the earlier communist systems. Thus when authorities destroyed a Uighur cemetery in northwest China, as part of the larger repressive effort, they installed a recreation center that they revealingly named, "Happiness Park". Concerned about relatively low international rankings, the Chinese government, and many individual Chinese scholars, have worked to address the problem of advancing happiness by encouraging new consumer outlets – more feelgood films, amusement parks – and also by promotional rhetoric.

Further Reading

On the Soviet Union,

Balina, Marina, and Evengy Dobrenko, eds. *Petrified Utopia: Happiness Soviet Style* (London; New York; Delhi: Anthem Press, 2009).

Bonnell, Victoria E. *Iconography of Power: Soviet Political Posters under Lenin and Stalin* (Berkeley: University of California Press, 1997).

Boym, Svetlana. *Common Places: Mythologies of Everyday Life in Russia* (Cambridge, MA: Harvard University Press, 1994).

Communist Happiness 173

Koenker, Diane P. *Club Red Vacation Travel and the Soviet Dream* (Ithaca, NY: Cornell University Press, 2016).

Pisch, Anita. *The Personality Cult of Stalin in Soviet Posters, 1929–1953: Archetypes, Inventions and Fabrications* (Acton: Australian National University Press, 2016).

Polan, Antony J. *Lenin and the End of Politics* (Berkeley: University of California Press, 1984).

On China,

Pye, Lucian W. "Mao Tse-tung's Leadership Style." *Political Science Quarterly* 91, no. 2 (1976): 219–235.

Schram, Stuart R. (Stuart Reynolds). *Mao Tsê-Tung* (New York: Simon and Schuster, 1967).

Yu, Liu. "Maoist Discourse and the Mobilization of Emotions in Revolutionary China." *Modern China* 36, no. 3 (May 1, 2010): 329–362.

On more recent developments,

Fong, Vanessa L. *Only Hope: Coming of Age under China's One-Child Policy* (Stanford, CA: Stanford University Press, 2004).

Stites, Richard. *Russian Popular Culture: Entertainment and Society since 1900* (Cambridge: Cambridge University Press, 1992).

Tang, Wenfang, and William L. Parish. *Chinese Urban Life under Reform: The Changing Social Contract* (Cambridge: Cambridge University Press, 2000).

12 Comparing Happiness in Contemporary Societies

Is it useful to try to compare levels of happiness from one country to the next? The answer is not entirely clear, for there is a real danger of juxtaposing apples and oranges. But it is certainly tempting to try, and the process can generate some important findings even if some basic questions cannot be definitively answered. While some duly cautious historians have shied away from the challenge, other social scientists have been eager to jump in.

This chapter focuses on regional developments concerning happiness since World War II, largely beyond the implicit debate between communist and Western approaches. For, even in decades in which global contacts increased notably, regional features continued to play a great role in both levels and conceptions of happiness. In turn, the regional factor highlights the opportunities for comparison – but also the complexities involved.

The obvious problem centers on the tension between features that can be juxtaposed with a fair degree of accuracy – like Gross National Product, or life expectancy – and cultural attributes that are much harder to pin down. Distinctive beliefs and values, and even particular political systems, can significantly evaluations of happiness quite apart from specific economic or demographic conditions. Differences in language often express this cultural component. The recent international happiness rankings cited in the introductory chapter already suggested some of these issues.

This chapter, though by no means suggesting a full global comparison, explores some dimensions of the challenge in two ways. First, we will briefly consider the results of two elaborate research efforts undertaken in the late 1950s/early 1960s and mid-1970s, respectively. Then we will venture two case studies, for India and Japan, respectively, where distinctive cultural factors play a substantial role in shaping the expectations and experiences of happiness.

Projects in the Social Sciences

While polling data explicitly targeting happiness on a cross-national level did not develop until recently, social scientists in the postwar decades eagerly measured closely related topics like hopes and fears or anticipations of the future. Two major projects found significant but not fully predictable

Comparing Happiness in Contemporary Societies 175

differences among a number of different nations. One, led by Hadley Cantril on the "patterns of human concerns", offered an elaborate survey covering various nations drawn from wealthy/capitalist, communist, and other countries including Brazil, India, the Philippines, and Nigeria. The survey was conducted in the late 1950s and early 1960s, in a period of considerable global economic growth and, in some societies, great optimism about the promise offered by recent political change (national independence in Nigeria, the recent communist revolution in Cuba). A second study in the early 1970s, on anticipations of the year 2000, surveyed ten countries representing similar global clusters.

Both studies concluded that national patterns tended to override internal differences. Everywhere, to be sure, distinctions based on living standards and educational levels mattered, as did age and (more rarely) gender. Internal variations were more evident in some cases than others: more in India and the Philippines, for example, than in the United States or Cuba (with the important exception, in the United States, of African Americans, whose frustration levels were unusually high). But something of an overall tone could be captured nevertheless, which is where the national component predominated.

Around 1960. Several conclusions can be drawn from the ambitious effort to categorize major concerns about 15 years after World War II.

First, very broadly speaking, people in different countries reflected similar characteristics relevant to happiness. Almost always, economic factors loomed largest when people tried to evaluate hopes and anxieties. Health and family issues followed closely. Personal concerns of this sort always outweighed larger topics such as political structure or international conditions. People in a few countries did project some larger interests. West Germans, fresh from defeat in war and caught in the midst of the Cold War, worried about peace when they assessed their individual situation; recent instability pushed political concerns up on the agenda in the Dominican Republic and Brazil. Nowhere, however, did larger issues outweigh the primacy of more personal criteria.

Further, Cantril and his colleagues concluded that almost everywhere, at this point in time, hopes outweighed worries. They also noted that growing global knowledge was contributing to shared aspirations for a better life.

Second, some of the key differences among countries were entirely predictable based on levels of economic development. Thus, when West Germans or Americans talked about their standard of living aspirations, they referred to bigger cars, possibly a boat, opportunities for travel, or (in the United States) the ability to send the children to private schools. References to health, and hopes for better health, were also more common in the prosperous nations. Americans frequently noted their expectation that their children would be able to do better than their parents – usually with considerable confidence.

176 *Happiness in Contemporary World History*

The conversation was far different in Egypt, or Nigeria, or India, where more widespread poverty clearly constrained aspirations. An Egyptian noted, "I would like to have more sons to help me with my farming"; he also wanted a cow. Two times more Indians than Americans talked about outright inadequacy or economic deterioration. Indians often mentioned hopes for enough land to avoid starvation; one respondent went a bit further in talking about the desirability of running water and maybe even access to electricity. Often these narrow, though completely understandable concerns spilled over other domains: Indian respondents, for example, expressed few specific fears or hopes regarding their children, for immediate issues seemed more pressing. In the Philippines, comments or expectations concerning health were impressively infrequent, compared to the predominance of references to the economy or the family. Fatalistic statements like "I can only hope that God will help me" were not uncommon.

Key attitudes in communist countries fell in between what was then often called the "first" and "third" worlds – mirroring their intermediate position in economic development. Poles talked about hopes for better housing – rather than discussing either starvation or the need for a bigger car. They were careful to note that they had made great progress in the previous five years and expected more in the five years to come, while recognizing that they had a long way to go.

All this said, the most impressive conclusion to draw from the studies of the Cantril team was the real unpredictability of many crucial attitudes – the lack of full correspondence to any economic development scale. A number of key contrasts, particularly within the category of wealthy, intermediate, or poorer nations, highlighted cultural preferences independent of material standards.

Thus references to the role of the family in happiness varied greatly: far more common in the United States than in West Germany, or in still-Catholic Poland than in more secular Yugoslavia. Within the less-economically developed category, only in Egypt and the Philippines did a large minority of people report that they valued wealth for its own sake, rather than linking it to other goals.

But the most important unpredictability centered on hope. Nigerians, newly independent though on average very poor, looked forward to great personal and national advancement in the future. Indians and Brazilians, in contrast, seemed apathetic and resigned. They conveyed little sense of either individual or social progress. Indians, particularly, frequently used religious references to explain how they must accept their lot in life during their present incarnation.

Levels of aspiration varied, another element in defining hopes. Americans were far more complacent than West Germans, or Yugoslavs, or Nigerians. They were not apathetic so much as satisfied. They did discuss progress in their personal lives, but they essentially took it for granted. Yugoslavs,

Comparing Happiness in Contemporary Societies   177

under unusually competent communist leadership, Israelis, Nigerians, and West Germans were more ambitiously hopeful.

Again, this was not directly a study about happiness. One can debate whether complacency or hope for a brighter future is a better measure of happiness. But the differences the Cantril group uncovered, and particularly the areas where national distinctions clearly reflected some special political or cultural factors, clearly highlight the complex variables involved in personal attitudes and expectations.

Looking toward 2000. A cluster of social scientists surveyed ten countries in the early 1970s, asking people how they anticipated the upcoming new century, just 25 years away. Two questions, touching, on happiness explicitly, revealed a great deal about expectations, offering further evidence about the complex role of hope.

Thus in India, 52% of those polled argued that happiness would be greater in 2000 than it was at present. And a full 46% said that the present was so unhappy that only the future mattered. In contrast, Czechoslovaks, under communist rule, while even more hopeful about the future (57%), were noticeably less glum about the present (31% saying that things were so bad today that only the future mattered).

In contrast, probably predictably given their greater average prosperity, Britons, Norwegians, and Dutch were notably less focused on the future. Only 10% of Norwegians, for example, thought that happiness would be greater a quarter-century out. But very few of this group had soured on the present: only 17% of the Norwegians said that things were so bad today that all they could do was think about the future.

Data of this sort are not entirely clear-cut. Were the majority of Indians really optimistic at this point (in contrast to the apathy that seemed to prevail, in the Cantril study, just 15 years earlier)? Or did their expectations about 2000 mainly reflect their sense that things were really bad right now: how, in other words, did optimism and pessimism balance out? Were Norwegians less convinced that the future would be better because they were so pleased with the present, or because they had greater doubts about whether new technologies and further economic development really brought progress? The scholars involved in the project wondered whether people in some highly developed societies, like Norway, had somewhat soured on the magical prospects of future technologies.

Data from Japan suggested further complexity in the role of economic development in shaping evaluations of happiness. While the Japanese expressed more hopes for the future than the West Europeans did, at 36%, they were markedly uncomfortable with the present despite the rapid economic growth around them. Almost as large a group as in India, at 42%, said that the current situation was so bad that only the future mattered – raising the same question as in India about whether their ratios really reflected optimism or rather the high levels of contemporary unease.

178 *Happiness in Contemporary World History*

Both the Cantril and the Year 2000 studies are now more than a half-century old. They do not reflect current material or cultural realities – much has altered since then, and we already know that beliefs about happiness can change, sometimes quite rapidly. But the data are worth remembering both as a bit of a benchmark that can be used to evaluate particular national situations more closely – such as, for example, the elusive topic of happiness in Japan; and as a wider reminder that there is simply no ready formula that can fully anticipate values and expectations in this aspect of the human experience. Regional conditions, offering distinctive combinations of beliefs and standards of living, continue to shape evaluations of happiness even in a globalizing world.

Happiness in India

Since gaining independence in 1947, India's contemporary history has been a considerable success story. Unusually among former colonies, the nation has preserved democratic forms – becoming the largest democracy in the world. Despite ongoing inequality, the caste system has been outlawed and considerable efforts undertaken to undo its legacy. Conditions for women have improved – again, despite continuing problems; rates of child marriage, for example, have dropped. While considerable child labor persists, levels have fallen, and education has spread. The economy has expanded; agricultural production now limits the risk of famine, and in recent decades overall economic growth rates have soared, creating a large middle class. The nation has avoided major war.

To be sure, India's development has been more modest than that of neighboring China. Urban growth has been considerable, but the nation maintains a rural majority. Poverty levels have dropped and access to modern amenities such as electricity and running water has improved, but deep problems persist. Endemic political tensions include difficult relationships between the Hindu majority and a large Muslim minority.

India's trajectory over recent decades raises some basic questions about happiness: have improvements in levels of satisfaction followed from the substantial changes that have occurred – or have these been too rapid, or not rapid enough? How do contemporary trends interact with more traditional views about happiness, including those espoused by people like Mohandas Gandhi in the decades before independence? Interpretation is further complicated by the vast size and internal regional and social differences amid the Indian population. It is unsurprising that no one size fits all.

Hedonism. All societies, from the formation of civilization onward, have offered opportunities for material pleasure, particularly of course for the upper classes, and despite its deep religious traditions India has been no exception. Classical India in fact produced an exceptionally elaborate manual concerning sexual pleasure, the *Kama Sutra*, and there were philosophers

Comparing Happiness in Contemporary Societies 179

as well who advocated sensual enjoyments. The region has also generated some of the world's most sophisticated culinary traditions.

During the past several decades, urbanization and economic development have produced wider opportunities for pleasure. India does not lead the world in consumerism, but consumer interests have expanded, particularly in the growing middle classes. New customs, such as beauty pageants, have been imported with considerable success, while also drawing traditionalist criticism.

India has also generated the world's largest movie industry, particularly around the productions collectively known as Bollywood, and while Indian films are quite varied, an unabashedly escapist tone has predominated since the industry began to take hold in the interwar period. Bollywood movies typically combine music, action, and romance (often with considerable sexuality), adapting traditional Hindu stories to a modern setting. Bollywood films draw large audiences, eager for their money's worth from performances that often last three hours; they are usually rewarded with tales of individual heroism, star-crossed lovers, and appealing show tunes. The importance of this form of pleasure translates into great fame and considerable fortune for the leading Bollywood stars, male and female alike.

More recently, television has amplified some of the pleasures available from going to the movies. While only 10% of all Indian households had a TV set in 1990, by 1999, after a decade of rapid economic growth, this figure soared to 75%. Entertainment fare now broadened to include a wide variety of dubbed Hollywood movies – which provoke a mixture of delight and disapproval. Interestingly, reflecting growing consumerism, advertisements in India are even more likely than those of the West to claim that their products will increase happiness.

A variety of efforts during the past several decades have sought to blend Indian consumerism with more traditional entertainment forms. Bollywood's reliance on older storylines provides one example of this. A number of programs designed to increase happiness feature popular presentations of customary music and dance styles. Some efforts, admittedly, fall flat: an effort to combine a beauty pageant with expertise in regional culture failed because the people who knew the culture refused to compete for beauty, while the contestants who did present themselves knew little about the culture. But in other cases, the combination has worked well and can mediate between newer forms of pleasure and older values.

Traditional themes. Deep commitments to Hinduism among India's majority provide opportunities for vigorous assertion of older ideas of happiness, from a variety of thinkers and popularizers. Often, these play against the trappings of modernity, with insistence that happiness does not come from social mobility or consumer pleasures but must center on spiritual growth. A number of advocates urge in fact that Indian values offer international inspiration for genuine well-being, against the shallower ideas of happiness generated by consumer societies.

180 *Happiness in Contemporary World History*

Quotes from several recent essays on happiness reflect the Hindu framework. "Happiness lies deep within us, in the very core of our being. Happiness does not exist in any external object, but only in us, who are the consciousness that experiences happiness." "Whatever turmoil our mind may be in, in the center of our being there always exists a state of perfect peace and joy, like the calm in the eye of a storm....Happiness is thus a state of being – a state in which our mind's habitual agitation is calmed." Ideas of this sort, explicitly conveying values expressed in the great Hindu epics, have a substantial audience in India and indeed beyond. The themes of detachment from the illusions of the external world, and the importance of inner cultivation, continue to be emphasized by a variety of Indian thinkers.

This approach also highlights the importance of collective well-being, and not just health and happiness for the self. Everyone should have the opportunity for a happy life, and not simply a few particularly spiritual leaders. A traditional prayer thus gains new attention: "May all be happy, may all be free from disease. May all perceive good, and not suffer from sorrow."

The centrality of family. A recent anthropological study of happiness India, by Steve Derné, stresses the strong hold of a rather traditionalist commitment to family, and while this is not unrelated to the more spiritual approach it offers different emphases and tensions. The focus here is on group support and connectedness, heavily centered on relationships between adult children and their parents. Evidence in this particular study comes from upper-class Hindus, and it is not clear how widely representative the findings are. The happy family, according to these respondents, is based on a distinctive, or at least decidedly non-Western, approach to love. Families are formed on a sense of duty, and love derives from this rather than the other way around; nor is love focused on the spouse alone. Indeed, the spouse may not seem to have any special qualities at all, but simply serves to anchor a family that is judged primarily in terms of pleasing older parents. Too much purely spousal love is in fact dangerous, because it might induce a couple to become "careless" and "forget their duties to their (wider) families." Further, the love involved is not confined to family but spills over into a love for the whole society. Always, there is an abiding concern about how one's behavior will be judged by others – and particularly the family elders. As one man put it, nothing should be done "without asking father". "Our mental state is that all problems are solved in the way father says."

This approach to happiness explicitly prioritizes custom and group approval, with no interest in individual self-fulfillment. The importance of arranged, parentally approved marriage remains central; polls show that over two-thirds of all Indians believe in arranged marriages, including a majority even in the lower classes – though in an urbanizing society the matches are not always easy to orchestrate. Some men, frankly stating that they do not like the wives their parents found for them, nevertheless

Comparing Happiness in Contemporary Societies   181

say they are happy because they are fulfilling their duty to their elders. More generally, many Indians feel very uneasy in situations where senior authority figures are not involved or where their support cannot be determined. At most, there is some admission that individual wishes cannot be entirely subordinated, that a person should be able to make some decisions on his or her own – an example used was wanting to go to the movies whether parents approved or not.

The family-centered definition of happiness allows many Indians to filter the entertainment fare now available to them, allowing many Hollywood themes, such as rampant sexuality, to be either ignored or disapproved. As one man put it in 2001, "Love marriages are only stories in films. In real life they are not possible.... I know I'll marry according to my parents' wishes." At the same time, there is real concern that the television fare now available may undermine family values. This can lead to outright protests, as in riots that chased couples from a restaurant when they were trying to celebrate Valentine's day (an obvious foreign import). In a changing society, India's approach to happiness and family could become an active source of anxiety or contestation.

The puzzle. When international happiness polls began in the 21st century, it was striking – and to some, truly surprising – that India ranked extraordinarily low. In 2019, it stood at 140 out of 156 countries tallied, just barely above societies in clear crisis like Syria or South Sudan. This was obviously well below levels of nations that might otherwise seem roughly comparable in terms of economic development, like China or Russia.

Most observers seeking to interpret the results tended to focus on short-term issues, in particular a rash of new problems in India – a recently slowing growth rate, new levels of political turmoil around a controversial though popular president – that pushed the nation's low rankings even lower (from 133 to 140 in the most recent polls).

Surely, however, recent deterioration was far less significant than the low position in the first place – and this brings us back to some of the basic problems in interpreting the Indian case. Possibly the lags in Indian development were simply not matching the expectations of key segments of the population, who could see that societies that were changing more rapidly, like neighboring China, were doing better. (Remember how a majority of Indians, in the mid-1970s, had assumed that happiness would be greater by 2000.) Or, the change that was occurring seemed too great for many Indians, given more traditional ideas of happiness – there was too much strain on family values, too much distraction from the older ideals of spiritual development. Or, the mixture of Indian ideas of happiness simply did not comport well with an internationally based questionnaire that tended to highlight an individual's state of mind – in which case the poll results, though interesting, were not really indicative of Indian happiness at all. Is this fundamentally another case of a distinctive, valid approach to happiness that just does not fit currently conventional notions?

182 *Happiness in Contemporary World History*

It is frustrating for a student of happiness not to be able to pick definitively among these options. It would be far tidier to be able to say, 35% of India's lag results from the inappropriateness of the polls, 35% from inadequate modernization, and the remainder from excessive modernization. Obviously, this kind of precision is impossible. It is clear that India maintains a distinctive approach to happiness, while sharing in some of the newer global interests; and that there seem to be significant issues about the levels of satisfaction that currently result.

Japan

Several building blocks for happiness in modern Japan were clearly set before 1945, though the devastating loss in war inevitably raised new challenges (including a postwar plunge in happiness levels). The Japanese had already moved toward an approach to happiness that was less individualistic than its Western counterpart. However, to the extent that the alternative had involved a heavy emphasis on nationalism, it had to be rethought after 1945 when defeat in war raised inescapable questions about the nation's priorities. Further, greater exposure to American influence during the postwar occupation, and even more the steady advance of the Japanese economy that created greater opportunities for consumerism, introduced new factors as well.

There is little question that postwar adjustments encouraged several relevant changes in Japanese culture. The decline of aggressive nationalism did not eliminate national pride – there was still great celebration, for example, for success in international sports competitions – but adjustments did occur, and certainly a military value system ebbed considerably. Religion also shifted. Japanese regimes before the war had strongly emphasized the traditional Shinto religion, but this was now partially discredited. While a number of vigorous Buddhist groups arose, and the Japanese generally continued to use Buddhist and Shinto rituals for occasions like funerals, religion came to play a lesser role in daily life. Changes of this sort might well impinge on happiness, potentially affecting some meaningful options.

Finally, as discussed in Chapter 1, the recent advent of global happiness surveys highlights another parameter: the fact that the Japanese, despite their economic and political achievements over the past 70 years, tend to score in the middle of the range – noticeably lower than one might expect. As with India, it is not easy to determine how meaningful these results are, but they certainly suggest, from another angle, a distinctive Japanese take on happiness.

The concept of ikigai. One anthropologist, trying to explain the relationship between Japanese approaches to happiness and patterns in the United States, or the West more generally, emphasizes the central importance of the term *ikigai*, which centers on the question of what makes one's life

Comparing Happiness in Contemporary Societies 183

worth living, or which seeks to identify the focus in life that creates this sense of worth. The Japanese often discuss the term – more often than they discuss happiness directly, resulting in statements like "my *ikigai* is my family" or "mine is mountain climbing." The term crops up frequently in book and magazine titles throughout the postwar decades, and it is also the subject of national polls, as when 24% of all mothers claim that their *ikigai* is their children.

The word suggests something of a tension between a sense of individual fulfillment and a larger sense of obligation. Thus many Japanese men profess that work is their *ikigai*, but while in some cases this means that they find work rewarding, probably more often it reflects a deep loyalty to their employing company. Women similarly are often devoted to their family mainly in terms of fulfilling a sense of duty or obligation in that particular role. Here is one way that the Japanese approach to happiness is less likely to reflect a desire for self-expression than is true in the West. Where *ikigai* involves fulfilling a duty, it also indicates a commitment to a group and group norms – an older theme that persists in modern Japanese culture. It is relatively easy, for example, to shame a worker into staying late for overtime by asking about his loyalty. On the other hand, it is important to note that people have some choice in deciding their *ikigai*, often fairly early in life, even though some choices – like a predominant work focus for men – are particularly socially encouraged. This kind of tension between individual fulfillment and group norms arguably goes back to the Meiji era.

In postwar Japan, *ikigai* rarely has any religious connotations, in contrast, for example, to definitions of happiness for many Americans that often have a strong religious component. Here too, the Japanese dependence on a sense of group belonging and approval is particularly strong, displacing the need for religious validation.

During most of the postwar period, dominant expressions of *ikigai* have been highly gender specific. Men choose work, which means abundant devotion to the employer and typically very long hours, clearly at the expense of much family time. And while salary levels are not irrelevant, there is more focus on group performance; this contrasts with the more ambivalent, often instrumental approaches to work common in the West. Women, for their part, center on the family and the extensive duties of a good mother, which involve not only childrearing but careful oversight of a child's educational progress. Needless to say, this male/female contrast can generate significant tensions within the family itself, where annoyed wives have to come to terms with the fact that their husbands' commitment lies elsewhere.

Pleasures. Satisfactions in Japan are not captured by *ikigai* alone. The nation offers robust opportunities for enjoyment, ranging from somewhat traditional and distinctive outlets, such as the famous public baths, to some of the more standard pursuits of a consumer society. It is no accident that Japan, along with the United States, has led the world for many decades

184 *Happiness in Contemporary World History*

in the creation of new toys and playthings for children, or has pioneered in entertaining forms of animation. Many Japanese children, carefully encouraged to do well in school, are often given extensive compensatory play times.

Some distinguishing features apply even in this category. The Japanese are ardent consumers, but they also save more than their American counterparts. Drinking plays a noticeable role in Japanese male culture. The Japanese baths have few counterparts elsewhere; one study argues that they involve more acute sensory pleasures than most Westerners seek, and they certainly provide opportunities for family engagement, as when fathers play with their sons in a public bath. As noted earlier, even gift-buying can express somewhat distinctive values. When the Japanese visit the Disneyland gift shop near Tokyo, they typically buy presents for friends and family; their American counterparts, in California or Florida, buy items for themselves.

Still, it is important not to overdo the distinctions. Japan plays a strong role in global consumer culture, which means that it shares in and helps guide widely popular forms of entertainment. A study around 2010 showed that Japanese rated entertainment a slightly greater priority than the British did, though both were a bit lower than American levels. A focus on the family is another broadly common feature, despite gender distinctions. While the same 2010 study showed a much lower priority for marriage or romantic love in Japan, commitment to family itself was almost as strong as in the West – everywhere heading the list of factors regarded as essential to happiness.

Deterioration? Early in the 21st century, 65% of the Japanese rated themselves happy or somewhat happy compared to 84% in the UK and 88% in the United States. A similar, and revealing, gap involved hope: 49% of the Japanese, but 60% and 65% of Britons and Americans, respectively, said they were hopeful about the future, and there were even greater disparities in degree of confidence about whether hopes would be realized.

Some of these distinctions can be fairly readily explained. Japan's lower levels of religious commitment contrast with the role of religion in supporting American hopes, and we have seen that the challenging relationship between *ikigai* and happiness complicates polling results whenever Japan is involved.

But almost all observers believe that happiness levels in Japan have been dropping in recent decades, despite the nation's affluence and some of the highest life expectancy levels in the world. Two or three factors are involved.

First, the Japanese economy fell into prolonged doldrums by the 1990s, after decades of gains; this stagnation objectively limited living standards and also dented any sense of optimism about the future. Even a still-prosperous society, in the industrial age, may depend on a sense of continued advance.

Second, many Japanese are rethinking *ikigai* or transferring it to a greater sense of self-realization. While working hours for men remain long, the stress this causes has become more visible. Further, in the troubled economy, more employers are offering only short-term employment arrangements, rather than lifetime guarantees; why, then, commit one's sense of obligation to the company? For their part increasing numbers of women are pushing back at the idea of primary family commitments. They seek jobs; they are often reluctant to have children; many even avoid marriage – all in the interest of gaining opportunities to carve out their own course in life.

Third, Japan's rapid aging creates its own stresses. Many older people, having devoted adult life to work or family, find it hard to define happiness once their active period has passed. And large numbers are simply alone, in a society that values group context.

The overall result is a society that is visibly reevaluating what life is all about, and this, more than any objective deterioration, seems to be responsible for the challenge to happiness. We will see that some of these issues carry over into other advanced industrial societies as well, but they have been particularly marked in Japan.

★★★

Four points emerge clearly from a focus on regional approaches to happiness – apart from the obvious fact that it would be desirable to be able to include even more parts of the world in this kind of analysis.

First, as noted above, dealing with happiness cross-culturally is very difficult, precisely because of crucial differences in language and meaning. Comparisons are revealing, but they also show how difficult it is to evaluate definitions of happiness that are unfamiliar – as with the distinctive familial component in Indian evaluations, or the idea of *ikigai* in Japan. Even amid globalization, vital regional distinctions remain.

Second, happiness does not correlate precisely with objective criteria such as Gross National Product, though these are relevant in comparative analysis to some degree. Almost every student of happiness knows this, but it is important to emphasize given the importance many economists continue to place on what seems easy to measure.

Third, it is simply not clear whether happiness *levels* can usefully be compared. One recent scholar, Eunkook Suh, juxtaposing East Asia and the West, explicitly argues that Westerners are happier; and there is no question that they say they are, through comparative polling. Most anthropologists, however, are more cautious.

Fourth, compounding the challenge: happiness does not hold still, in any region in the modern world. It really seems that Japanese happiness is currently encountering new challenges, which may among other things increase its differentiation from countries like the United States (though

186　*Happiness in Contemporary World History*

American happiness is probably becoming less robust as well). Indians strive in various ways to accommodate new influences while keeping contact with more traditional thinking. The different levels of hope that could be identified in polling data a half-century ago no longer describe contemporary reality. Analysis of change has to be factored into any comparative statement.

For all the challenges, however, comparative analysis remains essential precisely because regional frameworks retain such importance. Sweeping formulas are impossible, but empirical analysis can pick up definable differences around common components of happiness such as family, religion or hope, and aspiration. The combination of cultural and material factors is more difficult than the standard of living alone, but it can be addressed. And even the fraught topic of *levels* of happiness, though unquestionably complex, deserves attention. Closer to home, an appreciation of different regional approaches offers perspective on our own ideas about happiness, one of the standard benefits of comparative insight. Globalization itself, the focus of Chapter 14, promotes a mixture of regional influences where happiness is concerned.

Further Reading

On the classic polling data:

Hastorf, Albert H., and Hadley Cantril. "They Saw a Game: A Case Study." *Journal of Abnormal Psychology* 49, no. 1 (January 1954): 129–134.

Ornaver, Helmut, Haykan Wiberg, Andrzej Sicinsky, and Johan Galtung, eds. *Images of the World in the Year 2000* (Berlin: Walter De Gruyter Inc, 1976).

On Indian tradition,

Kumar, S.K., "An Indian Conception of Well-being." In J. Henry (Ed.), *European Positive Psychology Proceedings* (Leicester: British Psychological Society, 2003).

On Indian families,

Derné, Steve. *Culture in Action: Family Life, Emotion, and Male Dominance in Banaras, India* (Albany: State University of New York Press, 1995).

Freeman, James M. *Untouchable: An Indian Life History* (Stanford, CA: Stanford University Press, 1979).

Moore, Erin. "Moral Reasoning: An Indian Case Study." *Ethos* 23, no. 3 (September 1995): 286–327.

Osella, Filippo, and Caroline Osella. "From Transience to Immanence: Consumption, Life-Cycle and Social Mobility in Kerala, South India." *Modern Asian Studies* 33, no. 4 (October 1, 1999): 989–1020.

On Japan,

Genda, Yuji. "An International Comparison of Hope and Happiness in Japan, the UK, and the US." *Social Science Japan Journal* 19, no. 2 (2016): 153–172.

Hendry, Joy, and Gordon Mathews. "What Makes Life Worth Living? How Japanese and Americans Make Sense of Their Worlds." *The Journal of the Royal Anthropological Institute* 3 (June 1, 1997).

Kavedzija, Iza. "The Good Life in Balance: Insights from Aging Japan." *HAU: Journal of Ethnographic Theory* 5, no. 3 (January 1, 2015): 135–156.

Comparing Happiness in Contemporary Societies 187

Kitanaka, Junko. *Depression in Japan: Psychiatric Cures for a Society in Distress* Princeton, (Princeton, NJ: Princeton University Press, 2012).

Mathews, Gordon, and Bruce White. *Japan's Changing Generations Are Young People Creating a New Society?* (London: Routledge Curzon, 2004).

Roberson, James, and Nobue Suzuke, eds. *Men and Masculinities in Contemporary Japan: Dislocating the Salaryman Doxa* (London: Routledge, 2002).

For both India and Japan, see:

Mathews, Gordon, and Carolina Izquierdo, eds. *Pursuits of Happiness Well-Being in Anthropological Perspective* (New York: Berghahn Books, 2009).

Roland, Alan. *In Search of Self in India and Japan: Toward a Cross-Cultural Psychology* (Princeton, NJ: Princeton University Press, 1988).

See also:

Baumeister, Roy F. *Meanings of Life* (New York: Guilford Press, 1991).

Diener, Ed, and Eunkook M. Suh, eds. *Culture and Subjective Well-Being.* (Cambridge, MA: The MIT Press, 2000).

13 Western Society in Contemporary History

Even Happier?

A recent international survey, published in 2015, asked parents in many countries what their most important goal was when it came to their children. Western societies uniformly responded, with substantial majorities, that the answer was happiness. France led the parade with 86% opting for happiness, Canada rang in at 78%, the United States with 73%. Other societies chose differently: Mexico and India rated success at the top, Chinese parents chose good health. Robin Berman, a childrearing expert who travels widely in the United States, confirms the American preference: "When I give parenting lectures around the country, I always ask the audience 'What do you want for your children'...The near-universal response I get is, 'I just want my kids to be happy.'"

Happiness goals are alive and well in Western culture. The happiness revolution marches forward, with some additional features but without many new directions. Hesitations that cropped up in the decades of war and depression were largely cast aside, at least until recently, and the search for a fascist alternative was abandoned. As the childrearing poll suggests, the Western commitment not only extended earlier trends, but stood apart, at least to some extent, from the approaches of many other societies. Along with basic economic and political conditions, the combination of cultural continuity and additional enhancement readily explains the West's distinctive position in international happiness surveys.

At the same time, the pervasive interest in happiness began to surface some new issues, or at least to bring them to wider attention. Several features of the contemporary Western commitment generated some troubling constraints. While the problems involved did not unseat the basic culture, they did raise important questions for the future.

Signposts

A number of indices confirmed the Western commitment to happiness from the postwar decades onward, and often suggested further intensification. Books and articles urging happiness and suggesting surefire paths to attain it proliferated steadily, particularly in the United States. The titles told much of their story: *The Ladder Up: Secret Steps to Happiness*;

Western Society in Contemporary History   189

33 Moments of Happiness; *One Thousand Paths to Happiness*; *Baby Steps to Happiness*; and *Everlasting Happiness*. Two sources of happiness guidance were particularly interesting, and they sometimes overlapped: many Protestant leaders now urged that they had the keys to the kingdom of happiness, as with the evangelical guru Billy Graham and his *Secrets to Happiness*. Business advocates claimed that theirs was the road, as with *7 Strategies for Wealth and Happiness,* by "America's foremost business philosopher".

Connections with specific domains abounded. People seeking sexual guidance could turn to the *Joy of Sex*; foodies had the best-selling *Joy of Cooking*. Teenagers had special books showing them how to be happy; so did African Americans.

While this varied literature offered a wide range of recommendations, from religious faith to the importance of vegetarianism or *feng shui*, they tended to agree that individuals could and should craft happiness on their own: happiness was not a matter of luck, or divine selection, or the wider social environment. Norman Vincent Peale, a radio evangelist, was a particularly important spokesperson for this kind of thinking, and his book, *The Power of Positive Thinking* (1952) gained wide influence, selling millions of copies. The central message was clear: "Our happiness depends on the habit of mind we cultivate. So practice happy thinking every day. Cultivate the merry heart, develop the happiness habit, and life will become a continual feast." At times, Peale's advice recalled earlier philosophical approaches, as he urged the importance of modest expectations, humility, and a capacity to appreciate small pleasures and cultivate "inner peace". At other points, however, he was less guarded: "No matter how dark things seem to be or actually are, raise your sights and see possibilities – always see them, for they're always there." "If you paint in your mind a picture of bright and happy expectations, you put yourself in a condition conducive to your goal." Most obviously, positive thinkers could expect financial success; happiness and worldly ambition were perfectly compatible. But the main point was the individual's power and responsibility for the achievement of happiness.

Books, magazine articles, and radio shows were not, of course, the only signs that the commitment to happiness was running strong. The Disney empire expanded its reach with a number of theme parks, modestly proclaiming one of them "The Happiest Place on Earth." Television shows won popularity with titles like "Happy Days." Bars began featuring "happy hours", a time to drink before dinner or as a transition from work to home. The idea of happy hours may have originated around American naval bases as early as 1913, but they gained much wider notice with a number of articles in the popular press during the 1950s, about drinking practices among the military. The happy hour idea spread widely in the English-speaking world during the final decades of the 20th century, although it also attracted efforts to regulate – in Ireland, for example – in hopes of curbing excess.

190 *Happiness in Contemporary World History*

Happiness and advertising became inextricably linked. Studies in the early 21st century suggested that 7–12% of all print and television ads explicitly linked products and services to happiness. Happiness might come through investing in a new bathtub, or obtaining proper dentures, or getting that new car, or buying a variety of stylish clothes or cosmetics. The John Lewis department store chain in the United Kingdom regularly sponsored happiness advertising in anticipation of Christmas, drawing wide attention.

A wide variety of Happiness Foundations were established from the 1980s onward. Some had particular religious connections, with movements like Scientology. Others aimed at greater awareness of the dangers of alcohol or some other specific target. The obvious point was the seemingly irresistible temptation to associate a considerable range of causes with the notion of obtaining happiness.

In 1963, an American advertising executive named Harvey Ball created the yellow smiley-face happiness image, which became an instant international hit. The year was not a particularly happy one in the United States, as the Kennedy assassination and growing involvement in the Vietnam War dampened spirits. But this new image suggested that happiness was available even so; an individual could express it by using the icon, and the image in turn might spread cheerfulness to others. By 1971 yellow smiley-face buttons were selling over 50 million copies annually, and the image spread as well to tee shirts and other items. While Ball did not copyright his creation, an outfit called the World Smile Corporation stepped in to fill the void. By the 21st century, happy faces (with as many as three dozen versions available) became the most popular emojis for online communications, taking at least four of the top ten slots; by 2019 a "tears of joy" symbol ranked as number one.

Happiness had become ubiquitous. Almost anyone in the contemporary West was surrounded by opportunities to obtain happiness in various ways; to express happiness; and of course to wonder if one was happy enough.

Consumerism and the Lure of More

The Western link between happiness and consumerism was hardly new, but it unquestionably gained new importance as economic growth created "affluent societies" throughout virtually the entire Western world between the 1950s and 1980s. Particularly noteworthy was the ability of many manufacturing workers to win high standards of living. Studies of "affluent workers" showed that instrumentalism was advancing to new levels, with difficult working conditions accepted in return for rising consumer lifestyles. In the United States, opportunities to create more interesting job conditions were sometimes rejected because they might constrain high wages. At another social level, the late 20th century saw

Western Society in Contemporary History 191

the emergence of a group called "Yuppies" – young urban professionals, usually in two-career marriages, who were focused on fashionable, affluent lifestyles. An intriguing British study, *The Symmetrical Family,* argued that the purpose of family life (often without children) now centered on a shared commitment to consumerism.

The growing attachment to consumerism showed in many ways, as more and more people were able to explore this as a path toward happiness. Motor bicycles and cars began to replace walking or mass transit for many workers. In Europe, attendance at trade union meetings began to drop in part because so many members were either working overtime to pay off their vehicle – or enjoying the vehicle itself. Vacations became more elaborate. New organizations like Club Med, in Europe, sprang up in the postwar decades to facilitate more exotic holidays, particularly to tropical destinations; it was increasingly possible to enjoy Western-style amenities from Malaysia to Mexico.

The rise of the mall was symbolic of the newest stage of consumerism in advanced industrial societies. Beyond department stores, malls offered an unprecedented array of goods and services, mixing food and browsing, often with a movie theater thrown in, and allowing literally day-long absorption in the process of shopping. Then in the 21st century the rise of online opportunities, though reducing the ritual of the shopping experience, made quick access to goods more abundant than ever before.

Much of the new consumerism simply involved more. Spending on Christmas gifts more than doubled in Western societies between the 1960s and the year 2000. Low-income families in the United States were committing up to 5% of total income on birthday gifts, while on the more affluent end some children's birthday party invitations by 2000 were specifying that presents under $35 would be unacceptable. In between, a host of organizations arose largely to cater to more elaborate parties. Average home sizes increased in the United States, despite a low birth rate. So-called McMansions offered huge spaces, sometimes to couples working such long hours that they were actually not home much during most days; the average size of the American home rose by 55% between 1971 and 2000, even as family size dropped. Interest in furnishings rose accordingly. A *House and Garden* editor sought to explain the meaning involved: "Sure, shopping and arranging (and hoarding) are materialistic pursuits, but they also connected to deeper passions…they nurture our souls." Many of those involved clearly believed that they were pursuing happiness. Always an option in discussions of happiness, materialism loomed larger than ever before.

Innovations. New products were vital to this newest stage of consumerism, and some of them changed the fundamental rhythms of life. Regular television viewing became a basic leisure form from the 1950s onward, and the array of entertainment and sports options steadily expanded. Even more than with radio, television allowed viewers a deep association with

192 *Happiness in Contemporary World History*

some of their favorite shows, finding fear in ubiquitous presentations of crime but enjoying vicarious joy in a make-believe world where happy endings usually predominated.

With the rise of the Internet from the 1990s onward, along with increasingly permissive legislation, access to pornography became more widely available than ever before, and this form of sexual pleasure undoubtedly began playing a greater role in many people's lives. By the 21st century, the porn industry was a $12 billion operation in the United States alone, $95 billion worldwide.

The growth of attachment to pets was another intriguing manifestation of rising consumerism, deeply attached to notions of happiness particularly in societies with declining birth rates. Spending on pets went up steadily, with increasingly elaborate toys, pet "hotels", and other accoutrements. The expansion of pet cemeteries was another sign of growing emotional commitment, the flip side of the happiness pets provided during their lifetimes. By the 21st century, a third of all American pet owners said they preferred pets over children. Disaster relief officials, beginning with a major hurricane in 2005, found that people were increasingly unwilling to abandon pets even for personal safety, and national evacuation procedures had to be altered as a result. A rise of the notion of companion animals, vital to emotional well-being, further extended the meaning of pet ownership for many people, and here too, laws had to change as a result, for example to accommodate furry friends on airplanes.

The surge of electronic products, from the 1990s onward, was the final new category that commanded growing attention as part of the larger rise in consumer commitments. The need to have the latest gadgets, and the devotion of more and more waking attention to such gadgets, became a basic part of life by the 21st century, from childhood onward.

Always, with new products and old, there was a constant felt need to get more. By 1995, 66% of all American households had at least three television sets, often with a separate one for each child. Home computers were supplemented by more portable laptops. The impulse for more, and for the latest version, had been part of modern consumerism all along, but it became steadily more pronounced. One of the reasons that home sizes increased was to accommodate the profusion of things; and even with this, a California study revealed that a growing number of people had to park cars on the street because garages were needed for piles of consumer goods including toys and games.

Contemporary consumerism was not of course a uniform experience across the Western world. Living standards continued to vary greatly by social class, and in many countries inequalities increased after the 1980s. Even aside from this, personal preferences varied greatly; one of the vital ways consumerism could connect with happiness involved opportunities to indulge particular personal tastes, even though there were some widely shared interests such as passionate sports spectatorship.

Western Society in Contemporary History 193

Families and regions also varied in the extent to which they modified consumerism through personal savings; American consumers were particularly noted for their willingness to go heavily into debt for consumer pleasures.

The most interesting division may have involved choices between things and experiences, though most consumer families enjoyed some of each. European consumer patterns after 1945 featured a remarkable expansion of vacation time, often upwards of five weeks per year for many working and middle-class sectors. This kind of leisure growth did not spread to the United States, where formal vacation time increased very little during the same decades, and where a commitment to material acquisitions seemed to command greater attention.

Sexuality and drugs. Growing interest in sexual pleasure amplified consumerism in emphasizing the hedonistic aspect of contemporary happiness. Several developments combined in this domain. A variety of experts, and some feminists, increasingly emphasized the female capacity for pleasure, countering more traditional prudery. New contraceptive products, particularly the birth control pill, enhanced the possibility of purely recreational sex. Religious and legal restrictions on sexuality loosened, though in the United States an effort to promote abstinence among young people persisted. Most important, behaviors changed. The so-called sexual revolution of the 1960s lowered the average age of first sexual experience, a striking change particularly for women. Premarital sex became increasingly common. And, though evidence here is less clear, sexual expectations within marriage increased as well. Correspondingly, representations of sexuality in the popular media became steadily more graphic, quite apart from explicit pornography. These developments added an important component to popular expectations for happiness.

From the 1960s onward, a number of groups in Western society also experimented with drugs designed to produce happiness highs. By the 21st century pressures mounted to legalize marijuana. Even government could get into the act, sponsoring medical panels on such topics as "Beyond Therapy: biotechnology and the pursuit of happiness." Here was another somewhat uneasy frontier.

Consumer emotions: loneliness, envy, boredom – and happiness? We have seen that modern consumerism always had emotional components, beyond the quest for happiness; but many of these increased, or at least became more obvious, after 1945. Several raised some challenging questions about the continued association between consumerism and happiness.

Reports of loneliness began to increase, particularly by the early 21st century. A growing old age sector helped explain the new concern, as some elders outlived their closest family contacts or simply found themselves neglected. But changing consumerism contributed as well. Television made spectatorship a more isolating experience for some viewers, compared to earlier sociability, as participation in voluntary groups dropped. Growing reliance on social media, displacing person-to-person contacts, seemed to promote loneliness as well from the 1990s onward.

Envy, long a part of the consumer package, became more unpleasant for some. The phrase, "keeping up with the Joneses", had been introduced to the English language earlier in the 20th century, but it gained new currency particularly by the 1970s, to refer to competitive consumerism in suburbia. Even more interesting was the impact of social media on envy in the 21st century, as it revealed a perverse aspect of the commitment to happiness. Individuals on Facebook and other sites were eager to emphasize their own happiness in their self-presentations, complete with the smiling selfie; onlookers, aware of problems in their own lives, sometimes found this emphasis discouraging – it was easy for a viewer to think that friends or acquaintances were happier than oneself.

Even more interesting, and potentially problematic, was the apparent rise of boredom. Here was another modern emotion linked to consumerism since the mid-19th century, but now it became both more common and more pressing. References to the word increased steadily. A 1986 study claimed that boredom had become "America's number one disease". The growing availability of almost constant entertainment seems to have increased impatience with any lull – and then the advent of devices like cell phones, instantly accessible, heightened the problem still further. A new idea of "micro-boredom", in brief intervals between games or contacts, suggested the new standard. Generational differences widened. Older parents, raised to see boredom as a challenge to find something creative to do, were nonplussed by their offspring's complaints. "I'm bored" in fact became a childish weapon, now implying that some adult – a parent, a teacher – should step up with something fun (Figure 13.1).

As always, the relationship between boredom and happiness was double-edged – as with so many aspects of consumerism. On the one hand, it suggested the desire for more, for some means of gaining even greater diversion and happiness. On the other, particularly as levels of boredom

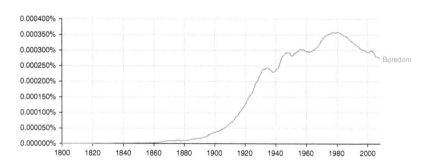

Figure 13.1 Frequency of the word "boredom" in English, 1800–2008, Google Ngram Viewer, accessed June 15th, 2020.

Western Society in Contemporary History 195

seemed to increase, it might suggest a dissatisfaction that outweighed happiness. In 2020, amid the regulations limiting social interaction instituted in response to a global pandemic, some observers argued that Western, and particularly American, individuals faced unusual difficulties in handling the crisis because so many were easily bored, seeking escape hatches in bars and parties despite the dangers of contagion. More widely, the apparent intensification of boredom translated a classic concern about happiness – that expectations might make happiness harder to find – into some novel specifics, in this case about the need for constant entertainment. Here, as with envy and loneliness, the broader emotional offshoots of contemporary consumerism suggested new concerns. Changes here could link with some wider problems in the contemporary Western version of happiness.

Positive Psychology and Well-being

Consumerism and the desire for constant entertainment were not the only translations of the growing emphasis on happiness in the Western world. Industrial psychologists and personnel experts continued to consider ways to make work a happier experience. Efforts to promote worker morale and reduce stress continued. A great deal of effort went into protecting the "work/life balance". A number of programs allowed some employees to work from home at least a day a week, to allow a change of pace. Widespread adoption of "casual Fridays" reduced customary style requirements. A growing tendency to refer to employees as "associates" tried to put a happier face on inequalities in the workplace.

Colleges and universities, particularly in the United States, increased their investments in programs designed to make education a happier experience, though college students had long managed to combine education and fun. Student life staffs expanded. Orientations became more elaborate, featuring a variety of games and even camping experiences (with little reference to education). Several dozen American campuses built rock-climbing walls, and in general student unions became more elaborate as part of the competition for student interest. In the early 21st century a number of schools began to bring puppies to campus during examination periods, to provide comfort.

As with the experiments with work, it was not always clear how effective these efforts were; reports of student anxiety and stress continued to mount. But there was no question that a number of agencies were eager to expand the promotion of happiness in new ways, beyond the narrowest kinds of hedonism.

Campaigns for well-being. The most important specific change in this context emerged from 1998 onward, with the introduction of what was called positive psychology. This movement built on the more general impulse toward "positive thinking" and on an earlier interest in "humanistic" psychology within the discipline itself. As announced in a 1998 speech by a leader of the new movement, Martin Seligman, positive psychology aimed

196 *Happiness in Contemporary World History*

at using careful research to enhance the understanding of the ways that individuals could learn how to increase their own happiness. A new array of experts and popularizers worked hard to shift efforts in the discipline away from a focus on problems like mental illness, toward new opportunities to build what many of them now called "positivity". In the process, they also sought to expand attention to a wider definition of happiness, away from a primary emphasis on hedonism. While the movement had particular traction in the United States, it soon built enthusiasm in Western Europe, Canada, and Australia as well.

The movement oscillated in its use of the word happiness. Pronouncements from people like Seligman emphasized the interest in "the scientific study of human flourishing." "Well-being" often seemed a better term than happiness, since the latter so often seemed to focus on material pleasures that could have rather fleeting effects. But the focus on a broad concept of happiness was in fact reasonably clear. Seligman talked of promoting a "good life" defined in terms of "authentic happiness and abundant gratification." The emphasis on positive emotions involved contentment with a person's past, happiness in the present, and hope for the future.

Always supported by explicit research projects, recommendations for individuals aimed at expanding their well-being had several components. Often, guidance repeated ideas that went back to the classic philosophers. The importance of attention to physical health and moderation, for example, reiterated longstanding advice. Seligman and others, while granting the importance of pleasures found in entertainment or relationships, urged that transient enjoyments formed the least important part of real happiness – another case where a finding first articulated by the classical philosophers was being placed in a contemporary context. Further, the basic notion that individuals could and should advance their own happiness confirmed older themes in the history of happiness.

Other findings arguably translated the interest in a broad and durable kind of happiness into some newer emphases. One study, for example, concluded that while having children can add meaning to life, this is not necessary for happiness. This claim meshes with contemporary behavior and the strong interest in individual decisions about happiness, but it was hardly traditional wisdom. A number of positive psychologists also invited people to pay more attention to experiences than to the acquisition of material objects if they sought to maximize happiness, an interesting new caution for a consumer society.

Positive psychology placed great emphasis on urging people to identify their strengths and learn to play these up, rather than spending a lot of time addressing deficiencies. This was consistent with stressing the importance of moral and generous behavior, but again it departed somewhat from earlier ideas about happiness which had usually involved greater attention to character improvement.

Attitudes toward gratitude were revealing. Research in positive psychology urged the role of gratitude in improving well-being, helping a person identify the good things happening in life. But implementation of gratitude could take some novel forms. People were urged to begin keeping "gratitude books", recording things that they were thankful for on a daily basis. Here again, the emphasis on an individual approach to defining and promoting happiness was striking. Researchers granted that more conventional expressions of gratitude, by actually thanking other people, might be even more effective, but this kind of interaction took a back seat to what an individual could do on his own – part of a larger surge in the emphasis on individualism over social connection.

Critics most commonly contend that positive psychologists are overoptimistic, downplaying real problems that make some people unhappy or depressed in their insistence that individuals can create a happier life. There is also concern that the movement exaggerates the importance of explicitly aiming for happiness, of active planning, in contrast to simply trying to live a good and useful life. The movement hardly monopolizes discussions about happiness in the contemporary world.

In response, advocates insist on their recognition that real happiness must involve a range of emotions, including periodic sadness. And they point to research findings that seem to confirm the contention that pursuing a positive psychology agenda has measurable effects, including reducing the incidence of depression.

Positive psychology has stimulated programs beyond strictly academic study or approaches in individual therapy. Since 2000, it has contributed actively to efforts by many employers and university administrations to develop programs that will increase happiness in their areas of endeavor.

Thus a 2019 study found that the number of American companies offering well-being programs had doubled over the preceding decades. Employers were increasingly eager to use such programs not only to reduce health care costs, but also to improve morale and productivity. Many employers found that well-being programs were becoming vital to attracting and retaining a talented workforce.

Many universities also eagerly signed on to a well-being approach, which enhanced the existing interest in making college life a more agreeable experience. Several universities and private secondary schools in Australia, for example, began to highlight a well-being emphasis. Institutions in a number of countries began to attempt measurements of student and staff well-being – the Gallup Organization even developed a "Wellbeing Finder" – and to promote programs that ranged from improving physical health to introducing techniques of mindfulness and meditation. It seemed particularly important, for student audiences, to promote decisions that would maximize long-term happiness over short run satisfactions.

198 *Happiness in Contemporary World History*

The well-being movement did not transform contemporary approaches to happiness, or contemporary constraints. It did however add an important new component, with its intriguing mixture of classic and innovative approaches.

Problems: Sadness and Frustration

Several observers in the later 20th century began to identify several clear limitations in the Western approach to happiness, that reflected important complications in the contemporary experience. One involved a measurable lack of correlation between economic gains and perceived happiness; the other, more dramatic, highlighted an increasing tension between happiness and sadness. These issues developed alongside the growing academic interest in well-being, though positive psychologists did recognize some of the issues involved. Some of the problems added substance to the concern that too many contemporaries in Western society, including some of the positive psychologists, were placing undue emphasis on the importance of striving for happiness.

The Easterlin paradox. Growing prosperity after World War II created a measurable gap between objective improvements in the human condition – in health conditions as well as living standards – and the level of happiness articulated in polls and other self-reports. Westerners were not gaining in happiness as rapidly as had been expected.

Richard Easterlin, an economist, using United States data between the 1940s and mid-1970s, argued that whereas at one point, increasing average income generated roughly equivalent improvements in reported happiness, after a certain juncture that correlation ceased. In the American case, even as prosperity continued to rise, reported happiness became flat or dipped slightly. This finding has been confirmed for the United States over a longer period of time, into the 21st century, and also for other developed nations. Various critics have tried to counter the finding, including some psychologists eager to emphasize improvements in happiness, but on the whole it has held up fairly well. Economic growth does produce greater happiness but not constantly, and the linkages weaken over time.

Several factors contribute to this important caveat about modern happiness. First, inequality colors the picture; average national levels conceal great disparities and the resentments that can result. Second, people's memories fade: one generation does not recall the conditions of a century past, and so has no active appreciation of how much better things are in their own time. The same applies to memories of health gains: how many contemporaries actively remember the time, just over a century ago, when virtually every family would experience the death of an infant? Something of a gratitude gap results. Third, people often place greater weight on hopes for further improvements in living standards, and frustration that these are not arriving more quickly, than on current levels: this is an

Western Society in Contemporary History 199

old dilemma in the happiness field. Finally, the feeble correlations remind us that after a certain point, people do not define happiness primarily in terms of material standards; they look to other measurements. These four factors can readily combine.

Evaluations similar to the Easterlin finding have also been applied to individuals. In 2010 *Time* magazine highlighted another research report which claimed that once a person had reached an income level of $75,000 a year, further improvements did not increase happiness. This confirmed that up to a point, higher salaries do generate more happiness, because of pride in the achievement and appreciation for the goods and services available. But again, after a certain level the quest for happiness turns more to other criteria; or to frustrations that salaries are not rising even faster; or to resentment that a coworker enjoys an even higher salary – or some combination of the above. And it is clear that most people earning $75,000 still want more, which adds to the complexity of interpreting the happiness levels involved.

The $75,000 plateau has been even more widely disputed than the Easterlin paradox. A fancy magazine, *Town and Country,* did its own calculation of what it takes to be happy (which included a private plane) and concluded that a really happy person needed at least $100 million. Another critic more sensibly suggested that the income needed for happiness would vary with the individual. And it is vital to remember, when looking at national happiness more generally, that most Americans have never made $75,000 a year.

Still, both national and individual data suggest that the income/happiness correlation is real but incomplete, and that, particularly in contemporary history, trends in happiness tend to be flatter than purely economic data would suggest. Rising consumerism and comfort had more impact in earlier periods, for the world's most affluent societies, than they have had in recent decades. Many people want something more, or something different, and they do not always find it.

Sadness. The second vulnerability in contemporary Western approaches to happiness involves the pressure that expectations of happiness place on the evaluation of sadness. Robin Berman, the pediatrician, argues that the greatest weakness of American parenting centers on an unwillingness to tolerate a sad child or periods in which many children will naturally be sad. Cultural standards push parents to believe that a sad child must reflect badly on them – a good parent should have constantly happy children – or, to deflect their guilt, to assume that the sad child must be ill, requiring medical attention and, often, some kind of medication.

The issue may go beyond childrearing. The steady intensification of Western happiness culture may make sadness, or even temporary dips in happiness, feel like personal failure. Positive psychology, though recognizing in principle that sadness is normal, may enhance a belief that any well-balanced individual should be able to generate happiness. We have

200 *Happiness in Contemporary World History*

seen that even earlier in the 20th century, new tensions began to apply to expressions of grief. On another front, some categories of service workers, such as flight attendants, reported that the pressures to present a cheerful front to surly customers ended up confusing them about their own real emotions. Happiness standards, in other words, can be intolerant, making a real or imagined deficiency in happiness harder to manage.

There is little question that since the 1930s, rates of psychological depression have been increasing in Western society, affecting a growing minority of individuals; by the 1990s, up to 15% of all Americans were reporting at least one depressive episode in their lifetimes. These rates surely reflected the growing clinical interest in depression, increasing the frequency of diagnoses. They also seem to result from some of the larger tensions of industrial, urban society; at least until recently, rural regions seem to generate lower rates. But happiness expectations may enter in as well, causing some people to believe they are depressed when they cannot measure up and prompting doctors more readily to identify happiness inadequacies with illness. A 2008 study found that up to 25% of all depression diagnoses in the United States actually involved a non-clinical level of sadness which, in a happiness culture, could not easily be accepted.

★★★

Developments in contemporary history demonstrate the strong hold that the earlier "happiness revolution" maintains in Western culture. Many of the basic features of consumer society continued to rest on claims and expectations for happiness, including cheerful salespeople. Western society did feature tensions between hedonism and a broader approach to happiness, a new version of a dilemma identified by philosophers early on. The rise of positive psychology obviously reflected a desire to find new ways to widen approaches to happiness. The discovery of new and troubling byproducts of the commitment to happiness, from mounting boredom to the challenge of sadness, confirms the distinctive Western commitment to happiness but also highlights some troubling complications.

Further Reading

On consumer affluence,

Goldthorpe, John H. *The Affluent Worker in the Class Structure* (London: Cambridge University Press, 1969).

Lebergott, Stanley. *Pursuing Happiness American Consumers in the Twentieth Century* (Princeton, NJ: Princeton University Press, 2014).

Samuel, Lawrence. *Happiness in America: A Cultural History* (Lanham, MD: Rowman and Littlefield, 2018).

Stearns, Peter N. *Satisfaction Not Guaranteed Dilemmas of Progress in Modern Society* (New York: New York University Press, 2012).

Western Society in Contemporary History 201

Young, Michael Dunlop, and Peter Willmott. *The Symmetrical Family*. (New York: Pantheon Books, a Div. of Random House, 1973).

On the Easterlin paradox,

Easterbrook, Gregg. *The Progress Paradox: How Life Gets Better While People Feel Worse*, 1st ed. (New York: Random House, 2003).

Easterlin, Richard A., Holger Hinte, and Klaus F. Zimmermann. *Happiness, Growth, and the Life Cycle* (Oxford: Oxford University Press, 2010).

Stevenson, Betsey, and Justin Wolfers. "Economic Growth and Subjective Well-Being: Reassessing the Easterlin Paradox." *Brookings Papers on Economic Activity* no. 1 (2008): 1–87.

On boredom and loneliness,

Alberti, Fay. *A Biography of Loneliness: The History of Emotion*. (Oxford: Oxford University Press, 2019).

Dalle Pezze, Barbara, and Carlo Salzani. *Essays on Boredom and Modernity* (Amsterdam: Rodopi, 2009).

Fernandez, Luke, and Susan J. Matt. *Bored, Lonely, Angry, Stupid: Changing Feelings about Technology, from the Telegraph to Twitter* (Cambridge, MA: Harvard University Press, 2019).

Putnam, Robert D. *Bowling Alone: The Collapse and Revival of American Community* (New York: Simon and Schuster, 2000).

For a history of the wellbeing movement,

Horowitz, Daniel. *Happier?: The History of a Cultural Movement That Aspired to Transform America* (New York: Oxford University Press, 2018).

On well-being,

Compton, William. *Introduction to Positive Psychology*, 1st ed. (Boston, MA: Cengage Learning, 1994).

Seligman, Martin E. P. *Flourish: A Visionary New Understanding of Happiness and Well-Being* (New York: Free Press, 2011).

On emotional constraints for service workers,

Hochschild, Arlie Russell. *The Managed Heart: Commercialization of Human Feeling* (Berkeley: University of California Press, 1985).

On sadness,

Berman, Robin. *Unhappiness: The Keys to Raising Happy Kids* (Santa Monica, CA: Goop, 2016).

On depression,

Good, Byron, and Arthur Kleinman. *Culture and Depression: Studies in the Anthropology and Cross-Cultural Psychiatry of Affect and Disorder* (Berkeley: University of California Press, 1985).

14 Happiness Goes Global

Accelerating globalization, particularly over the past half-century, has promoted an expansion of interest in happiness, among a variety of groups and nations. To be sure, deep cultural distinctions have not been erased, and while regional economic inequalities have diminished, huge differences in living standards remain. Some global features of happiness have emerged, however. They have involved more than the importation of Western standards to other societies, though this occurred to some extent. They have also reflected some standard reactions to urbanization and improvements in standards of living and health. And they have highlighted contributions to ideas about happiness from other regions, particularly South Asia, which have increasingly enriched global discussions and even amplified recommendations emanating from positive psychology.

Any serious student of globalization must note the often complicated combination of regional and global forces, and this certainly applies to happiness: there can be no argument that a single global standard of happiness has emerged. Moreover, the political aspects of contemporary global happiness pose a further complication. A wide variety of governments in recent decades have found it useful to talk about their contributions to happiness; indeed, happiness became a more explicit part of many political agendas than ever before, even in comparison with the 18th century, and in a wider regional array. This is in itself an interesting global phenomenon, but it also entails a great deal of political manipulation, with states claiming new programs and commitments without much attention to definitions and experiences of happiness in the population at large. At the same time, political showmanship is not the only feature of global approaches to happiness. Wider commitments to consumerism, to happy holidays, and even to experiments with well-being programs suggest other interests. A number of individuals and societies are struggling to figure out what happiness consists of in contemporary life, and trying to move it forward.

"World Happiness Day" and the Global Promotion of Happiness

In 2012, the United Nations established March 20 as an annual International Day of Happiness, intending it as a regular global celebration.

"Conscious that the pursuit of happiness is a fundamental human goal... Recognizing also the need for a more inclusive, equitable and balanced approach to economic growth that promotes sustainable development, poverty eradication, happiness and the well-being of all peoples," the General Assembly expressed the hope that the Day would be acknowledged through programs aimed at raising overall awareness.

The Day was the brainchild of Jayme Illien, who had been born in South Asia in 1980, orphaned and ultimately raised in the United States. Illien headed a movement advocating "Happytalism," urging the importance of a broad approach to economic development that would have maximum public happiness as its goal and outcome. The annual World Happiness Report, also launched in 2012, noted in Chapter 1, was an outgrowth of the same basic impulse.

The movement, for all its gimmicky aspects, sought to recognize the important changes in global economic structure that were occurring as more and more societies industrialized, but also to make sure that these combined with an appreciation of the wider components in human happiness. The combination of motives: political propaganda, Western influence including the notion of the pursuit of happiness itself, but also the need to recognize other approaches to happiness, underlay much of the global commitment to happiness that emerged by the early 21st century. Happiness began to be considered an appropriate policy goal and the real measure of human progress.

Programs and agencies. New initiatives abounded, in a variety of world regions. A *Journal of Happiness Studies* was founded in 2000 by a group of American and Dutch psychologists, aiming to promote research in the field. A separate initiative, called the Happy Planet Index, launched in 2006, aimed at using environmental impact as the basic criterion of happiness, generating a very different set of international rankings from that provided by the United Nations or the Gallup organization. David Cameron, British Prime Minister in 2010, directed his government to devise new ways to measure happiness beyond Gross National Product. A variety of British writers and politicians regularly addressed what they called a "happiness agenda", usually seeking to promote various conservative policies including limitations on immigration. On the other hand, it was another Conservative government, just a few years later that set up a major program to deal with loneliness in one of the British ministries. Happiness was in the air, but it embraced a variety of goals.

In 2019, New Zealand made an even more explicit move, unveiling its first-ever "well-being budget." Targets included mental health, child poverty, rights of indigenous peoples, plus developing a low carbon-emission economy and promoting flourishing in a digital age.

Initiatives of this sort remained rather tentative. Many Western governments had yet to buy into the idea of promoting well-being, sticking to older, and more purely economic, definitions of national policy; the United States fell clearly into this category, riveted on criteria such as

204 *Happiness in Contemporary World History*

Gross National Product and stock market indices, despite important initiatives in the private sector.

On the other hand, interest now spread well beyond Western societies. In 2016 the United Arab Emirates set up a Ministry of Happiness, linked to entrepreneurial initiatives. Ohoud Al Floumi, appointed as the first Minister, proclaimed, "What is the purpose of government if it does not work toward the happiness of the people?" Claiming that happiness was a "science," she argued that it touched on "medicine, health, social science." "We're trying to bring it from a broad framework into daily practice in our society." The operation worked closely with a Happiness Research Institute in Denmark, though the results remained at best rather vague. "Happiness meters" were installed in offices so that people could register their levels of happiness, while police officers gave well-being badges to good drivers instead of focusing on issuing tickets to bad ones.

Similar offices were established elsewhere, some of them clearly intended for propaganda purposes at home and abroad – as in Venezuela in 2013, when the country was in economic freefall. Other governments, however, consulted Danish and other experts, sincerely hoping to figure out programs that could address regional issues relevant to happiness: thus South Korea sought advice on dealing with its stubbornly high suicide rate, which persisted despite, or because of, its rapid economic growth. While the Chinese government continues to chart its own path, its explicit interest in happiness fits into the international pattern in some respects.

Whether for show or distraction, or out of genuine concern, or from some sense of global competition around devotion to happiness and its rankings, politicians were devoting more attention to happiness than ever before in world history.

Well-being initiatives. Growing international interest in positive psychology was both cause and symptom of new global interest, as well-being programs spilled well beyond Western societies. In 2018 the government of New Delhi, India, launched a series of "happiness classes" for 11-year olds, seeking to shift focus from academic achievement alone to include emotional well-being. The official in charge noted that India had long been turning out top professionals, but now needed to focus on turning out top human beings as well. After a first class, one seventh-grader noted, "We should work happily. When you work sadly, your work will not be good."

Tecmilenio University, a large private system in Mexico, introduced an elaborate well-being program in 2016. The President realized that training for jobs was not enough; a university should also help train for positive purpose and happiness in life. All first-year students began to take a well-being course designed to emphasize character strengths and "mindfulness", and each was expected to be able to answer a question about his or her purpose in life.

Happiness Goes Global 205

Programs of this sort, spreading through most major regions of the world to some degree, blended a recognition of the growing importance of happiness, and the steps that psychologists were urging to enhance it, with specific concern about stress and anxiety levels among students. The problems, and at least some of the possible solutions, now seemed global.

Context: Living Standards

The growing interest in happiness built on major changes in material conditions for much of the world's population, particularly after the 1980s. Rapid industrialization in places like China and Brazil combined with growing economic opportunities for many people in East Africa or Southeast Asia. Improved public health measures also spread widely.

Best years in world history? By the early 21st century rapid reduction of poverty, infant mortality, child labor and other traditional constraints prompted some observers to argue that global progress was occurring at an unprecedented rate. The data were striking.

Thus between 1990 and 2018, child mortality dropped, on a global basis, by 59%, and by the latter date fewer than 4% of all children born died before reaching age 5. Between 2000 and 2016, life expectancy improved by 5.5 years, again on a global basis, reaching an unprecedented average of 72 years at birth. Improvements in medical care by this point insured that urban health was better than rural, even as the majority of the world's population was living in cities, again for the first time in history.

Poverty dropped. One estimate held that 137,000 people *per day* moved above the extreme poverty level, during every year since 1990. Access to running water, toilets, and electricity expanded rapidly. Famines declined, except in a few regions, and average stature increased – another sign of greater access to a viable food supply.

Claims of this sort masked continuing regional inequalities, to be sure. Average life expectancy in Africa, at 62 years, obviously fell below the global standard; but rates of improvement were particularly great precisely in some of the most disadvantaged regions. Global inequalities – aside from a few areas in dire crisis – were dropping.

Gains of this sort – not always widely understood, amid the crises that dominated the media and a certain degree of fashionable pessimism among many academics – prompted some observers to contend that Enlightenment anticipations of progress were finally being realized.

Global consumerism. Evidence of expanding consumerism on the whole matched the basic indices of material progress, at least for a growing global middle class. Tourism expanded, as masses of Chinese and Russian tourists joined the more established streams from the West and Japan. By 2019 it was estimated that 5 billion people around the world, the vast majority of the population, now had cell phones. Interest in spectator sports grew massively, thanks to instant access provided by satellite television but

206 *Happiness in Contemporary World History*

also the spread of professional teams. Basketball became the second most widely watched sport in the world, after soccer football, with networks of professional teams in Turkey, China, and elsewhere.

The surge of interest and emotional investment in pets was another intriguing global development. Japanese pet ownership was particularly striking, with rapid expansion both in the number of pets and in the levels of spending on their comfort. But devotion to pets also spread in China and elsewhere.

Something like a global youth culture expanded on the basis of shared consumer interests. Hip-hop, K-pop, and other musical styles spread widely. In 2000 a new word, "teen", was introduced into the Vietnamese language, to designate young people devoted to popular music, fast foods, blue jeans, and other staples; and soon a second word, "teen-teen", was added to single out those who were especially avid.

Happy holidays. A growing interest in highlighting happy holidays was another sign of global change. Celebration of Christmas as a consumer event spread in places like the United Arab Emirates or Turkey, shorn of religious connotations. The word "happy" was increasingly applied to holidays that originally had far different meanings. Thus in English *Ramadan Mubarak*, or "blessed Ramadan" was increasingly rendered as Happy Ramadan, even though the holy month actually emphasized self-sacrifice; and a practice of sending commercial greeting cards to accompany Ramadan spread widely. Chanukah was increasingly embellished among American Jews, to provide a Christmas-like sense of happiness. Newer holidays, like the growing recognition of Juneteenth in the United States, almost always had the adjective happy tacked on from the outset.

Most revealing was the increasing internationalization of the birthday, as a time for celebration and gift-giving for children and adults alike – usually accompanied by a translation of the song Happy Birthday. (The song is available in at least 30 languages.) Organizations offering to help arrange birthday parties sprang up in Cairo, Shanghai, and Dubai.

What might be called happy consumerism was far more common in cities than in the countryside. It attracted people who were particularly open to Western influences. But Western styles now commonly combined with more local flavors: McDonalds fast foods thus offered a wide array of vegetarian options in India, *Iftar* meals in Morocco, wine and beer in France, and teriyaki burgers in Japan. Consumer innovations from places like Japan and South Korea, in music and animation, rivaled Western initiatives. A link between consumerism and expectations of happiness was increasingly global.

Syncretism

As with consumerism, global happiness initiatives increasingly combined Western-inspired themes with influences from other regions. This blending of concepts, called syncretism, became an increasingly important

Happiness Goes Global 207

aspect of discussions of happiness, among experts like the positive psychologists and a larger popular audience as well. It remains valid to see many of the happiness themes in contemporary world history as an extension of priorities developed first in the West, but this is not the whole story. Western authorities themselves increasingly valued other practices as they sought to enrich their own approach and modify the association of happiness with hedonism.

South Asia. Hindu and Buddhist practices provided an increasingly important component of global happiness initiatives. Interest in Indian spirituality, as a means of enriching or even replacing a Western approach, developed early. It became an important feature of the 1960s youth rebellion against Western values. In 1968 the famous Beatles singing group made a pilgrimage to India to learn more about transcendental meditation, a trip that both symbolized and promoted wider interest. In turn, various Indian spiritual leaders developed centers and training programs in many parts of the world.

Mindfulness and meditation were the themes that gained particular attention, increasingly incorporated into a variety of well-being initiatives in the West and elsewhere. Both involved practices that were designed to focus the mind on a particular thought, to improve awareness and achieve a calm and stable emotional state. The values and techniques involved were not new, but they contrasted with some of the more materialist, activity-oriented impulses in Western ideas of happiness. Many people found that meditation, whether associated with religious interest or not, provided tranquility and even a sense of bliss. Following Indian tradition, many well-being practitioners began recommending at least two 20-minute meditation sessions per day. By 2017, according to one study, at least 10% of all Americans were regularly practicing meditation (with a variety of specific techniques).

Bhutan. The small Himalayan nation of Bhutan developed an outsized global role in discussions of happiness by advocating national measurements of well-being that would go beyond purely economic criteria (criteria by which the small country, relatively poor, fared badly). From 1971 onward Bhutanese leaders began advocating a Gross National Happiness (GNH) measurement that would take into account spiritual, social, and environmental factors. The idea that well-being should gain precedence over economic growth hardly won universal acclaim – most developing countries proceeded resolutely to expand industry and trade – but it did gain growing attention. Many of the happiness initiatives favored by governments in the 21st century, from Britain to the Emirates, reflected substantial interest in trying to go beyond material standard of living alone – particularly given the increasing realization that living standards and happiness did not fully correlate. And while the United States government stayed away from the happiness issue, focused more conventionally on economic criteria, American well-being programs actively embraced the wider agenda.

208 *Happiness in Contemporary World History*

Bhutanese values also gained attention as part of growing concern about environmental deterioration. Its minister of education put it this way:

We believe that you cannot have a prosperous nation in the long run that does not conserve its natural environment or take care of the wellbeing of its people, which is being borne out by what is happening in the outside world.

Some Bhutanese teachers went on to contend that the commitment to GNH must go beyond environmental concerns, to provide a "philosophy for life." True to form, Bhutanese schools include regular meditation periods, soothing music to replace clanging school bells, and other efforts to promote serenity.

The Bhutanese model hardly conquered the world. The nation itself struggled with poverty and growing environmental change which threatened water resources, with an uncertain future. But the notion of an alternative model did win some global attention. Specific Bhutanese ideas – like the notion that one cannot live a truly happy life without thinking of death at least five times a day – did create small initiatives in other countries, even including online apps like WeCroak, to provide reminders of deeper themes in life.

Japan. South Asia was not the only region to contribute to the growing global diversity of ideas about happiness. Key Buddhist movements in Japan established global outreach to promote world peace and nuclear disarmament, often highlighting their commitment to programs that would allow people to find "prosperity and happiness."

Another fascinating initiative emerged in 2011 that soon caught global attention. A woman named Marie Kondo, long fascinated with the importance of tidiness and influenced also by youthful service at a Shinto shrine, published the first of several discussions of what she called the Konmari method. The method centered on urging people to gather all their possessions, in relevant categories, and then decide which items truly "sparked joy" – while getting rid of the rest. Kondo claimed that cleaning and organizing things properly conveyed spiritual values in Shintoism, which can be more widely shared. "Treasuring what you have, treating the objects you own as disposable, but valuable, no matter what their actual monetary worth, and creating displays so you can value each individual object are all essentially Shinto ways of living." Here was a new take on happiness and joy in a consumer age.

Kondo's publications, quickly translated into many other languages, were followed by an array of television appearances and a flurry of initiatives in individual households in the United States and elsewhere. A Netflix series in 2019 won wide attention.

★★★

Happiness Goes Global 209

Global contributions to discussions of happiness cut two ways. On the one hand, they could directly counter dominant Western approaches to happiness, including consumerism. On the other, they could combine, in the West and elsewhere, potentially enriching approaches to happiness by introducing additional values and practices. A variety of voices were contributing to an increasingly global, if diverse, conversation.

Happiness Trends: The World Values Survey

Measuring global happiness is an inexact art at best, and for better or worse it has not been undertaken very often. Earlier chapters discussed some relevant initiatives in the 1960s and 1970s, as well as the recent United Nations effort, stemming from the discussions surrounding the International Day of Happiness, which provides some challenging comparative data. Only one project has covered a sufficient time period to venture generalizations about trends over time – within the contemporary period – while also offering comparative evidence. The World Values Survey offers some interesting material, along with explanations that, as with any ambitious venture on global happiness, need careful assessment.

The Survey. The World Values Survey (WVS) is an ambitious international social science undertaking, headquartered in Sweden but with investigators in a growing number of countries. The Survey aims particularly at identifying national trends toward greater democracy; happiness is not the primary focus. But the Survey has generated findings about happiness over time, since its inception in 1981, and also explanations both for trends and for comparative differences.

The principal findings run as follows: human values in countries around the world divide according to two axes: one contrasts primary reliance on tradition, including religion, with commitment to a more modern secular-rational approach; the other contrasts societies or groups emphasizing survival and security, with those more eager for self-expression, with high levels of tolerance and trust. Happiness is lowest in societies where tradition and survivalism combine; highest in the secular/rational plus self-expression group. A few societies fall in the middle, for example, secular-rational but concerned about security.

WVS scholars further emphasize that while these divisions can be found within societies, as with poorer groups stressing survival over more affluent self-expressers, divisions *among* countries are much stronger. In other words, cultural combinations exercise a powerful influence over whole societies.

Implications for happiness: comparisons. The results of this ambitious analysis generate comparative patterns very similar to those of the World Happiness Survey, which is somewhat reassuring except for critics who simply distrust polling results. The happiest countries include the Scandinavians

210   Happiness in Contemporary World History

and similar cases, with a Protestant tradition, deep impact from the Enlightenment, and advanced industrialization. Many Middle Eastern countries rank low, because of the combination of tradition and survival concerns. China does somewhat better in these rankings than in the Happiness Survey; India remains fairly low.

Several Latin American countries – Mexico, Brazil, Argentina – do better than expected. Their economies have been improving, at least until recently, but they also have been enjoying greater democracy and tolerance; yet sociologist Marita Carballo notes they also value religion, and this cultural combination (modern but religious) may be an advantage compared, say, to cases like China where greater secularism predominates.

Trends. The most important conclusion is that the vast majority of the countries in the initial group of 54 saw happiness levels improve markedly between 1981 and 2007. Only 12 lagged, and these were particularly concentrated in Eastern Europe where the fall of communism introduced an overwhelming survival/security concern.

Most countries generated improvements: in the West, in Asia, in Latin America, and parts of Africa. And WVS scholars rush to emphasize the combination of factors involved. Economic development – industrialization – plays the greatest role in encouraging a shift to secular/rational values and away from traditionalism. But along with this, growing democratization and tolerance promote a sense of freedom and agency, and opportunities for self-expression. A wider variety of societies have moved to the positive side of the values ledger, though comparative differences still contrast happiness levels in regions like Latin America or China from those in the West. But the gaps may be narrowing – as they have been in economic development.

Caveats. Several cautions attach to these intriguing findings – the best evidence available for trends in recent decades. Modern culture may encourage people to believe they should *say* they are happy, particularly when so many varied governments are trying to promote happiness as a political goal. Whether they actually are, or not, could be another matter – though even a trend of trying to claim happiness would be an interesting development.

The Western values bias of the WVS may be troubling, a problem we have encountered before in dealing with cases like Japan. Some countries, otherwise "modern", may simply rate self-expression and individual agency less vividly than their Western or Latin American counterparts, but at the same time may have alternative definitions of happiness that do not show up as clearly in a global poll.

The most dramatic red flag, however, involves questions about what has happened, globally, since 2007. The Great Recession of 2008 set back economic growth in some countries, though not all. For this and other reasons, a number of societies have become less democratic and tolerant, more authoritarian, in the same recent timespan: this includes China,

Happiness Goes Global 211

Turkey, Brazil, the United States, and Russia, though in varying degrees. Has happiness suffered accordingly?

Several countries, further, including the United States and Britain, have experienced additional setbacks to measurable happiness in recent years. Stagnating incomes in parts of the United States have reduced hope, and modern happiness may depend strongly on a belief in achievable personal and social progress. Symptoms such as growing opioid use and rising suicide rates, quite apart from political disarray, suggest that something is amiss. More recently still, in 2020, the challenge of the coronavirus pandemic and economic dislocation have reduced happiness levels still further, though the setback may be temporary; 2020 was not a happy year. These developments must be factored into any equation that argues for a definitive global pattern of rising happiness.

★★★

Several global strands over the last half-century or more produce a messy pattern – but possibly a pattern. Global interest in happiness has increased, on the part of governments but also businesses and universities. This may generate more happiness in fact, or at least a greater belief that happiness should be emphasized. Definitions of happiness have expanded in some cases thanks to a mixture of global influences. Economic development and health improvements provide a plausible basis for expecting rising satisfaction. And one massive data effort – the World Values Survey – suggests that, on the whole, trends over time confirm the expected results: happiness has been increasing.

None of this should neglect continued variety. A few countries, torn by war and environmental damage, have seen happiness decline, as with an Iraqi refugee who noted plaintively, in 2018, "I have forgotten what happiness is." Cultural factors, as well as differences in economic development levels, continue to complicate the picture. Eastern Europe has become a bit of a puzzle, with a growing regional turn away from the patterns of liberal democracy and happiness rankings in the second quartile internationally. But parts of the West, including the United States, are generating new questions as well, with happiness was already stagnating despite economic advance but with further dislocations in recent decades that have begun to push levels downward; a 2020 survey (reflecting additional problems resulting from the virus pandemic and economic collapse) found levels of happiness in the United States lower than at any point since 1972.

Even for observers who take some understandable comfort in contemporary global trends, it would surely be rash to project into the future. Global changes over the past several decades, definitely; a measurable pattern at least until very recently, probably; a clear path forward? Wait and see.

212 *Happiness in Contemporary World History*

Further Reading

On global happiness initiatives,

Boddice, Rob. *A History of Feelings*, 1st ed. (London: Reaktion Books, 2019).

For data on material progress,

Pinker, Steven. *Enlightenment Now: The Case for Reason, Science, Humanism, and Progress* (New York: Viking, an imprint of Penguin Random House LLC, 2018).

Roser, Max. "Economic Growth." Published Online at OurWorldInData.org (2013).

On meditation,

Shear, Jonathan, ed. *The Experience of Meditation* (New York: Paragon House, 2006).

On global trends and comparisons,

Carballo, Marita. *La Felicidad de Las Naciones*, 1st ed. (Buenos Aires: SUDAAMERICANA, 2014).

Welzel, Christian. *Freedom Rising: Human Empowerment and the Quest for Emancipation* (New York: Cambridge University Press, 2013).

15 Conclusion

Happiness has changed a great deal over the course of human history, though in somewhat different ways in different regions. There is no question that historical analysis improves our understanding of this human emotion, even for observers primarily interested in contemporary patterns. People may indeed have always wanted to be happy, but what they have meant by this, and how they have been able to shape their experiences, has varied greatly and depended on particular historical circumstance. Happiness today is the product of past religions, the Enlightenment, commercial capitalism, and the massive modern entertainment industry, psychological advice, plus whatever personal, familial, and local variables add to the mix.

Complexities

The history of happiness is unquestionably complex: there is no tidy master narrative to trace a steady evolution in any particular direction. Even the question "are you happy?" would make no sense in certain cultures and time periods. Here are some of the key problems encountered in this historical sketch:

Relevant historical research is still widely scattered, with a disproportionate focus on the West. The conclusion, for example, that high levels of reported Latin American happiness result from a unique combination of Enlightenment ideas with continued religious support is intriguing, but far more historical work is needed to flesh out how this combination developed after the end of the colonial period. Many other key regions are underserved, and even for the West ample room exists for much more explicit research. There are a host of inviting opportunities, but in the meantime, comparative conclusions must often remain rather speculative.

For the sheer variety of regional approaches to happiness is clearly a challenging aspect of the history of happiness – at any given period of time, including the present. Approaching alternative cultural systems and linguistic preferences accurately is not an easy task. For the contemporary period particularly, some of the most ambitious efforts to chart happiness, as with the World Values Survey, remain suspiciously Western in orientation.

214   *Conclusion*

For any period and any region, the tension between formal writing about happiness, from philosophers or religious authorities or, more recently, psychologists, and actual popular beliefs and practices is a fundamental issue. It is clearly easier to seize on the writings, but it is always vital to look at what groups of more "ordinary" people seem to be saying and doing. The two domains often relate, as with religious ideas and practices, but they are rarely identical.

The challenge here may be particularly great in the more recent historical periods, even though we have a great deal more direct information on popular concepts. For, from the Enlightenment onward, a variety of modern systems have worked hard to tell people they should be happy and cheerful. Corporations promote seemingly happy workers; Disney and other consumer organizations preach happiness; communist governments and, more recently, some of the well-being programs in contemporary societies push in the same direction. All of this plays a valid role in the history of happiness, but it also can distort results, even in polling data. It is hard to sort out modern happiness from a modern encouragement to seem to be happy. Another complexity to be aware of.

Religion clearly plays a central role in the history of happiness – but its impact is not easy to determine. It may veer away from happiness in this life to hopes for the next; it may promote fear or melancholy or outright self-sacrifice. But it may also provide vital solace, even moments of transcendent joy. The variety of religious approaches, and changes in major religions such as the modern Christian embrace of happiness, complicate the picture. In the contemporary period, available data on the relationship between religion and happiness point in several directions. A number of highly religious societies do not score well on happiness reports, and some secular societies actually head the list. Attempts to explain these disparities are helpful but not fully satisfactory. Thus rich secular countries, like those in Scandinavia, build on prosperity, democracy, and tolerance to sustain happiness without much need for religion, while societies that are religious but poorer understandably fare less well. Economic performance, in other words, not religion is the key variable. But this distinction may overlook the special role of religion in reported happiness in the United States and especially in Latin America, or, by contrast, the complex combination of religion, economic development, and low international scores in several prosperous Islamic countries or in India. At the same time, a variety of studies continue to cite religion as a positive contributor to happiness, particularly *within* individual societies, and many religious-like practices, such as meditation, are gaining new emphasis. Again, generalization is difficult, with different regional patterns and significant changes over time.

Finally, no dominant trend line can be established for a world history of happiness. Some optimists, in the Enlightenment and again around 1900, tried to argue that happiness had steadily increased from past to present (perhaps with a bow to a primitive Golden Age), but this schema does not

Conclusion   215

fit the available facts. Fluctuations, rather than tidy trajectories, may best capture reality – particularly at a moment, in 2020, when happiness in many societies seems to be taking a nosedive.

Recurrent Themes

From the classical philosophers onward, and very much in the present day, several general themes have intertwined with the history of happiness, even at the popular level, and this can offer some coherence for the subject across various time periods.

The tension between hedonistic definitions of happiness and those that seek other, arguably deeper themes has affected discussions of the subject, and actual choices, since the early civilizations. It remains a lively topic today, as the efforts of the well-being advocates suggest. But it also affected the balance between religious emphases and more popular pleasures in key periods. A related theme, again recurrent both in philosophical treatments and in real life, balances short-term, sometimes intense, pleasures against a focus on more lifelong satisfactions, or possibly hopes for greater happiness in a life to come or in a post-revolutionary world.

Another dilemma, noted early on, involves levels of aspiration. We have seen that hunting and gathering groups may seem particularly happy because they live in the here and now. Correspondingly, many authorities from the early civilizations onward urged modest expectations as a crucial component of happiness. On the other hand, some people have always sought more than they currently have – whether in material and social standing or in spiritual fulfillment, and this might be a vital component of happiness (or unhappiness) as well. Choices here may have become more pressing in modern societies, when the idea of personal or social progress burns brighter, but with greater potential frustrations as well. Individuals may shoot too high but so, arguably, can some social movements such as communism. The philosophers might have been surprised at the modern specifics, but they would have recognized the problem.

A different topic, but again a recurrent one, juxtaposes luck versus human agency in the quest for happiness. Here too, the debate has involved varying details, and some cultures have preferred one option over the other. Some observers argue that groups or regions that today display unusual interest in gambling provide yet another contemporary indication of an older emphasis on luck as the only real path to happiness. Modern Western culture has tended to argue more for personal agency. But this can leave some individuals convinced that their unhappiness must somehow be their own fault. And new data, as with genetics, complicates this ongoing discussion in additional ways.

Family looms large in most popular definitions of happiness. Here is an aspect that the philosophers sometimes had less to say about, and which some contemporary students of happiness bypass as well; most of the

216   *Conclusion*

explicit international happiness polls, for example, stay away from family issues. It looms large in real-life assessments of happiness, however. This said, the variety of family emphases complicates any easy generalization. In many agricultural societies, sheer family size seems to have been the most obvious component of happiness (at least in male-dominated rhetoric), and philosophers sometimes mentioned this as well. In many modern settings, more explicit emotional fulfillment or shared consumer interests play a greater role. The importance of attachment to parents provides yet another approach to family happiness, apparently linking traditional and more contemporary values in some regional societies. We have also seen that ideas about children's happiness and play constitute another important variable over time.

Themes of this sort help organize comparisons among different regional approaches to happiness, or changes from one period to the next, even though they yield no tidy formulas. They also highlight the importance of choice. One way to assess happiness today, as in the past, is to consider whether different individuals and groups could opt for a version of happiness that best suited their situation and temperament – even though others, in the same region and time period, might pursue other preferences. Even today, for example, in societies that for the most part do not equate family happiness with lots of children; some individual couples happily – they claim – opt for the older standard. Those modern societies that are fairly tolerant have also added options to choose among religious and secular approaches to happiness, which may contribute to a positive overall outcome as well.

Major Changes in the History of Happiness

At this point in our historical understanding, and in trying to develop a relevant world-historical framework, it has not been possible to mark off tidy chronological periods for every stage in the history of happiness. There have, however, been some particularly important turning points.

The transition from hunting and gathering to agriculture, and then the advent of formal civilizations, clearly denote a major watershed. Whatever conclusions one draws about levels of happiness in hunting and gathering societies, there is no question that agricultural civilizations introduced several new and challenging issues in defining and achieving happiness, which is why philosophers began to spend so much time discussing the subject and why new words for happiness had to be introduced. High levels of disease and death, frequent poverty, heightened work requirements, patriarchal gender systems all added complications. In contrast to industrialization (at least in the West), no prior buildup of new attitudes toward happiness had arisen to cushion the impact of agricultural innovations or disruptions.

Conclusion 217

Within the long agricultural period, the advent of more complex religions, most of them emanating either from India or the Middle East, suggests another set of adjustments. Chronology here varies, but after the collapse of the classical civilizations, that is, from the 5th or 6th century CE onward, religions began to play a particularly powerful role in helping to shape happiness in much of Asia, Europe, and parts of Africa. Religion was never the sole factor in happiness, save for some individuals; it must be balanced against other aspects of popular culture. But it could definitely establish directions and constraints.

The "happiness revolution" in the West highlights major change, from the 18th century onward. This was a striking departure in many ways, from smiling cheerfulness to definitions of family happiness to new challenges in reconciling happiness and death. It needs careful treatment, both because it did not erase earlier approaches in the West and because its global influence was gradual and remains incomplete to this day. From Russian communism to contemporary well-being programs in the Middle East to gestures such as the International Day of Happiness and the very idea of trying to measure happiness globally, however, some themes from the happiness revolution turn out to have wide impact.

The challenge of industrialization. The advent of industrial society, first in the West and now more widely, raises a fundamental question about happiness and historical change: if agricultural civilization reduced or complicated happiness in fundamental ways, compared to earlier human society, what about industrialization compared to its agricultural predecessor?

The response is not easy, in part because of the impact of different regional cultures: industrial Japan, for example, compared with the industrial United States, or industrializing India compared to China. But some suggestions can be ventured, and recent optimists like Steven Pinker have plausibly argued that industrialization, and the cultural changes it has promoted, does increase human happiness, though probably not as much and not as steadily as would be expected from a simple standard-of-living contrast between a mature industrial society and its agricultural counterpart.

This argument can certainly be contested. Many historians would shy away from a big generalization of this sort, arguing that modern historical reality is more complex – particularly given how difficult it is to agree on a definition of happiness. Others would point to the undeniable miseries and injustices in the contemporary world, including persistent racism, and disclaim any overall optimism; Pinker himself was explicitly attacked in 2020 on precisely these grounds.

Yet evidence relevant to happiness can be offered, without denying persisting problems. Certainly, after some growing pains, industrialization corrects some of the damage brought by agriculture: the quality of food supply improves; average stature increases, and the stature gap between upper and lower classes eases; health and life expectancy gain massively and contagious diseases decline; and gender inequality lessens. The duration of

218 *Conclusion*

work drops notably, though this category is complicated because the pace, and sometimes the monotony, intensify.

To be sure, some problems persist from the agricultural age: social and economic inequality, for example, does not decline much, persisting despite new social systems. Family life and leisure life do change – as with the decline of festivals and a reduction of spontaneous play for children: but assessing the quality of the results is not a simple matter, though most modern people, easily bored, would probably find it difficult to adapt to the more occasional rhythms of the festival tradition. There is, on the other hand, a vague "good old days" theme in contemporary culture that suggests some doubts about recent trends in family life or entertainment.

Unquestionably, some new issues are also added in as the industrial society matures. Religion does not disappear, but it undeniably becomes more complicated in a more secular framework, and this may affect happiness for some. Accommodating death in a more modern context may generate new tensions. Environmental changes may affect happiness, and this will probably loom larger in the near future.

Industrial societies almost certainly produce new levels of stress. In Western society, this problem began to be noticed in the late 19th century, under various names, and it has certainly persisted. Industrial societies also encourage cultural changes that, in turn, promote rising expectations: for social mobility, for greater wealth, for a better society, and these can lead to various signs of frustration. In Western culture particularly, the pressure to seem happy can itself generate tension, especially to the extent that it fails to accommodate sadness. These are some of the reasons that happiness does not increase as steadily as might be anticipated – along with the fact that people understandably fail to recall the past conditions against which the present might be measured.

With all this, and with due caution about the uses of polling data, surveys do fairly consistently suggest that the happiest societies are ones in which industrial levels have been achieved and accepted; where a culture encourages recognition and expression of happiness (but not, perhaps, undue cheerfulness); and where welfare measures and high levels of social trust add to a protective environment – a combination that, it must be added, not all industrial societies fully achieve. And the comparative rankings do not seem to change very rapidly, even as global reports of happiness may have been improving overall.

Finally, the history of happiness also reminds us of fragility. Classical philosophers and religious authorities long warned of this for individuals. Well-being advocates, trying to promote attitudes that can override setbacks, do the same in the contemporary context. But fragility applies to societies as well as individuals. Major political collapse, an epidemic surge, the aftermath of destructive war – developments of this sort have recurrently disrupted general happiness, in agricultural and industrial societies alike.

Conclusion 219

In a year – 2020 – in which some major societies have been buffeted by disease, economic collapse, and massive social protest – a really unusual combination of crises – and in which happiness is measurably on the decline in many places, it does seem appropriate to end on a cautionary note. Various suggestions, over the past 3,000 years, can help individuals define happiness constructively and work to achieve it. History helps us understand where our particular ideas about happiness have come from, and what some of their strengths and limitations are as against other approaches. But happiness also depends on the social environment and on actively paying attention to the greater good. This is where the challenge lies, for the foreseeable future.

Index

Abrahamic religions 34, 54
Achebe, Chinua: *No Longer at Ease* 142
"active intellect" 64
active temperance movements 129
adaptations and inequalities 30–32
"affluent societies" 190, 199
age of imperialism 135
aggressive nationalism 182
agricultural age 21, 35, 77, 218
agricultural civilizations 30, 35, 36, 40,
    83, 216–217
agricultural economies 21, 29, 37, 39
agricultural societies 8, 22–24, 71,
    75–77; adaptations and inequalities
    30–32; anthropologists 25–27;
    causes and complexities 28–30;
    characteristics of 27–28; golden age
    33–36; religion 54
agriculture 7, 21–23, 27–32, 35, 37, 38,
    150, 216, 217
The Alchemy of Happiness (Al-Ghazali)
    64
Alcott, Louisa May 111
Alger, Horatio 121
American culture 5
"American Dream" 123
Anatomy of Melancholy (Burton) 92
Antoinette, Marie 95
Aquinas, Thomas 62, 65
Arab Golden Age 74, 84
Aristotle 41–44, 48, 49, 51, 62, 64,
    74, 117
Art of Contentment 91
Ataturk, Kemal 151, 160, 161
Augustine of Hippo 60–62
Aurelius, Marcus 51
Australian aboriginal culture 26

Ball, Harvey 190
Beccaria, Cesare 94

Beethoven, Ludwig van 110
Bentham, Jeremy 94
Berman, Rachel 199
Berman, Robin 188
Beveridge, A.J. 137
Bhutan 9, 207–208
Bitzer, G.W. 108
Bolivar, Simon 140
Breughel, Pieter 71
Britain 1, 92, 94, 100, 108, 113–115,
    125, 126, 140, 157, 207, 211
Buddhism 54, 57–60, 66–69
Buddhist movements in Japan 208
Burton, Richard: *Anatomy of
    Melancholy* 92
Byrom, John 100

Calvinism 84
Calvin, John 68
Cameron, David 203
Canterbury Tales (Chaucer) 67
Cantril, Hadley 175–178
Carballo, Marita 210
"carnal desire" 63
Carnegie, Dale: *How to Win Friends and
    Influence People* 155
caveats 24, 198, 210–211
Chastellux, Marquis de 35, 94
Chaucer, Geoffrey: *Canterbury Tales* 67
childhood 66, 74–76, 118–120
Chinese culture 42, 168
Chinese Empire 135–137
"Chinese flowers" 78
Chinese philosophy, happiness in 45–48
Christianity 34, 44, 47, 52, 54, 55,
    59–62, 64, 66–68, 95, 110, 136,
    138, 142
Cicero 43, 44
"civilizing mission" 134
collective happiness 103–104, 166, 170

222 *Index*

collective programs 166–167
collective well-being 180
comfort 2, 5, 30, 40, 49, 56, 59, 67, 68, 88, 96, 97, 102, 110, 139, 195, 199, 206, 211
communism 149, 164, 170, 210, 215
communist China 168–170
communist happiness 164; communist China 168–170; Soviet commitment 165–168
community solidarity 79, 82
competitive consumerism 194
"complete virtue" 41
complexities 4, 13, 88, 174, 213–215; causes and 28–30; class divides 128–129; great expectations 130–131; sex and death 129–130
Condorcet, Nicolas de 98, 109, 131; *Sketch for a Historical Picture of the Progress of the Human Mind* 98
Confucian fascination 46
Confucian happiness 47
Confucianism 45, 47, 52
Confucius 34, 39, 45, 46, 49
consumer emotions 193–195
consumerism 2, 16, 88, 90, 91, 97, 104, 119, 122–125, 135, 139, 142, 143, 145, 157, 158, 167, 182, 202; competitive 194; contemporary 192, 195; global 205–206; and happiness 96, 193; Indian 179; individualism and 146, 159; sexuality and 101–103
consumer-oriented societies 17
contemporary consumerism 192, 195
contemporary societies: happiness in India 178–182; Japan 182–186; projects in social sciences 174–178
conventional happiness 158–159
cultural revolution 96, 170
culture 16, 18, 126, 130; American 5; Australian aboriginal 26; Chinese 42, 168; consumer 149; East Asian 47; Egyptian 38; global youth 206; Greek 43; of happiness 152; Japanese 182–184; modern 210; preindustrial 123; regional 2, 179, 217; Russian 143, 165, 166; signs of good cheer 112–114; Western 95, 98, 188, 200, 215, 218; Western happiness 199
customary economic patterns 141

dance activities in festival traditions 82
Daoism 45
Darwin, Charles 12, 111

The Decline of the West (Spengler) 152
depression 15, 151, 152, 157, 161, 188, 197, 200
Derné, Steve 180
desire theory 17
Dhammapada 57
Diamond, Jerrod 28
Dickens, Charles 114
Diener, Ed 15
disputed happiness: fascism and happiness 158–159; nationalism 159–162; new frontiers 152–158; World War I 151–152
"domestic felicity" 119

early civilization 29, 32, 37–39, 215
Easterlin, Richard 198–199
economic dislocations 135, 152, 159, 211
Egyptian culture 38
Egyptian religion 54
emotional satisfaction 42, 115, 117
emotional well-being 192, 204
endemic political tensions 178
Engels, Friedrich 110
English Protestant intellectuals 90
Enlightenment beliefs 96
Enlightenment optimism 97
Enlightenment thinking 139
Enlightenment tradition 99
Epictetus 44, 45, 49
Epicureans 43–44
Epicurus 43, 44
eudaimonic approaches 14
"eudaimonic" happiness 14
"euphoria" 169
European consumer patterns 193
European imperialism 137

facial expressions 13, 99, 154
family-centered definition of happiness 181
fascism 151, 158–159
"feeling right" 19
"felicity" 50, 51, 62, 63
festivals 2, 8, 24, 31, 113, 114, 124, 125, 218; athletic 50; Christian 66; consumer 171; periodic 79–85, 114; traditional 2
fin de siècle 111
"First and Perfect" age 33
Al Floumi, Ohoud 204
Fourier, Charles 110
Franklin, Benjamin 121, 123

Index 223

French revolutionary radicals 98
Freud, Sigmund 111
frustration 8, 17, 25, 97, 111, 175,
 198–200, 215, 218

Gallup organization 4, 197, 203
Gandhi, Mohandas 151, 160, 161, 178
gender inequality 28, 130, 217
genetic predisposition 12
genetics 16–17, 215
Al-Ghazali 63; *The Alchemy of Happiness*
 64
Gibbon, Edward 52
Gilbert, Dan 3
global consumerism 205
globalization 186, 202
global promotion of happiness 202–205
Graham, Billy 189
Great Leap Forward 168, 169
Greco-Roman tradition 9
Greek approach 40–45
Greek cultural legacy 42
Greek religion 50
Guy Fawkes Day (England) 81

Han dynasty 52, 78
"happiness agenda" 203
"happiness meters" 204
"happiness of hope" 61
happiness revolution 87, 143, 217;
 assessing 104–105; causation 96–97;
 collective happiness 103–104;
 consumerism 88; fundamental
 change 91–93; individual happiness
 101–103; new concepts of happiness
 93–95; preparatory developments
 90–91; smiling 99–101
happy families 115–120, 123, 130, 180
Happy Planet Index 203
"Happytalism" 203
heaven 1, 54, 55, 59–63, 66, 72, 98,
 136, 138
"hedonic" happiness 14
hedonism 43, 178–179, 195, 196,
 200, 207
Hesiod: *Works and Days* 33
Hinduism 54, 55–56, 66, 69, 80, 84,
 146, 160–161, 179
Hitler, Adolf 158, 159
Hong Xiuquan 136
hope and aspiration 18
Houghton, Walter 111
How to Win Friends and Influence People
 (Carnegie) 155

Huizinga, Johann 75
"humanistic" psychology 195
hunting and gathering 7, 22–24, 26–29,
 31, 32, 34–36, 72, 77, 83, 215, 216
Hutcheson, Francis 93, 94, 99

ikigai 182–185
Illien, Jayme 203
"immediate sensual enjoyment" 94
"imperfect happiness" 62
imperialism and happiness 137–142
India 39, 54, 55, 59, 68, 137, 160–161,
 175, 177, 204, 206, 207, 214, 217;
 festivals 80, 82; happiness in 178–182;
 Hinduism in 56, 84
Indian consumerism 179
individual happiness 19, 101–104, 151,
 170
individual violence 24
industrialization 29, 108, 109, 112,
 114–116, 121, 123, 128, 131, 134,
 142–145, 150, 155, 165–167, 169,
 172, 210, 216, 217
industrial life, divisions of 114;
 happiness and new emotional
 context 127–128; happy child
 118–120; happy families 115–118;
 leisure 123–127; work 120–123
industrial societies 23, 87, 108, 127, 128,
 131, 150, 156, 168, 217–218
inequalities 192, 195; adaptations and
 30–32; economic 24; gender 28, 130,
 217; global 205; regional economic
 202; social 128
instrumentalism 122–124, 190
"intermedial" happiness 91
International Day of Happiness 202,
 209, 217
Irving, Washington 114
Islam 34, 52, 54, 55, 62–68, 134, 146

Japan 5, 142–146, 208; concept of ikigai
 182–183; deterioration 184–185;
 pleasures 183–184
Jefferson, Thomas 165
Johnson, Samuel 105
Journal of Happiness Studies 203
joy 26, 45, 46, 55, 65–69, 71, 90, 92, 95,
 103–104, 110, 127, 138, 139, 142,
 143, 157, 159, 180, 192, 208, 214
Judaism 34, 59

Kant, Immanuel 105
Keys to Happiness (1910) 143

224   *Index*

Kharji 64
Khrushchev, Nikita 168

Latin America 35, 60, 135, 138–142, 210, 213, 214
leisure 31, 72, 108, 114, 115, 123–131, 159, 169, 191, 193, 218
Lenin 165
Lequinio, Joseph-Marie 103, 104
Lewis, John 190
"life satisfaction" 14–15
Locke, John 90, 91
loneliness 17, 67, 144, 193–195, 203
Longfellow, Henry Wadsworth 114
Lotz, Max 121
"lower middle class" 122
Luther, Martin 68

Maoist approach 168
Mao Zedong 168–171
Marcus Aurelius 44, 51
Martineau, Harriet 154
Marxism 164
Marxist happiness 164
Marx, Karl 109, 121
Mayo, Elton 155
Mazzini, Giuseppe 109
McMahon, Darrin 35
"melancholic demeanor" 1
Mencius 45, 47
middle-class codes 129
middle-class parents 1
Mill, John Stuart 109
"mindfulness" 58, 197, 204, 207
Moore, Clement 114; *The Night Before Christmas* 114
Morris dancing 81–82
Muhammad (Prophet) 62, 68
Mussolini, Benito 158, 159

nationalism 103, 109, 135, 144, 146, 159–162, 171, 182
Nazism 152, 158–159, 167
negative emotions 12, 34, 63, 157
neologism 101, 128
The Night Before Christmas (Moore) 114
Nirvana 58
No Longer at Ease (Achebe) 142
Norse traditions 81
Nuwwas, Abi 78

Ottoman Empire 135–137, 142, 160
overindulgence 61

Ovid 33
Owen, Wilfred 151

patriarchal gender system 37, 216
"peaceful happiness" 61
Peale, Norman Vincent: *The Power of Positive Thinking* 189
"perfectibility of society" 98
Pericles 52
periodic festival 79–85, 114
Persian mythology 34
philosophy: competing options 49–51; and legacies 51–52; philosophers and ordinary people 48–49; and science 109–112
physical self-discipline 56
Pinker, Steven 217
Plato 33, 40–42, 48, 49
poetry recitals, tradition of 77
Polan, A.J. 165
Pope, Alexander 93
positive psychology 8, 9, 12, 195–200, 202, 204
The Power of Positive Thinking (Peale) 189
preindustrial society 114
Protestantism 84, 90, 115, 145
psychological basics: desires and state of mind 17; downsides of happiness 19; facial expressions 13; genetics 16–17; "hedonic" & "eudaimonic" happiness 14; hope and aspiration 18; "life satisfaction" 14–15; preliminary list 17–18; psychological work on happiness 12; psychology and history 19–20
psychological depression 8, 200
psychological work on happiness 12
psychology 94; dependent on 2; discipline of 7; and history 19–20; "humanistic" 195; industrial 155; positive 8, 9, 12, 195–200, 202, 204
"public felicity" 35, 103
"pursuit of happiness" 1, 103, 143, 203
pursuit of wisdom 40
Putin, Vladimir 172

Qur'an 63

radical protesters 90
Ramadan Mubarak 206
rapid industrialization 166, 169, 172, 205

Index 225

regional approaches to happiness 39,
 185–186, 213, 216
regional diversity 3
regional economic inequalities 202
regional religious traditions 134
relative affluence 157
religion 218; Abrahamic 34, 54;
 Buddhism 54, 57–60, 66–69;
 Christianity 34, 44, 47, 52, 54, 55,
 59–62, 64, 66–68, 95, 110, 136,
 138, 142; Egyptian 54; Greek 50;
 Hinduism 54–56, 66, 69, 80, 84, 146,
 160–161, 179; Islam 34, 52, 54, 55,
 62–68, 134, 146; question of impact
 65–69; Roman 50, 54; traditional
 Shinto 182
"religious age" 69, 71, 82
religious approach to happiness 65, 69, 79
religious joy 65–67, 71
religious movement 136
"right to happiness" 93
river-valley civilization 21, 37, 38
Roman religion 50, 54
Romantic approach 110
Romantic intellectuals 110
Romantic movement 110
Roosevelt, Franklin 153, 157
Rousseau, Jean-Jacques 95
Russia 93, 97, 135, 142–146, 165, 166,
 171, 172, 181
Russian culture 143, 165, 166

sadness 6, 25, 26, 38, 46, 62, 101,
 105, 110, 135, 138, 139, 154, 197,
 198–200, 218
Schiller, Friedrich 110
"selfish indulgence" 119
Seligman, Martin 195, 196
Seneca 44
sexual abstinence 31
sexual activity 63; and interest 74;
 before marriage 102
sexual indulgence 50, 59
sexuality 61, 126; attitudes toward 63;
 and consumerism 101–103; and
 drugs 193; graphic 78; rampant 181
sexual revolution of 1960s 193
Shelley, Percy 110
Siddhartha Gautama 57
*Sketch for a Historical Picture of the
 Progress of the Human Mind* (de
 Condorcet) 98
Smiles, Samuel 111, 121

Smith, Adam 94
social class distinctions 84
social framework 39–40
Socialist Realist style 166
social sciences 94, 96, 174–178
Socrates 40–42
Song dynasty 78
South Asia 202, 203, 207, 208
Soviet commitment 165–168
Soviet tourism 167
Spengler, Oswald: *The Decline of the West*
 152
spiritual joy 66
Stakhanov, Alexy 166
Stakhanovite movement 166
Stalin 165, 166, 171
standard of living 17, 175, 186,
 207, 217
state-sponsored vacations 167
Stoics 44, 49, 51
Strength through Joy 159
subjective well-being (SWB) 14, 15
sub-Saharan Africa 77, 141
Suh, Eunkook 185
Summa Theologica 62
SWB *see* subjective well-being (SWB)
syncretism 206–209

Taiping movement 136
Taiping rebellion 136
Tang dynasty 69, 78
Tanzimat reforms 136
temporary happiness 56
Tolstoy, Leo 143
traditional Hindu approaches to
 happiness 55
traditionalism 210
traditional Shinto religion 182
traditional wisdom 93, 171, 196
"true" happiness 84

"ultimate happiness" 64
United Arab Emirates 9, 204, 206
United Service Organizations (USO) 158
United States 17, 108, 110, 113, 116,
 118, 123–127, 137, 140, 144, 151–157,
 164, 167, 168, 175, 176, 182, 183–185,
 190, 195, 196, 198, 200, 203, 206–208,
 211, 214; British colonies of 102;
 childrearing manuals in 112; leisure
 growth 193; low-income families in
 191; middle-class parents in 1
utilitarian school 94

226   Index

"virtuous" behavior 17

well-being 5, 56, 179, 202, 203;
collective 180; emotional 192, 204;
initiatives 204, 207; movement 9;
positive psychology and 195–198;
programs 214, 217; subjective 14, 15
"Wellbeing Finder" 197
Western happiness culture 199
Western intellectual life 109
Western society: consumerism
190–195; positive psychology and

well-being 195–198; sadness and
frustration 198–200; signposts
186–190
Western-style happiness 164
Western-style optimism 144
Works and Days (Hesiod) 33
"World Happiness Day"
202–205
World Values Survey (WVS)
209–211, 213

Yukichi, Fukuzawa 144